W9-BYA-093

FRAMING INNOCENCE

FRAMING INNOCENCE

A Mother's Photographs, a Prosecutor's Zeal,
and a Small Town's Response

LYNN POWELL

THE NEW PRESS

NEW YORK
LONDON

© 2010 by Lynn Powell
All rights reserved.
No part of this book may be reproduced, in any form, without written permission
from the publisher.

Requests for permission to reproduce selections from this book should be mailed to:
Permissions Department, The New Press, 38 Greene Street, New York, NY 10013.

Published in the United States by The New Press, New York, 2010
Distributed by Perseus Distribution

LIBRARY OF CONGRESS CATALOGING-IN-PUBLICATION DATA

Powell, Lynn, 1955-
Framing innocence : a mother's photographs, a prosecutor's zeal, and a
small town's response / Lynn Powell.
p. cm.
ISBN 978-1-59558-551-6 (hc)
1. Child pornography—Ohio—Oberlin—Case studies. 2. Photography of
children—Ohio—Oberlin—Case studies. 3. Photography of the
nude—Ohio—Oberlin—Case studies. 4. Custody of
children—Ohio—Oberlin—Case studies. 5. Stewart, Cynthia, 1951- I.
Title.
HV6570.3.O24P69 2010
364.1'74—dc22   2010010894

The New Press was established in 1990 as a not-for-profit alternative to the large,
commercial publishing houses currently dominating the book publishing industry. The
New Press operates in the public interest rather than for private gain, and is committed
to publishing, in innovative ways, works of educational, cultural, and community value
that are often deemed insufficiently profitable.

www.thenewpress.com

Book design and composition by The Influx House
This book was set in Goudy Oldstyle

Printed in the United States of America

2 4 6 8 10 9 7 5 3 1

For Dan, Anna-Claire,
and Jesse

CONTENTS

PART THREE

Author's Note

This is a work of nonfiction. I have told this story as accurately and factually as I could. There are no invented scenes and no composite characters. Since this case received local and national media attention and is a matter of public record, I have changed no names, with the exception of the "Guardian Angel" and "Deep Throat." The child at the center of this case is now nineteen years old; both she and her parents have given their permission for this story to be told. All my interviews for this book were tape recorded and transcribed for accuracy.

This book would not have been possible without the generosity of the many people who shared their recollections, notes, letters, e-mails, documents, and opinions about this prosecution with me. And I am indebted to Cynthia Stewart and a number of people who read passages of my work or the entire manuscript to verify its accuracy. Nevertheless, *Framing Innocence* is my own attempt to make sense of the experiences of an embattled family, and of our community, in the years 1999–2000. Although this is Cynthia, David, and Nora's story, it is my book, and no one asked for or was given approval of the manuscript. I alone bear responsibility for any errors this work may contain.

FRAMING INNOCENCE

Snapshot

When my son was three years old, he had a mix-and-match ward-robe of invincibility. Before nursery school each morning, he could turn into Superman, Robin Hood, a lion, a pirate, or a policeman in the costumes I improvised out of old pajamas, swaths of dime-store cloth, and my daughter's outgrown tights. But one February after-noon, intrigued by the cherubic boy he'd seen on Valentine's Day cards, my son shed his clothes, slipped into his sister's room, put on her large, pink fairy wings, and sidled up to me in the kitchen holding his plastic bow and suction-cup arrow. "Guess who I am, Mommy!" he exclaimed. It was one of those moments when I wanted the world to stand still and let my child always stay so impish and innocent.

I guessed who the little god was, and as he ran off, I called after him, asking if I could take his picture. He agreed. So I stood him before a window where the light streamed in, as if he were indeed an emissary from the clouds. I framed his pink body against the gray sky. Then just as I snapped, I thought, *Oh, my God! Could this picture get me into trouble?*

I had heard news reports of parents getting arrested for taking snapshots of their naked children—pictures the parents considered innocent but the police considered obscene. Could the police see my picture as obscene, too?

I looked back through my lens. No, I thought, nobody could mistake this cute picture for porn. I thought of the large hand-colored photograph framed on the wall of our living room—my husband's father as a naked baby lying bottom up on a bearskin rug in 1925. Reassured, I snapped a few more shots of my Cupid.

When I sent off the film to be developed, I did feel a second twinge of concern. But the prints came back on time, and I was delighted with how they had turned out. I knew that someday, when it was hard to recall my son's exuberant nakedness and lopsided wings, I would be grateful to have those pictures. In the meantime, I tossed them into a box of family photos waiting to be put into albums.

A few years later, however, a mother just down the street, the mother of one of my son's best friends, would be arrested for pictures she hadn't thought twice about taking.

PART ONE

The citizen's safety lies in the prosecutor who tempers zeal with human kindness, who seeks truth not victims, who serves the law and not factional purposes, and who approaches his task with humility.

—Robert H. Jackson,
Attorney General of the United States,
in a speech to federal prosecutors, 1940

1

A Knock at the Door

The first two photographs of Nora Stewart were taken by her father, David Perrotta, in 1991, on the day she was born. In one, the midwife is hefting and weighing her, as if hefting and weighing a good-sized fish, in the sling of a portable scale. In the other, her mother, Cynthia Stewart, is lying back on a pillow looking exhausted but pleased, with a "Gonzo's Garage" T-shirt pulled up above both of her breasts. The baby is wearing a bright Guatemalan cap. Her eyes are closed, and her tiny hand is half-clenched, with one of her fingers reaching up and almost touching the nipple her mouth is about to latch onto.

Cynthia's own first snapshot of her daughter was taken a week later. Cynthia's father had come for a visit bearing one of his famous whole-wheat fruitcakes, triple-soaked in bourbon and wrapped in a sheet of Mylar. He presented the cake as Nora's "dowry," then whisked up his new grandchild and draped her over his shoulder. Cynthia picked up her hand-me-down Nikon—a parting gift from an old boyfriend—and snapped.

By 1999, motherhood had transformed Cynthia Stewart from a casual to a passionate photographer. Early in her daughter's life, Cynthia had decided to take pictures of Nora on the last day of every month to record her growth and changes. Soon the photo sessions were weekly. And as Nora grew, so did the reasons to bring out the camera: puddle splashings, tree climbings, tea parties, bubble baths, picnics, birthdays, family friends, playmates, grandparents, fields of wildflowers, sunsets, pets. Nora took Suzuki violin lessons and Scottish dance lessons, played on a city soccer team, sang in a children's chorus, and performed with a children's drama troupe. Wherever her daughter went, Cynthia went, too, always with her Nikon around her neck.

Cynthia annotated, numbered, dated, and filed with its negative every photograph she took. Those photos were stored in a few dozen cardboard boxes—hatboxes, fruit boxes, shoe boxes—stacked in columns against the family's dining room wall. Cynthia dreamed of someday publishing a photojournalistic book that chronicled their family's life. But her larger goal was to bequeath to Nora a photographic memory of her childhood. In the eight years since Nora's birth, she had taken a staggering 35,000 photographs. Not all of those pictures were of Nora, but she was in the frame more often than not.

Cynthia, David, and Nora lived in a hundred-year-old farmhouse about a mile from the center of Oberlin, Ohio. Their house—the next-to-last before the neighborhood petered out into fields and farmland—was little, but with a big yard filled with forsythia, apple saplings, and a vegetable garden. Cynthia was a school bus driver. Now in her late forties, she was tall with ruggedly beautiful features and a mass of bushy brown hair that flowed down her back. There was a sureness to her bearing, a down-to-earth elegance and an expansive warmth. David telecommuted to New York City, working as a consultant for *The Nation* magazine, managing their digital archives. He was shorter than Cynthia, more reserved, and very handsome, with dark hair, a dark goatee, and a mordant sense of humor. Nora had grown into an articulate, precocious eight-year-old with her father's large, dark eyes and her mother's lighter brown hair, which almost touched her waist.

The family lived in a kind of cozy, whimsical disorder: piles of books teetered on tables and the piano bench, sweaters and scarves occupied comfy-looking chairs, issues of the *New Yorker* rose in knee-high stacks, colorful bird feathers were taped to kitchen cabinets, old holiday decorations hung about like domesticated ghosts. A large aquarium with fluttering fish stood in the small living room, where several cats lounged on the clutter. The most orderly precinct of the house was David's office, which shared the tiny upstairs with his and Cynthia's bedroom.

Cynthia usually took her film to be developed to Drug Mart, a large chain drugstore on the town's edge. On July 6, 1999, spotting an ad for a film processing sale, she scooped up eleven rolls and drove to Drug Mart. As usual, she scribbled the date and a few notes to herself on the receipts.

When Cynthia stopped by a few days later to pick up her prints, the clerk could find only ten envelopes with her name. Cynthia showed her the eleventh receipt, and, after searching the bins, the clerk promised to call the processing lab and track down the missing roll. But after a week of calling with no results, the clerk gave Cynthia the lab's number and wished her better luck.

Cynthia began calling the lab, fifty miles away in another Ohio town, every few days. Each time she called, her query was met with silence. Then the customer service agent would say, "That roll of film has not left the premises." Yes, Cynthia would explain, she had been told that before, but since her roll of film was clearly lost in their facility, could they keep looking for it? The agent would respond, "We have a tracer out on it." At first, this reassured Cynthia. But as she called repeatedly over several weeks, she grew frustrated: no one seemed concerned that her pictures had been lost, and no one could explain what this "tracer" process involved.

The date on Cynthia's receipt indicated that the missing roll had been shot in early June. The receipt's note—"Three in bath with crossed arms"—meant that the last three shots were similar and, since the third one was probably best, she should make sure the lab printed every frame. Cynthia was not concerned that the missing roll contained nude pictures of a child. She had taken photos of Nora naked—both in and out of the bathtub—since she was born, and most of those had been developed through this same lab. Cynthia's concern was that thirty-six of her pictures might be lost for good. Once before, another lab had lost one of her rolls, and she had spent two years calling, trying to track it down. Cynthia could never remember what was on the roll, which was exactly what pained her.

Over the following weeks, Cynthia kept calling, and, one by one, jotting down the names of the employees she had spoken with—Shelly, Jody, Minnie, Janet.

On the morning of August 11, two policemen knocked on the family's front door. One of the officers introduced himself as Detective Anadiotis from the Oberlin police department. He said they had some of her photographs down at the station.

"You've found my pictures!" Cynthia interrupted, delighted.

"Yes," he said, "and there are serious questions about those pictures, ma'am."

The detective's stern tone surprised Cynthia. He seemed tense, as if his efforts to be polite were being taxed by something unsaid. Then she thought of the bathtub shots. He must have gotten a wrong idea about them, she realized. Confident she could straighten out any misunderstanding, she invited the officers into the house.

As the men came in, Cynthia explained that she was a mother and an amateur photographer. Her missing roll—the roll they had found—was part of an ongoing project to document her family's life. She pointed at the boxes stacked in the dining room as proof.

The detective glanced at the boxes and said, "Ma'am, we'd like you to come down to the station right now and answer some questions."

Again Cynthia was taken aback by the officer's brusqueness. But she quickly agreed to go to the station—whatever it took to bring those pictures home. First, she would need to tell her partner, who was upstairs working, where she was going.

David had studied Law and Society in college and had interned with a lawyer; he had a broad and somewhat jaded understanding of the legal system. When Cynthia told him of the conversation downstairs, David was alarmed: "You're not talking to the police—not without a lawyer, you're not!"

"The police just misunderstood," she assured him. "It's no big deal."

David was incredulous. "It's *always* a big deal when the police want to talk!"

Cynthia said she could explain everything.

"Not without a lawyer, you won't!" David insisted that an attorney was needed anytime you said *anything* to law enforcement, no matter how innocent you were.

But Cynthia didn't see why she couldn't just go down to the police station and set the matter straight. She didn't need anyone's help to tell the truth. Their disagreement escalated down the stairs and continued in the living room in front of the officers until Cynthia turned to Detective Anadiotis and asked him to explain the situation to David.

The detective looked straight at her and said again, "There are serious questions about those pictures, ma'am."

David blanched. And for the first time, Cynthia felt concerned, too—not about the police, but about David. Fighting was not something she and David often did, and this sudden vehemence between them unsettled her. She didn't want to push their fight any further, especially with the policemen watching. "All right," she conceded. "We're going to call a lawyer." The detective urged her to have the lawyer contact him at the police station as soon as possible.

As the officers drove away, there was no disagreement about what to do next. Cynthia picked up the phone and dialed Tom Theado.

2

Lawyers in Their Life

Tom Theado was one of Cynthia's oldest friends. They had met in 1970 as freshmen at Oberlin College and had both ended up settling in the town. In their young adulthood, they had socialized often. When Tom had visited the Stewart family farm in West Virginia, he had been astonished to learn that Cynthia's father did not change his clocks when the rest of the country went on daylight savings time: Bill Stewart considered daylight savings time *unnatural*. And Tom had been nonplussed when he had learned firsthand what Cynthia had meant by, "We'll go swimming at The Farm." She had meant they would be skinny-dipping in the Ohio River with barges going by.

Tom had gone on to become a successful lawyer in the large county Oberlin was part of: Lorain County. Through the years, he and Cynthia had stayed in touch, mostly by phone. Now he listened to her description of the police visit with more concern than Cynthia had anticipated.

As a class-action attorney, Tom said he couldn't be of much help. But he did know an attorney whose specialty was family law and who would be just right: Amy Wirtz. Though only in her early thirties, Amy had already served as public defender in a nearby county, had extensive experience with Children Services, and was earning a reputation as a feisty advocate. Tom promised, "Amy will fight for you 100 percent because that's the kind of lawyer she is."

As soon as they hung up, Tom called Amy himself. He wanted to assure her that she could believe everything Cynthia and David told her. "I knew Cindy way back when she was Cindy," Tom said. "I can vouch for these parents."

When David and Cynthia called Amy, she agreed that it had been prudent for Cynthia not to go down to the station. She did think, however, that the situation could be easily resolved. For a parent to get into trouble, usually the photos had to show sexually graphic or explicit material, a sexual act. Their first appointment would cost $40. Cynthia and David scheduled that appointment for the next day.

Amy Wirtz was in private practice in Elyria, the county seat. She shared a tidy suite of offices—and a secretary and a legal assistant—with another female attorney. A blindfolded, scales-and-sword-wielding Lady Justice towered on each side of the office's large window that looked out on the green town square and the county courthouse.

Amy had short brown hair and wore a trim dark suit and pumps, all of which made her look to Cynthia and David like a textbook lawyer. But they liked that her conference room was furnished with a dining room table. Amy believed that the best talking in a family happened around meals, so a law office ought to have a table where people can open up as they do at home.

To Amy, Cynthia looked like an attractive, aging hippie. She was braless and wore a loose blouse, flowing skirt, and Birkenstocks. David looked younger than Cynthia, and Amy quickly learned that he was younger—by thirteen years. He and Cynthia had never married, but they had been together a dozen years and were raising their daughter nuclear-family style. As David detailed his concerns about a police interrogation, Amy found him well-informed and ferociously articulate.

Cynthia wanted to describe to Amy the beginnings of her passion for photography. After the birth of her daughter, she said, she had been flooded with postpartum *elation*. That had not surprised her. What *had* surprised her was an accompanying feeling: a sharpened sense of her own, and her daughter's, mortality. That overwhelming sense of the transience of life made her marvel at her camera: a box she could put a moment inside of; a contraption that could catch and keep what was fleeting. Cynthia had begun to document her family's life in an almost daily way. Her interest was not in filling up scrapbooks. Her interest was larger: she wanted to give her daughter a vivid, permanent memory of her childhood—to save from oblivion the ordinary days of her growing up. Every picture she took, Cynthia felt, was a moment she had snatched away from death.

Amy listened to Cynthia carefully. She knew something about the art of photography: her own father had taught the subject at a state university, and he had worn a camera around his neck much of the time. Still, she had never heard anyone talk about photographs in such an ardent way. Concerned, she asked Cynthia to describe what was on the confiscated roll.

Based on the date and the note on her receipt, Cynthia said, the roll probably contained end-of-school-year pictures and pictures of Nora in front of a weeping cherry tree. Most of her photographs were spontaneous, she explained, but sometimes she took pictures in annual series. For example, each spring, when the neighbor's weeping cherry or the peonies in a professor's yard bloomed, she would pose Nora in front of those flowers.

The roll also definitely included some nude shots. In June, Cynthia had taken Nora to see a photography exhibit at a local art gallery. Nora had been mesmerized by a black-and-white photograph, shot from above, of a woman rising out of a claw-foot tub with her head thrown back, her eyes closed, and her long hair swirling in the water behind her. When Nora had asked if they could re-create the picture at home, Cynthia had agreed.

Later that afternoon, at the end of Nora's bubble bath, Cynthia brought her camera into the bathroom. She stood above the tub and aimed her camera down as Nora closed her eyes, threw her head back, and lifted slowly up from the filmy water. Cynthia took several shots as the water drained out. Then Nora stood up to rinse herself with the shower sprayer as she always did.

When her daughter was small, Cynthia had started a bath-time game to make sure she had washed and rinsed properly. Nora would stand in the tub, and Cynthia would name each part of her body, asking if she had rinsed there. Nora would answer by pointing the showerhead at that part of her body and spraying. The rinsing went from head to foot, including her buttocks and genitals. Sometimes as she rinsed, pretending to be a Power Ranger, Nora would assume poses that made her look like a superhero. A couple of times in the past, Cynthia had photographed the rinsing game. That afternoon, Cynthia thought to document the game again.

She finished up the roll by taking some waist-up shots of Nora out of the tub with her arms crossed and a towel wrapped around her long, wet hair. Those shots were a test of various lighting conditions—some had flash and some did not. None of the pictures was a close-up. "So, you see," Cynthia concluded, "those pictures are really no big deal."

Amy was not so sure. The police were not going to look at those pictures the way a mother would, she pointed out. The police were going to look through the eyes of men who had been charged with the job of rooting out crime, and in the past dozen years or so, child pornography and the sexual abuse of children had become crimes on everybody's minds—so much so that children were now often viewed primarily as potential victims.

Amy knew of two cases in other Ohio counties where parents had been prosecuted for what they claimed were innocent pictures of their children. In one case, the parents had taken a video of their infant son touching his penis. The parents had thought the video was funny; the police had not. In the other case, a wealthy, single mother had been arrested for snapshots her naked six-year-old daughter and her daughter's friend had taken of themselves with a disposable camera, without the mother's knowledge. Against all evidence, the county prosecutor indicted the mother for taking the pictures herself. Although she was eventually acquitted, the prosecution dragged on for months, the headlines were sensational, and the mother spent a couple hundred thousand dollars on her defense.

Anything out of the ordinary could arouse suspicion, Amy warned, and Cynthia's pictures did sound out of the ordinary. Yes, many people had snapshots of their *toddlers* in the bathtub, but not of their eight-year-olds. And even though Cynthia felt confident she could explain her pictures to the police, those officers might not be as comfortable as she was with nudity in the home, or cameras in the bathroom, or taking a child to photography exhibits with naked women rising up out of claw-foot tubs. If the police thought the pictures looked like porn, Cynthia's explanations would be irrelevant. The police were trained to focus on hard evidence, not character assessments or motives.

But Cynthia couldn't imagine how to assuage the policemen's concerns without talking to them and explaining why she had taken those pictures. Amy argued that a policeman could turn Cynthia's honesty against her. "Don't you think a pedophile could become aroused by your pictures?" he might ask. Cynthia might answer, "Well, yes, but I would never show them to a pedophile." And the policeman would seize upon the "Well, yes" as evidence she had created child porn.

Amy did agree, though, that Cynthia needed to explain the context of her pictures. So she suggested an alternative: Cynthia could write a statement, and Amy would review it, have it notarized, and deliver it to the police. By submitting an affidavit, Amy hoped to allay the detective's concerns. But, she warned, if the detective passed along the pictures to the prosecutor, the prosecutor might send them on to Children Services for evaluation. If a social worker there thought follow-up was needed, an informal case could be initiated, with the agency working with the family to assess Nora's well-being. If the social worker's concerns about Nora deepened, then Children Services might file official charges and hold a court hearing. In the worst-case scenario, if Children Services were convinced that Nora was in immediate danger, the agency could apply for Emergency Temporary Custody—a swift removal of a child to foster care for ninety days while an investigation was pursued. Amy thought all this was unlikely, but she wanted to prepare Cynthia and David for every eventuality.

Cynthia and David had read terrible stories about children being harmed in foster care and families being traumatized by family service investigations. But Amy had an upbeat assessment of Lorain

County Children Services. Before coming to Elyria, she had worked in a different Ohio county where the family services agency had been too quick to separate children from their parents and even to dissolve family bonds and put foster children up for adoption. Moving here, Amy had been pleasantly surprised to discover that Lorain County's social workers did not rush to take custody or file charges; in fact, they routinely worked with families and their attorneys to resolve problems out of court.

Lorain County Children Services did have one troubling aspect, however, which differed from other counties. Instead of having in-house prosecutors who were accountable only to their agency and who were motivated solely by their social workers' concerns, they relied on assistant prosecutors assigned to them by the county prosecutor's office. The porous boundary between the prosecutor's office and Children Services made Amy nervous: the prosecutor might put pressure on Children Services to file charges against their own judgment.

Amy did not discuss with Cynthia and David the possibility of a criminal indictment. She did not imagine the situation developing that way. She did tell them, however, that the police might obtain a warrant to search their house and confiscate Cynthia's pictures and computer equipment. If they suspected she was creating pornography, they would assume she was scanning her pictures to post on child-porn Internet sites.

Cynthia panicked at the thought of her photographs being taken away. But she didn't own or even know how to use a computer. Amy asked if there were any other computers in the house. If so, they would be fair game in a police search. David's work for *The Nation* was entirely computer-based and having his computer confiscated would be catastrophic for him. He nervously wrote down Amy's instructions for what to say and how to behave if the police came back with a search warrant:

- "what can I do to assist you, what are you looking for?"
- READ THE WARRANT

- don't interrupt search
- take pix of damage afterward
- don't answer Q's, "attorney advised us not to speak"
- "YES SIR, NO SIR" keep mouths shut

Amy had one more warning for Cynthia and David. They did not seem to be the kind of troubled family who typically ended up with lawyers in their lives. Yet she knew even strong relationships could become undone by legal ordeals. "I'm going to be honest with you," she said. "Nothing can stress a relationship more than having your child's well-being called into question."

Cynthia and David agreed that an affidavit was a good way to proceed. They signed a contract and wrote Amy a check for $1,300— the flat fee she was charging for her services through the police investigation. Cynthia and David had been saving money to have their basement waterproofed. That check represented 10 percent of their savings. It was painful to give up the money, but they were grateful they had the money to give.

Amy's first impression of Cynthia and David had been positive. But as she closed the door behind them, she predicted to her secretary, "That woman is going to get screwed because she's unusual. The system is going to persecute her for her differences." Amy had been honest in her assessment of the strengths of Lorain County Children Services. Nevertheless, she was a realist who knew that human beings with biases, ambitions, and personal histories filled every position from policeman to prosecutor, from social worker to judge and jury—all sorts of people who might find Cynthia uncomfortably eccentric.

Amy also knew she had her own values and boundaries. In her stint as a public defender, she had had to represent a few parents who had done terrible things to children. Those cases had left her leery of adults who had innocent-sounding stories to explain away suspicious behavior toward children. She would feel uneasy until she had seen Cynthia's photographs. If the photographs alarmed her, she couldn't continue as their lawyer.

That afternoon, Amy called Detective Anadiotis. He seemed agitated, and their talk confirmed her belief that a police interview of Cynthia would not have gone well. Amy typed up brief notes from the conversation:

> Compromising positions—19 photos, at least one naked in shower with the shower spigot between her legs. He believes that they are over the line and needs to know who took the photos and for what purpose. Will take the pictures to the prosecutor's office to get their determination.

Back home, Cynthia hand-wrote the statement she wanted to give to the police. David typed it on his computer:

> I take pictures of my daughter so that when she is my age she'll have an aid to her memory of the way things were. Though I try to take good or artistic pictures, my aim is to keep a photographic journal of our family. . . .
>
> There are 3 things that I know I've taken pictures of that haven't turned up on any other roll, so I'm assuming they're on this one.
>
> The first is day one and two of a 31 day series that I did of Nora in front of a weeping cherry tree—from pre-bloom through full and on till there were no blossoms left.
>
> The second is of her in the bathtub. From the time she was about 3 years old, I would wash her in the bathtub, teaching her how to clean herself, including her yoni (our word for vagina) and her rosebud (ditto anus). Then I would leave her in the bathtub with the sprayer to rinse while the water ran out and go do whatever I had to do. When I came back I would say, "Have you rinsed your yoni?" My daughter, who will never give a simple answer when a dramatic one will do, assumes this posture (which has evolved over the years) with the sprayer pointing toward her vagina and shouts

triumphantly "Yoni!" Then I ask, "Have you rinsed your rosebud?" She switches the sprayer and the posture and yells "Rosebud!" Over the years I think I probably have two or three other sets of what we call "yoni-rosebud pictures."

The third thing that must be on this roll because I haven't seen it yet is another shot of Nora in the bathtub, possibly taken the same day. This spring I took Nora to the annual photography show at FAVA (Firelands Association for the Visual Arts) in the old Westervelt Building in Oberlin. There was a black and white photo, very dark and dramatic, that she was quite taken with of a nude woman in a clawfoot bathtub mostly filled with water with a soapy, milky surface. The woman was coming up out of the water with her long hair streaming down, her eyes closed—it looked almost birth-like. Shortly after we saw the exhibit, when Nora was taking a bath, she asked me if we could try to re-create the photograph. We did, but my memory is not very clear on how hard we tried, i.e., I don't remember whether there was one shot or six shots.

The accompanying photo album is something I came across recently that is a fairly good representation of the way I photograph my daughter and the occasions and frequency with which I have photographed her nude.

Cynthia Stewart

The album Cynthia planned to submit was one she had made when Nora was three years old. It was one of the only albums Cynthia had ever assembled. Taped to each page were one or two photographs of Nora, accompanied by handwritten captions: "Chaos Central or Find the Baby" (baby Nora on a cluttered bed in a cluttered room); "Doing Yoga" (toddler Nora bent over with her head on the floor and her arms outstretched); "Happy Family III" (three-year-old Nora and Cynthia and David smiling on a sunny, windswept promontory).

Of the sixty-five or so photographs in the album, eight showed Nora naked. The first was of Nora as a baby lying bottom-up on a quilt. The next six were a sequence of Nora playing naked in her grandmother's backyard. She looked about eighteen months old. In one, Nora was sitting with and talking to her grandmother; in another, she was gesturing happily; and in a third, at a considerable distance from the camera, she was squatting down slightly and looking at her toddler potbelly. The last naked picture showed Nora at a slightly older age, laughing and running around a room.

To give the police a context for the weeping cherry pictures, Cynthia added fifteen recent "Nora-with-flowers pictures" into a clear pouch at the back of the album. In none of these was Nora naked. She was often in outfits made by David's mother: Nora in a white dress in a field of Queen Anne's lace, Nora in a sunflower sundress in a crowd of black-eyed Susans.

Amy had been raised in a family where nudity was no big deal, and she treasured a handful of snapshots her father had taken of her naked when she was around four years old. When she read Cynthia's statement, she thought the "yoni-rosebud" language was strange and potentially provocative, but otherwise she thought Cynthia had written a good draft. But the lawyer who shared Amy's office and who had been raised much more conservatively than Amy read Cynthia's statement and gasped: "Oh, my God, you can't use this! This sounds like a sex game!" She helped Amy rewrite the affidavit to minimize language that might raise red flags for the police. The sentences were simple and blunt:

IN THE STATE OF OHIO:
COUNTY OF LORAIN:

AFFIDAVIT

Cynthia Stewart, being duly sworn according to the law, says the following:

1. I am Cynthia Stewart. I reside at [address], Oberlin, OH. My life partner is David Perrotta.

2. I am the mother of Nora Stewart.

3. Photography is my primary hobby. I enjoy taking pictures and have taken many pictures of my daughter since her birth. I took three photography classes in Brooklyn, NY in 1996/97. I enjoy going to photography shows and take my daughter to these shows, as well.

4. I think of the pictures of my daughter as a journal of my family and of her development. I have recorded her growth and beauty in various ways through photography. I have consistently taken pictures of her in front of flowers in clothing that her grandmother has made for her. I also take many photos of family events and milestones. I enjoy taking pictures of her playing with her friends, as well.

5. Throughout her life, I have chosen to take pictures of her when she is in various states of nudity to record the growth of her body and moments of silliness and play. With this affidavit, I am submitting to the Oberlin Police a blue, 3-ring binder containing samples of the kind of pictures I have taken since she was born.

6. I turned in multiple rolls of film to the Drug Mart located in Oberlin on July 6, 1999. When I went to collect the developed film, one roll was missing. Drug Mart did try to get the roll of film from the lab on several occasions and then gave me the phone number to try and retrieve it myself. The lab that develops Drug Mart's film told me the film had been checked in but had not left the facility.

7. On August 11, 1999, Officer Anadiotis and another officer came to my home to request that I go to the police station to discuss some photographs of my daughter. I decided not to go until I had contacted an attorney.

8. After discussing this situation with my lawyer, Amy Wirtz, I have decided to submit an affidavit rather than participate in a police interrogation. Officer Anadiotis describes the photographs in his pos-

session as naked pictures of an eight-year-old girl in a bathtub. I did take photographs of Nora in the bathtub naked. I have not received these photographs back from Drug Mart. In one of the photographs, Nora was recreating a picture that we saw at an annual photography exhibit.

9. The other naked photographs I took of Nora were of her washing herself. From the time she was about three years old after her bath she would play with the shower sprayer to rinse while the water ran out. This game became part of her bath time ritual and still continues. The pictures are taken to record this bath time game.

Cynthia was unhappy with the changes, which had stripped away every trace of her personality and any feel for their family's life. But after a lengthy meeting with Amy and David, she agreed to sign the rewrite. Amy had the affidavit notarized, and she delivered it, along with the photo album, to the Oberlin police department and into the hands of Detective Anadiotis. Afterwards, Amy left a message on Cynthia and David's answering machine reporting that the officer was "more low-key" than during their previous phone conversation and that he had told her that "once he reviewed the photo album and talked to the prosecutor, if they deemed it appropriate, he would have me come in and talk to him further."

The message reassured Cynthia and David. Still, David spent frantic hours backing up his computer files, and Cynthia readied all her boxes to be moved to Amy's office. Amy wanted to protect Cynthia's photos from seizure since they provided the context that could explain and normalize the prints already in the police's hands.

With the affidavit filed, the computer backed up, and all of Cynthia's photographs stored in Amy's office basement, the family began packing for a weekend trip to West Virginia. They were headed down to The Bash, an annual, old-fashioned family homecoming on the farm the Stewart children had grown up on. Cynthia's seven siblings would all be there, as well as Cynthia's mother, Gerry. Gerry had married and divorced Cynthia's father Bill twice, and she now lived in Oberlin. But Gerry always joined the summer and Christmas pilgrimages back to The Farm, where Bill now lived alone.

The Bash was a time of hand-cranked ice cream, banjo picking, camping out, and swimming in the Ohio River. Traditionally, Cynthia took The Bash family portraits, including the "Moon Shot" in which everyone in the assembled group bared their backsides. But Amy had warned Cynthia to take no nude pictures of anyone until things with the police got cleared up.

3

"Peculiar in That Which Is Good"

Cynthia harbored one regret about her own childhood: she couldn't remember enough of it. She could recite long passages from Shakespeare and sing every song she'd ever sung around a 4-H campfire. Yet Cynthia resented the human fact that she forgot much more than she remembered. And it grieved her that there were so few snapshots to help her recall her own young life. She longed for photographs of Chestnut, the old horse "full of piss and vinegar," and Barnsmell, the kitten her father found abandoned in their mailbox. She wished for pictures of her little brother riding on the back of a pig, of her big brother saving with his pocketknife a newborn calf sealed in its caul, of her mother whacking the pesky rooster with a broom. But the Stewart family archives were a couple of shirt boxes stuffed with school pictures, prom poses, and Olan Mills portraits—conventional images of a family that was anything but conventional.

In a black-and-white family portrait taken in 1960, Cynthia's four burr-headed brothers wear starched shirts, pleated trousers, bow ties, and suspenders. The two girls wear dresses made by their mother. Nine-year-old Cynthia has her hair pulled tightly in two long braids; her little sister's hair is neatly curled. Bill and Gerry Stewart smile broadly, surrounded by the beaming brood they've produced so far—a canonical 1950s all-American family. At the time of the portrait, the Stewarts lived in a former Appalachian oil boomtown on the south bank of the Ohio River. Soon afterward, Cynthia's father would move his picture-perfect family back to the land, and into the sixties.

~~~

Bill Stewart had served in World War II as a co-pilot of a B-17 Flying Fortress. He had been decorated with a Purple Heart, but the losses and horrors of that war had traumatized him. He returned from Europe convinced that his generation had been entrusted with a new mission: to make sure a war like that never happened again and to repopulate the world with children who would carry on that mission. He went to college on the G.I. Bill, married a fellow student, trained as a chemical engineer, and then went to work at the Union Carbide plant near his hometown in West Virginia. By 1959, Bill and his wife Gerry had six children. Early in their marriage, they had read the memoir *Cheaper by the Dozen*, about the autodidactic family of Frank and Lillian Gilbreth, pioneers of time and motion studies and efficiency experts. Like the Gilbreths, Bill believed there was a right way to do everything. And like Frank Gilbreth, he planned to sire a dozen children who would learn the right way to do everything, including save the world.

In 1960, Bill bought a farmhouse on a hundred acres of hilly pasture, old growth forest, and river bottomland. He shared the passion expressed in the West Virginia motto: *Montani Semper Liberi* (Mountaineers are Always Free). He wanted his children to breathe fresh mountain air, drink clean water, eat healthy food, and learn to be resourceful as well as book smart. Sitting on top of a ridge, the white farmhouse had one bathroom and was heated by a coal stove in the living room. A herd of milking cattle came with the farm, along with a scrappy rat terrier and copperheads sunning themselves on the hill's steep stone steps.

There was a strong conviction in the Stewart family that what was natural was best. The family produced much of their own food, and Gerry cooked everything from scratch. Cynthia's favorite lunch was a glass of milk from the cows and a bacon, lettuce, and tomato sandwich—made with bacon from a 4-H pig, lettuce and tomato from her mother's large garden, bread her mother had baked, and mayonnaise her mother had made from eggs laid by their hens. After school and chores, Cynthia and her siblings had the run of the farm.

They chased one another on the barn's rafter beams. They watched calves and kittens being born. They learned to drive tractors and to cut, winnow, and bale hay. In spring, they scouted for mayapple and trillium along Polecat Creek. In summer, they picked blackberries, skinny-dipped, and spent a week in the wilds at 4-H camp.

Unlike the *Cheaper by the Dozen* family, the Stewarts had no maid, cook, or handyman. Bill ran the farm in the evenings, after long days at Union Carbide. Gerry cooked, cleaned, gardened, sewed, laundered, mended, mothered, and curled her daughters' hair each night with strips of rag. After baby number six, a tired Gerry and Bill agreed that a half-dozen children was enough.

With only one bathroom in the house, it was impractical to be modest in a family of eight, and no one thought twice about skinny-dipping. Yet there was not much frank talk in the family about sex. When Cynthia heard from a playmate that "ladies pee blood and then they can't go swimming," her mother reassured her with the facts of menstruation. But when she later asked her mother what sex was, Gerry said, "You know, what the cows do." Since Cynthia had only seen cows artificially inseminated, her notions about sex remained hazy for a long time.

By the time Cynthia entered high school, the Vietnam War had escalated, and her father's politics had grown more dogmatically countercultural. Bill envisioned The Farm as an intentional community, free of sexism, racism, and militarism. He wrote antiwar letters to local and national newspapers and spoke against the war in Cynthia's social studies class. Most of her classmates thought her dad was "a weirdo," but Cynthia was proud when her father's passionate arguments changed her social studies teacher's mind about Vietnam.

Not everyone found Bill Stewart persuasive, though, even at home. As his boys entered their teenage years, he fought battles with them about the length of their hair and their interest in athletics. There were ample tensions in the marriage, too. Cynthia never forgot how once, as a child, she asked her mother what the word "brainwashing" meant. Gerry explained, "They torture you until you say two plus two equals five." And then, with anger rising in her voice, she added, "Your father, though, he'd rather *die* than say two plus two equals five."

In 1970, Gerry coaxed the family into the Olan Mills studio one last time. Months before, after an unplanned and difficult pregnancy, Gerry had given birth to twin boys. In the color portrait, the six oldest children, ages eleven to twenty-one, stand in a line behind their parents. Cynthia and her sister are dressed in slacks and sweaters, with their hair flowing down their backs. The boys have shoulder-length hair and are dressed in mismatched combos of jeans, plaid, paisley, and checks. Some of their shirts are untucked, and the fourteen-year-old is wearing a headband. Bill and Gerry each hold one of the twins, who are dressed in little overalls. Neither exhausted-looking parent seems quite able to muster a smile.

But Cynthia, at the center of the family, is radiant. She was about to leave home for college in Oberlin, Ohio—a small town with its own unconventional history of radical politics and utopian dreamers.

When Cynthia arrived at Oberlin College in the fall of 1970, cornfields buffered the town of eight thousand from the urban centers of Cleveland to the east and Lorain to the north. Townspeople and college students rubbed elbows in the two-block business district. Tappan Square served as the community's spacious green heart. Because northern Ohio had been scraped clean by a two-mile-high glacier during the last ice age, Oberlin was flat, with only a dip where Plum Creek cut through.

The colony and college of Oberlin had been founded on swampy woodland in 1833, as far from every vice-infested city as its little band of Christian visionaries could get. One of the founders famously declared: "Oberlin is peculiar. Oberlin is peculiar in that which is good." The community's strict social code required colonists to renounce tobacco, alcohol, coffee, spices, and tight-fitting clothes and to give their surplus money for the spread of the gospel. But the greatest peculiarity of the place was the school's student body: Oberlin was the first co-educational college in America and the first to admit students regardless of race.

Oberlin's radical politics were rooted in its piety. For decades, the renowned evangelist Charles Grandison Finney taught theology at the college and served as its president. Finney exhorted his flock to perfect themselves and perfect the world, and eradicating the sin of slavery became the community's first great cause. As the last stop on the Underground Railroad before the boat crossing to Canada, Oberlin attracted escaped slaves and freed blacks to the remarkably integrated town. Once slavery was abolished, Oberlin's zeal shifted to temperance and suffrage.

The activist community quickly earned both admiration and disdain. During the Civil War, satirists ridiculed Oberlin as a town of self-righteous do-gooders who were "the prime cause of all the trouble." After the war, even Mark Twain had acerbic words for the place. During an evening's entertainment in Oberlin's First Congregational Church, Twain was coolly received by an audience who much preferred the reading of his fellow performer, a writer of antiracist novels of Southern life. Later, Twain published a short story—"The Man That Corrupted Hadleyburg"—in which he skewered a "smugly conceited and reputedly virtuous" town that had kept its "reputation unsmirched during three generations, and was prouder of it than any other of its possessions." Contemporary readers recognized that town as Oberlin.

The settlers who killed the rattlesnakes and cleared a tract for Oberlin from mosquito-thick woods would not have recognized the campus where Cynthia unloaded her suitcases. Perhaps the political zeal of the place would have been familiar, as well as the idealism of their spiritual and intellectual heirs. But the country's first co-educational institution was now committed to bringing about social changes the original Oberlinians would never have dreamed of—or prayed for.

In November of 1970, *Life* magazine ran a cover story on the new phenomenon of co-ed dorms on college campuses. The cover photograph is of a pretty young woman with long hair and a long skirt sitting on the edge of an armchair and looking down into the eyes of a young man, in sideburns, vest, jeans, and sandals. She is holding a few books in one hand, and her other hand is resting in both of his. The magazine's headline reads, "CO-ED DORMS: An intimate revolution on campus." And the caption beside the photograph reads, "Rob Singler and Cindy Stewart in their dorm at Oberlin."

Inside the magazine, Oberlin is featured in ten pages of photographs. A two-page spread shows Cynthia and her boyfriend Rob in jeans and barefoot, relaxing in his tidy room, with a book by John Stuart Mill beside the bunk beds, a reel-to-reel tape player on the crowded bookshelf, and a sign taped up on the radiator that says, "are you RIPPLIN'?" The caption says that Rob and Cindy "live in a co-ed dorm housing 23 boys and 26 girls. Since meeting this fall, they have become very close."

The article trumpets the wholesomeness of the new living arrangements at Oberlin, where "the absence of traditional restraints has encouraged an ease and a naturalness enthusiastically endorsed by both students and faculty." An associate admissions director points out: "Some parents expect the Oberlin campus to be full of bomb-throwers, perverts and free-lovers. It's not. . . . Did it ever occur to you that boys in your daughter's dorm may look upon her as a sister instead of simply a sex object, and that she'll have a chance to accept them as human beings, too?"

Not surprisingly, many of *Life*'s readers in 1970 were not persuaded by the upbeat spin on what they feared was rampant sexual impropriety on liberal campuses like Oberlin's. Fresh from the farm, Cynthia achieved instant national notoriety as a poster girl for co-ed dorms and, implicitly, for the new sexual freedom. Hate mail poured into her college mailbox from across the country—sacks and sacks of letters vilifying her.

On campus, however, Cynthia became a celebrity. Boys had crushes on her because she seemed glamorous, and girls wanted the cachet of being her friend. For a while, Cynthia found it difficult to discern who her real friends were. She felt so shaken by her first fifteen minutes of fame that she never wanted another second of it.

Cynthia had gone to Oberlin College to become a teacher, but she dropped out of college in 1975 before finishing her degree. At the time, she had been renting the third floor of a large white house on one of the town's main streets—a bright attic apartment with big windows, a gambrel ceiling, and its very own turret. She loved her apartment and loved living in Oberlin, so she decided to stay put and become a townie. Cynthia slept in the turret, which had panoramic windows and no heat. In winter, she slept beneath a comforter she'd bought at a yard sale. In summer, she hung the windows with houseplants and felt as if she were living in a tree house. Cynthia nicknamed the apartment "82" after its street address.

Within a few years, Cynthia had settled into a job as a school bus driver for the Oberlin public schools. Driving a bus channeled Cynthia's schoolteacher instincts. She enjoyed talking to the children about their days at school and learning the names of their pets. Some children confided their worries or problems to her, like the little boy who spent months sitting behind her as she drove, obsessing about his fear of nuclear war. Driving a school bus quickly became more than a job for Cynthia; it became a mission. Her aim was to create a just society on her bus. She made seating charts, distributing children who had a tendency to make trouble among the more responsible riders, and she posted a placard with large letters at the front of her bus: "Racist, Sexist, Homophobic comments will not be tolerated. *Thanks.*"

When Cynthia met David Perrotta in 1987, she told her friends, "He knocked my socks off, and I didn't even have socks on!"

Raised with all the privileges of New York City affluence in the still-wild woods of the Hudson River Valley, David was a high-achieving child in a family that put a strong emphasis on education. The politics in the Perrotta household were liberal. After prep school and a B.A. from Brown, David showed no signs of going to law or business school, causing quiet consternation in the family. A zealous believer in cooperative ownership, David was, instead, thrilled to land his first post-graduation job as the education director of Oberlin's cooperative bookstore. David arrived in Oberlin and immediately organized a conference on "Investing with a Conscience," published a newsletter about injustice in the marketplace, and sat outside the bookstore exhorting customers to pay $5 to join its membership because, "If you're going to buy books at this store, you ought to *own* it!"

For three years, Cynthia and David lived in separate apartments but spent much of their time together. They read books aloud, traveled cross-country, named their cat after a Sandinista spy, and fought the demolition of historic buildings in Oberlin. Sunday mornings were spent at a local diner with a large crowd of friends and fellow activists—eating brunch, doing the *New York Times* crossword, and plotting strategy.

When in the summer of 1990, at the age of thirty-nine, Cynthia discovered she was pregnant, she embraced the unexpected chance to have a child. Twenty-six-year-old David, though, didn't feel ready for full-time fatherhood, and career considerations were urging him back to the East Coast. He moved to New York, where he landed his first job with *The Nation*. But David was in Oberlin for Cynthia's forty-five hours of labor and the birth of their baby on 82's living room floor on Easter morning.

For the first few years of Nora's life, Cynthia and David had a commuting relationship. Then, when Nora turned six, David switched jobs at *The Nation* to one he could do long-distance. Pooling their savings, Cynthia and David bought the little Oberlin farmhouse with a near-acre yard where David plowed up beds for tomatoes, beans, basil, collards, and melons. Cynthia couldn't bear to let go of her old, turreted apartment, so she renewed the lease and let her brother Jeffrey, back from the Peace Corps and other adventures, take up residence there.

Jeffrey christened Cynthia and David's new home "Campeloupe," a name he coined from "Camelot" and "cantaloupe." Campeloupe *did* have the feel of a kingdom set apart. The television received no signal from the outside world and was used for videos alone. Nora had never eaten fast food or even been inside a McDonald's. The family usually had the maximum number of books—fifty—checked out from the public library. And they shared an unusual verbal playfulness: Cynthia called David only by his Italian last name, Nora called her parents "Mom-o" and "Dad-o," and ever since Nora had misheard the word "heartthrob" in preschool, they had all called Cynthia's red, rusty Tercel—whose dashboard was piled with dried wildflowers, birds' nests, stones, and shells—"Heartfrog." On Campeloupe's answering machine, David's deadpan voice required callers to *sing* their messages. The best messages were always left by Cynthia or David for each other—Cynthia asking what she should bring home for supper in Gregorian chant or David asking who was picking up Nora in improvised Bob Dylan–esque rhymes. Nora loved the way her parents mimicked different voices as they read books or told her stories, so she liked to make her own young voice go deep and mysterious as she described Campeloupe as "a place of intrigue, danger, and large orange melons."

4

Arrest

As Cynthia, David, and Nora headed to West Virginia for the annual Stewart family Bash that August, all of Cynthia's siblings—from the yoga teacher to the NYU grad student to the owner of "Gonzo's Garage"—headed to The Farm, too. The animals were long gone, and the farmhouse had fallen into disrepair, but their father still lived there, baking his own bread and writing the occasional tirade to newspapers. When Cynthia told everyone about her recent brush with the law, her father joked, "We should all go get naked in the prosecutor's office. Or invite him to a Bash—that would loosen him up!" When someone else suggested they send the "Moon Shot" to the prosecutor, Cynthia bemoaned the fact that she couldn't take the group picture this year. But the girlfriend of one of her brothers piped up and volunteered to take the picture with her own camera. So everyone stood in front of the old homestead, turned their backs to the camera, and gleefully dropped their pants.

Back in Oberlin, school started, Cynthia settled into her routine of school bus driving, and Nora began third grade. Nora had been playing at her Gramma Gerry's house across town when the police had knocked on their door, so Cynthia and David had only later told her about the officers' visit, explaining that, with a lawyer's help, they were getting things straightened out. They also told her that a Children Services social worker might drop by sometime, at home or at school, to talk with her. Nora was a perceptive child and understood this was not business as usual. She quizzed her parents about when the police would come back and what the social worker might ask. Cynthia reminded Nora of what she had always told her: "The police are there to help." She assured Nora the same was true of social workers.

But the police did not reappear. No search of the house took place. Children Services did not rush in to ascertain whether a child was in danger, and no social worker dropped by school or their house to check on Nora.

On Monday, September 27, David finally called their lawyer to see if she had heard anything. No, Amy told him, no news. With more than a month gone by since they had submitted the affidavit, there was little chance now that anything else was going to happen: if anyone had real concerns about Nora, the police would have raided their house and Children Services would have been at their door long ago. Amy had a busy week ahead, but she promised David she would make some calls in the next few days and get this thing wrapped up.

Behind the wheel of her big yellow school bus, Cynthia was a familiar presence in Oberlin. Her long arm was always sticking out of the window to wave at someone she knew or someone she recognized from her daily route: shopkeepers sweeping their sidewalks, city trash collectors on their rounds, police in their cruisers. Out in the country, Cynthia never pulled away after dropping a child off until she had seen a parent come to the door and wave. An elderly farmer began waving at Cynthia after he had seen her stop her bus beside his field, turn on the flashers, get out, pick up a turtle, and carry it to safety in the roadside grass.

On Tuesday afternoon, September 28, just as Cynthia was grabbing her keys and rushing out for her after-school bus run, a sheriff's car pulled into the family's driveway and two deputies got out. One of them asked if she was Cynthia Stewart, and she said that she was. He informed her that he had a warrant for her arrest.

Cynthia was stunned. If a Children Services social worker had driven up, or if the police had arrived with a search warrant, she would have understood—they would be looking for more information. But how could they be arresting her? Based on what?

"You don't understand," she told the officer. "I'm a school bus driver. It's two o'clock. There's a bus waiting for me, and there are kids who need to get home."

The deputy assured her he understood. Nevertheless, he was arresting her now.

Upstairs, through his office window, David saw a patrol car in the driveway. He rushed downstairs and found a deputy watching Cynthia call her supervisor to report her absence. The other deputy explained to David how he could bail Cynthia out of jail.

As the officers escorted Cynthia to the door, one apologized, "If we don't handcuff you, we lose three days' pay." As a courtesy, though, he waited until she was inside the cruiser to snap her wrists into the stainless steel cuffs.

Riding to the county jail, Cynthia felt more angry than frightened. At the jail, the deputies took her into a holding room and left her standing alone for an hour, watched by a uniformed man behind glass. Cynthia had never been inside a jail before. She thought, *Well, this certainly is an interesting sociological experiment.*

Buzzed later into a larger room, she sat down next to a woman named Sherry who had been arrested for "menacing" but who insisted to Cynthia that she had only been protecting her child from a bully. Listening to her story, Cynthia became indignant on her behalf. Sherry didn't have money to buy a toothbrush from the jail store, and she wasn't going to be provided with fresh underwear with her prison jumpsuit. Cynthia thought everyone was supposed to be presumed innocent and that the jail should at least supply toiletries to those who didn't have the money or connections to get bailed out.

When Cynthia was called into the booking room, she eyed the height measurements marked on the wall and felt her photographer's interest stirred. Mug shots always made their subjects look grim and guilty. Would it be possible, she wondered, to take a *pleasing* mug shot? But when an officer shoved a black slate with a booking number into her hands and ordered her to hold the slate against her chest, Cynthia frowned, and the camera clicked.

David had called a friend to pick up Nora from school; then he had called Amy. Amy was infuriated by the arrest. The prosecutor had obtained a secret rather than a public indictment, which meant he had indicted Cynthia without discussing his concerns with Amy or informing her of the actions he was taking against her client. "A secret indictment is ridiculous!" Amy fumed to David, explaining that secret indictments were used when there was a flight risk for the suspect or a potential of more harm to the victim. "If Cynthia were a flight risk, she would have skipped town weeks ago! And if the prosecutor's so worried about Nora, why the *hell* has he left her unprotected at home for two months?"

Cynthia's bail was set at $10,000, so David could either come up with $10,000 in cash or he could put a $20,000 lien on their house. David went to the county recorder's office to request documentation of their property deed, to the sheriff's office to trade the lien for Cynthia, then on to the jail to await Cynthia's release. At every stop, David was struck by the quiet chasm between his own rising panic and the polite but disengaged efficiency of clerks for whom people getting locked up and people getting sprung was all in a day's work.

In the late afternoon, Cynthia walked out of jail feeling not panicked but lucky. Unlike her cell mate, she had a partner to bail her out, a house to put up for bail money, and a lawyer she trusted. Cynthia believed the worst was over for her. But she could certainly see how someone like Sherry might get steamrolled by the system.

Over supper, Cynthia told Nora what had happened in the jail. Nora got the impression that she didn't need to worry about her mother but that she should feel sorry for the woman in jail her mother was going to send $20 to the next day. Nora did notice, though, how quiet and upset her father looked.

After supper, as her parents talked on the phone in serious voices, Nora retreated to her bedroom with a box of markers and some blank paper. At bedtime, she presented her mother with a stack of drawings. One showed a smiling, long-haired Cynthia driving her school bus filled with stick children. Above the bus Nora had written, "You're the best bus driver there is!" Another drawing showed three flowers: two were small and featureless, while one was tall with bountiful petals and a smiling face. The caption read: "Mom you are 1 in a 1,000,000!!" In another, a policeman frowned as a forceful arm and fist came straight toward him, with its middle finger, decorated with a fancy ring, rising emphatically out of the fist. The last drawing showed a mother, father, and little girl surrounded by hearts and, across the page, a glaring policeman with a nightstick. Between them Nora had placed the barrier of a large X.

The night of her arrest, Cynthia called the superintendent of the Oberlin schools. He said he would consult with the schools' lawyer about whether her arrest would affect her job. In the meantime, he didn't see why she should be "presumed guilty until proven innocent."

The next morning, though, he called back with mixed news. The schools' lawyer had advised him to fire her. The superintendent assured Cynthia he would *not* fire her; however, he did understand that the school district could not have a person arrested for child pornography driving children around. He was sorry, but he would have to put her on unpaid leave—effective immediately.

That afternoon, Cynthia and David met with Amy. Cynthia asked how she could have been indicted when there had been no police investigation and no evaluation of their family by Children Services. Amy found the arrest very troubling, too. But, she explained, the law gave prosecutors enormous latitude in choosing when and whom and how to prosecute. That power—called "prosecutorial discretion"—was crucial to the functioning of the legal system because it allowed prosecutors, free from the oversight and influence of powerful people, to decide which evidence warranted criminal prosecution and which did not. Some prosecutors used that discretion wisely. Others exploited the lack of oversight by prosecuting too quickly or for the wrong reasons—to gain flashy headlines, votes, or political favor. Amy couldn't say why the county prosecutor had leapt into this prosecution. But if Cynthia's photographs were indeed as she had described them, then concern for Nora did *not* seem to be the motive.

Cynthia's indictment had been issued by a Lorain County grand jury. The words "grand jury" alarmed Cynthia. Amy agreed the situation was serious; a criminal indictment always was. But the fact that a grand jury had indicted Cynthia was probably a sign of division in the prosecutor's office, she thought. If there had been a disagreement among the assistant prosecutors about the legality of her pictures, then the prosecutor might have turned to the grand jury for a judgment instead of issuing an indictment himself. But in deciding whether or not there was probable cause for a person to be charged with a crime, a grand jury always made its decision based solely on the arguments of the prosecutor, the evidence the prosecutor offered, and the testimony of the prosecutor's witnesses. No evidence of innocence was offered, no judge was present, and the prosecutor did not have to clarify the law.

"Right," David smiled grimly. "That's why lawyers like to wisecrack, 'A good prosecutor could persuade a grand jury to indict a ham sandwich.'"

5

Suspicions

The evening after Cynthia's arrest, every child aged five to thirteen in the city soccer league gathered to have team pictures taken on the community playing fields. Scores of children in red and blue uniforms were running and kicking soccer balls while their parents chatted in the Indian summer evening.

My son, Jesse, was eight years old, and he and Nora were on the same soccer team. They had been classmates since preschool, they played together at recess, they went to each other's birthday parties, they took violin lessons from the same teacher. Jesse also rode Cynthia's school bus, and that morning he had tearfully refused to get on her bus when someone else had been in the driver's seat. When I ran into Cynthia on the soccer field that evening, I told her that Jesse hoped she'd be back on her bus the next day—and I did, too, so I wouldn't have to drive him to school again.

Her grave response alarmed me. She said she had something important to tell me, something she wanted the parents of Nora's friends to hear directly from her.

Was she seriously ill, I wondered? My mind raced so quickly in that direction that when she quietly explained that she had just been arrested for child pornography, I laughed with relief. What could be more absurd than mistaking Cynthia Stewart for a child pornographer?

But Cynthia did not smile. "You're kidding, right?" I asked. Cynthia assured me she was not kidding and described briefly what had happened.

"Oh, they'll investigate you, realize it's a big mistake, and drop the charges," I said breezily. I was not a close friend of Cynthia's, but I had observed her as a mother for more than eight years, and everything about her had always seemed loving and well-intentioned. And like everyone else in town, I knew Cynthia as a photographer. She always had double prints made from her rolls, and, as fiercely protective as she was of her originals, she was generous with her duplicates. She spent hours divvying up prints to share with whoever else was in the frame, and she was only half-joking when she told friends her greatest ambition was to have her pictures plastered on their refrigerators. My own refrigerator was decorated with pictures of my son playing goalie and playing his violin and performing as a wizard in a school play—all pictures Cynthia had taken and passed along to me.

But when I asked Cynthia to describe the pictures in question, she said her lawyer had instructed her not to talk about the photos, even to friends. Her lawyer's strict warning unnerved me. I noticed myself beginning to watch Cynthia, wondering if she did, indeed, have something to hide. Had she exercised terrible judgment, done something too shameful to discuss? It was impossible for me to imagine she had done something *intentionally* to exploit Nora. But what if, I wondered, despite good intentions, Cynthia's judgment had been truly impaired? What if she had not observed what I would consider the minimum proper boundary between parent and child? Cynthia was explaining something about the law, that the photographs had to be "lewd and graphic" for her to be convicted. Had she gone off some feminist deep end and taken Georgia O'Keeffe-like, orchid-inspired close-ups of Nora's genitals in some misguided celebration of femaleness? That was the worst thing I could imagine Cynthia doing, but that, I thought with a shudder, would be pretty bad.

"Well, I'm sure it will all work out," I said, this time with less conviction—and with a sudden recognition that I had no idea what I was talking about. I had had zero experience with the legal or criminal system and knew absolutely nothing about the county prosecutor, not even his name.

~~~

Twelve weeks had passed from the day Cynthia had dropped off her roll of film at Drug Mart to the day of her arrest. Except for the anxious week when she and David had been preparing a response to the police, all had been quiet from the perspective of Campeloupe. But that quiet had been misleading.

On July 7, the Police Department of Mansfield, Ohio, had received, from nearby Fujicolor Processing Inc., a roll of film that, according to the police report, "appear[ed] pornographic in nature." The suspect was listed as "Stewart." The police report classified the offense as "Child Pornography" and noted that the photos had been turned over to Mansfield detective R. Burks.

Mansfield was about an hour's drive south of Oberlin. Once the booming manufacturing center of an agricultural county, Mansfield now encouraged visitors who were "looking for a place with genuine American flavor" to look no further. Visitors could "wander down our all-American Main Street and stop for a piece of homemade pie" or hike along Johnny Appleseed's old trails. The small town had several things to boast about: for twenty-five years, Mansfield had hosted the Miss Ohio Pageant; its magnificent, abandoned reformatory had served as the film set for *The Shawshank Redemption*; and a local church housed Ohio's only wax museum with life-size figures, the Living Bible Museum, whose snack bar served Samson Burgers, Jonah's Tuna Sandwich, Eve's Fruit Salad ("in season—apples not included"), and Manna Fries.

Located on one end of Mansfield's Main Street, Fujicolor Processing Inc. employed more than one hundred workers at its film processing plant and another fifty drivers who picked up rolls and delivered prints to retailers throughout the area—including the Oberlin Drug Mart. Cynthia's roll of film had traveled by truck from Oberlin to Mansfield, where her prints had been flagged as suspicious by a worker at the Main Street lab.

On July 22, the Oberlin police received a phone call from Mansfield's Detective Burks informing them of the photographs, which he said he would Fed Ex to Oberlin that day. A report filed by Detective Anadiotis indicated that the package arrived on July 23 and that it:

> contained nineteen double print photographs of a young white female juvenile around the age of eight standing or laying [sic] in a bathtub in a state of nudity. Two of the photographs depict the juvenile having sexual contact with the pubic region and right side of her buttock with a running shower head. Two other pictures show the juvenile laying [sic] nude on her back in an empty bathtub with her pubic region in view. The remaining photographs show the juvenile in a state of nudity in various poses inside the bathtub.
>
> Enclosed with these pictures were eighteen double print photographs of unknown subjects including the unidentified juvenile female in normal settings. . . .
>
> The photographs have been retained as evidence. This investigation will continue.

Anadiotis showed the pictures to the lawyer-sociologist who taught at Oberlin College and moonlighted as the town's prosecutor. He told the detective that the photographs were not illegal and he would not prosecute. That's when Anadiotis took the photographs to Greg White.

Greg White had served as the Lorain County prosecutor for almost twenty years. A former Marine who had fought in Vietnam, White was a Republican in a Democratic county. As a young lawyer, he had first been elected prosecutor in 1980, when the local Democrats had been divided and mired in scandal. White burnished his image as the shiny new sheriff in town by zealously prosecuting both street and white-collar crime. Voters loved White's message that there was no double standard in Lorain County. Over time, admirers saw White as a "straight arrow" who backed up the police, cracked down on criminals, and was morally impeccable and politically adept. But critics accused him of being inflexible and overzealous, with a tendency to prosecute political opponents more readily than political friends. Defense lawyers complained that White over-indicted and, as one attorney put it, "He used a bazooka when a fly swatter would have been just as effective."

One difference between White and many other county prosecutors was that White refused to initiate a diversion program in Lorain County. Diversion programs gave first-time, nonviolent offenders a way to avoid trial and incarceration by pleading guilty and agreeing outright to the conditions of probation. After a successful probation period, their criminal indictments were often expunged, and, thus, first-time offenders were given another chance at a clean record and a law-abiding life. But White had never shown an interest in diversion programs or any other alternative method of handling a criminal case. His standard policy was: "We'll do our talking in the courtroom."

For almost a dozen years, Greg White's handpicked chief assistant prosecutor had been Jonathan Rosenbaum. Rosenbaum's reputation for ferocity far exceeded White's. Many in law enforcement appreciated Rosenbaum's caustic, uncompromising approach, but defense lawyers dreaded encounters with him in the courtroom, where he could be rude, vicious, and spectacularly effective. One colleague described Rosenbaum as "one of those people who was born to be a prosecutor—he just enjoys prosecuting people. Jon assumes everyone is *evil* until proven innocent."

Some people who admired White were baffled by his attachment to Rosenbaum, a man who seemed driven to get convictions at all costs. Others thought their relationship was the classic good cop/bad cop arrangement: White got to stay politically clean and above the fray, while Rosenbaum racked up the large number of convictions that enhanced White's reputation for being tough on crime.

Greg White had taken Cynthia's photographs to a county grand jury; the grand jury had indicted her on two second-degree felony charges, each of which carried a maximum penalty of eight years in prison. The first law—"illegal use of minor in nudity-oriented material or performance"—forbade the photographing of a minor child "in a state of nudity," except for "a bona fide artistic, medical, scientific, educational, religious, governmental, judicial, or other proper purpose." The second law—"pandering sexually oriented matter involving a minor"—stated that no person shall "create, record, photograph, film, develop, reproduce, or publish any material that shows a minor participating or engaging in sexual activity, masturbation, or bestiality."

What was not acknowledged in Cynthia's indictments, or even in the Ohio Revised Code itself, was that ten years earlier the "illegal use of minor in nudity-oriented material" law had been constitutionally challenged in a child-pornography case, *Osborne v. Ohio*, and that case had gone all the way to the U.S. Supreme Court. The Supreme Court had significantly narrowed the law's scope and had ruled that mere nudity was not enough to make a photograph of a child illegal.

In the late 1980s, an Ohio man, Clyde Osborne, was convicted of possessing four photographs of a nude male adolescent, including one in which the boy had an erection and one in which he was "lying down with a plastic object which appears to be inserted in his anus." After his conviction, Osborne's counsel appealed, arguing that the statute prohibiting the possession of nude photographs of minors was "unconstitutionally overbroad." The Ohio Supreme Court upheld Osborne's conviction, but they also narrowed the law's application to depictions of nudity, like those in Osborne's pictures, "where such nudity constitutes a lewd exhibition or involves a graphic focus on the genitals." The court also found that *scienter*—a deliberate, willful knowledge of one's wrongdoing—was an essential element of this offense. They reasoned that the "proper purposes" exceptions had been included in the law to allow the possession and viewing of nude photographs of minors "where that conduct is morally innocent."

In 1990, the U.S. Supreme Court agreed with the Ohio Supreme Court's reasoning. The majority opinion, written by Justice Byron White, made clear that the purpose of the Ohio law was to protect actual children from actual abuse and "to destroy a market for the exploitative use of children." Justice White wrote that criminalizing the mere possession of a lewd photograph of a child was permissible because it would disrupt the child-pornography market that had been driven, by this time, largely underground. But he affirmed that by limiting the statute's reach, the Ohio Supreme Court had correctly "avoided penalizing persons for viewing or possessing innocuous photographs of naked children."

Three U.S. Supreme Court justices dissented from the majority opinion in *Osborne v. Ohio*. In his dissent, Justice William Brennan argued that the state law, even as constrained by the Ohio Supreme Court, was still "fatally overbroad," and he predicted future problems with judging photographs by the new "lewd exhibition" and "graphic focus on the genitals" standards. This law, he argued, could end up criminalizing "toddlers romping unclothed" or even a "well known commercial advertisement for a suntan lotion [that] shows a dog pulling down the bottom half of a young girl's bikini, revealing a stark contrast between her suntanned back and pale buttocks." Justice Brennan wondered from whose perspective lewdness would be determined: "A 'reasonable' person's . . . ? A reasonable pedophile's? An 'average' person applying contemporary local community standards? Statewide standards?" He predicted that the vagueness of "lewd exhibition" could provide an avenue for "policemen, prosecutors, and juries to pursue their personal predilections." And "graphic focus" presented similar problems. Michelangelo's *David* might be said to have a graphic focus on the genitals, and, Justice Brennan presciently noted, even "a photograph of a child running naked on the beach or playing in the bathtub might run afoul of the law, depending on the focus and camera angle."

Grand juries are conducted in secret for a variety of good reasons: to prevent the flight of the guilty, to protect the privacy of the innocent, and to shield witnesses and grand jurors from outside pressure during investigations. Because their deliberations are secret, the transcripts of grand jury proceedings are sealed and not available to defense attorneys to scrutinize for errors or misleading statements made by the prosecutor. Thus, Amy did not know if the prosecutor had apprised the Lorain County grand jurors of the Ohio and the U.S. Supreme Courts' limitations on the Ohio law. She also did not know how many of Cynthia's photographs he had shown to the grand jury, but she assumed he had shown them only a few, with no indication of who had taken those pictures or when, where, or why they had been taken.

At her arraignment the day after her arrest, Cynthia pleaded innocent to both charges. Afterward, by a literal luck of the draw—all the judges' names were printed on cards, randomly stacked in a deck, drawn one at a time, and matched with upcoming cases—Judge Edward Zaleski was assigned to preside over her case. In Amy's opinion, that was indeed lucky because Judge Zaleski showed the most independence from the prosecutor's office. Many of the other judges and magistrates in the system had once served as assistant prosecutors in Greg White's office, and Amy believed that experience had shaped their outlook and now influenced their decisions. Zaleski, on the other hand, had never worked for Greg White.

But Amy did not assume Zaleski would be a pushover for the defense, either. Zaleski was Catholic, with a reputation for being especially sensitive to the plight of children. Amy had known him to leave his bench to cry in his chambers during a particularly horrific child abuse case. Not yet having seen the pictures herself, she had no way of guessing how Zaleski might react to them.

That night, Cynthia scribbled down the first of her soon-to-be innumerable lists: "QUESTIONS FOR AMY: At what point do I get to explain to the Judge what the shots actually are? At what point do we find out what they think the pictures are? . . . "

The next evening, Cynthia and Nora pulled into Campeloupe's driveway at dusk and noticed a small, dark lump in the road. Nora popped out of the car and realized that the lump in the road was her youngest cat Sammie. She sobbed inconsolably for hours.

The next day, the family performed the bittersweet ritual they had evolved for burying pets: they placed the cat's body in a backyard grave, sprinkled it with flowers, held hands and sang an old-time ballad, talked about the happy life Sammie had led, filled the grave, and planted a small tree on top. Sammie had been a fuzzy gray cat, so they had chosen a cottonwood—a volunteer sapling David had found growing close to the house.

Usually, Cynthia and David held to the view that you should get used to one cat being dead before getting another, but it was obvious this time that Nora was coping with more than a cat's death. A friend's cat had just had a litter, and Cynthia and David decided to bend their rules.

On the drive over to choose her new pet, Nora told her parents exactly what she was looking for: a kitty with gray and brown stripes, a white chest, and white paws. Among the kittens they found huddled in a box in their friend's kitchen, one perfectly fit Nora's description. Plus, she was the only kitten with her eyes open, and she was peering outside the box. "It's Jennie!" Nora squealed, claiming the kitten at once and naming her for the heroine of a children's book she loved.

In that book, *The Abandoned*, the main character becomes separated from his family. Alone and frightened in a world he's not prepared for, he's befriended by Jennie, a streetwise tabby, who saves him by teaching him how to think and act like a cat. It would be six long weeks before Nora could bring her own Jennie home to Campeloupe, but Cynthia promised they would visit the kitten every day.

6

Newsworthy

A couple of days after Cynthia's arrest, Amy called the prosecutor's office and told Rob Corts, the assistant prosecutor who had been assigned to the case, that she needed to see the pictures for which her client had been indicted. Having Corts assigned to the case was another lucky break, Amy thought. She saw him as the most laid-back of the assistant prosecutors. Even when they disagreed on issues, she found him collegial and respectful. Corts told Amy to come on over to his office. When she walked in, he handed her a small stack of color snapshots and said, "Aren't these weird?"

Flipping through the prints, Amy was relieved: the pictures were exactly as Cynthia had described them. A child lifting up out of soapy water. A child in the tub with the water drained out. A child rinsing off. No close-ups. No surprises.

Amy just said, "Rob, I need copies." Corts walked over to a Xerox machine, placed the prints four at a time on the glass, shrunk the copies down to half-size, and printed them in black-and-white.

On October 2, Elyria's newspaper the *Chronicle-Telegram* carried a small news item about Cynthia's arrest, without using her name. On October 5, the weekly *Oberlin News-Tribune* ran a front page story lumping Cynthia's arrest with the arrest of an Oberlin mother and father who had allegedly starved and beaten their five-year-old son. The headline read:

Bus Driver, Parents Charged with Abuse
School Employee Taken off Job

Cynthia's name was not used in the article "in order to protect her daughter, who is considered a sex abuse victim." But with only a handful of school bus drivers in Oberlin, it was easy for readers to figure out who she was.

On October 6, Cleveland's *Plain Dealer* reported the arrest, with a provocative description of the photographs: "A police report said two recent photos showed the child with a shower head near her genitals, and two others showed her genitals clearly." In the article, Amy defended her client: "I truly believe that she has been wrongfully charged. Prosecutors have to prove that the pictures are lewd, and that's not easy." Detective Anadiotis spoke for the police: "We consider these pictures to be obscene and pornographic." And Cynthia made a cameo appearance:

> The woman was holding a camera when she answered the door at her home yesterday afternoon. She said she was preparing to photograph her daughter, who was outdoors and clothed. The woman would not discuss the case.
>
> "I'm innocent of these charges, and we're going to fight these charges," she said.

Cleveland television stations quickly picked up the story. Unlike the newspapers, they used Cynthia's name and featured her full-screen mug shot: a photograph—with blank eyes and a sneering mouth—that made her look like a thug. A reporter from Cleveland's Fox News stood in the school bus parking lot and questioned Cynthia's fitness to be around children, solicited confirmation from the school superintendent that Cynthia had been suspended, and, arriving unannounced at Campeloupe, tried to question David through the half-opened front door. David repeated that Cynthia was innocent, but on camera he looked guarded and tense.

People who knew Cynthia and David were appalled at the coverage, and many called or wrote to tell them so. The farmer who had been waving at Cynthia ever since he saw her save the turtle even wrote a gentlemanly protest to the Channel 8 program manager:

"Could there be a desire for sensationalism at work here, because the truth has yet to be established?"

On October 10, Cynthia's case was the lead story on the front page of the fat Sunday edition of the *Plain Dealer*. The article quoted psychologists, child advocates, ordinary parents, and the case's adversaries:

> When Lorain County Prosecutor Gregory White saw the pictures of an 8-year-old girl in a bathtub, he knew what he thought. They were obscene.
>
> White, in deciding whether to prosecute such cases, said he considered the age of the child, the sequence of pictures, the type of poses and what was being done to the child. He said the Oberlin photos did not fall into a gray area.
>
> "They are well over the line. They are not anywhere near the category of normal," White said.
>
> [Amy] Wirtz saw the photos last week, and she said . . . "I'm more convinced than ever that there was no crime here."

When reporters had called Amy that week, her first impulse had been to clam up. During her work as a public defender, she had been taught by her superiors that the press was her enemy. The only statement she had ever been allowed to give reporters was, "My client has pled not guilty, and I will fight this case to the best of my ability to prove my client's innocence." Thus, when Amy picked up the *Plain Dealer* from her driveway that Sunday morning and found herself on the front page, she moaned, "Holy shit!" But as she read on, she calmed down and began to wonder whether this time the press might actually be a help, and raise as many questions in the public's mind about the prosecutor as about her client.

Amy heard through the courthouse grapevine that a controversy was brewing in the prosecutor's office. And indeed, within a few days of Cynthia's arrest, Rob Corts had been removed as prosecutor for the case, and Jonathan Rosenbaum, the chief assistant prosecutor, had taken over.

Amy's personal chemistry with Rosenbaum was dreadful. The first time they had met, they had ended up screaming at each other so loudly in the rotunda of the courthouse that bailiffs had to break them up. Amy now believed Rosenbaum had taken over Cynthia's prosecution because it had become high profile, and, as head of the criminal division, Rosenbaum handled the high-profile cases. But she also guessed he had stepped in to pursue the case more aggressively than Rob Corts would have done.

Amy filed a request for a Bill of Particulars, a document in which the prosecutor has to explain in more detail the reasons for the indictment. The Bill of Particulars that came back from the prosecutor's office was succinct, but it contained one new specific: it alleged that Cynthia's photographs—presumably the two with the shower sprayer near Nora's pubic area and buttocks—"showed a minor participating in or attempting to participate in, or simulating masturbation." Cynthia was shocked by the allegation, but it confirmed Amy's suspicion that Rosenbaum had come onto the case to play hardball.

Amy now realized that the black-and-white, size-reduced photocopies Rob Corts had given her of Cynthia's pictures would be insufficient for the preparation of her defense. For one thing, Corts had given her photocopies of only nineteen pictures—the ones shot in the bathroom. Almost half of the roll had been shot in other locations and contained no nudity. Viewed in the proper context of the whole roll, Amy thought, Cynthia's bathroom pictures would appear more normal. Potential expert witnesses were also indicating to Amy that they needed exact color duplicates in order to make credible assessments of the images.

Since the prosecutor's office had in their possession both sets of Cynthia's double prints, Amy asked Rosenbaum informally if she could have the extra set. Rosenbaum bluntly told her no: he would not give her the prints because if he gave them to her she would *show* them to people, and then he would have to indict her for pandering.

Amy was frightened by Rosenbaum's threat. She knew he had

no legal grounds on which to deny her access to the only evidence against her client. But she also knew that, even if he brought a worthless charge against her that the judge would summarily dismiss, any charge of pandering would generate enough headlines to seriously damage her reputation and career.

Amy called a mentor in a distant county for advice. He gathered a group of attorneys in his community to talk through her situation. They urged Amy to resign from the case since threats from a prosecutor—veiled or overt—would likely inhibit her ability to represent Cynthia and David vigorously. They were concerned that if the case did not turn out in her clients' best interest, then those clients could file a grievance against Amy for not zealously representing them due to her own anxiety about being prosecuted herself.

Amy saw the attorneys' point, but the more she thought about Rosenbaum's threat, the angrier she became. She complained to her mentor, "What a brilliant way to scare the *crap* out of the local defense bar!" She decided to keep the case.

Eager to tell her own story, Cynthia began drafting the testimony she planned to give in court. Amy warned that it would be unwise to describe the rinsing game in detail or to use the words "yoni" and "rosebud." Cynthia agreed to use more conventional language, but she didn't see how the photographs could be understood without describing the bath-time ritual. Her last working draft concluded with a list of other family traditions and private expressions, which she planned to describe to the judge and jury: "*nigh nigh nigh tucka roo roo roo*; after-violin hug; *lulla purr* in car on long trips; pulling courage from ancestors; wake-up panda; flounder of doom."

On the last page of her testimony, she wrote: "P.S. The first thing I looked for when these pictures were shown to me was whether or not we had cleaned the mildew off the bathroom wall yet (as you can see, we hadn't). I'm not at all embarrassed by the pictures of Nora; I'm embarrassed by the mildew."

In mid-October, a Cleveland PBS affiliate talk show host devoted a segment of his weekly roundtable to news of the Oberlin mother arrested for child pornography. His guest commentators were a county commissioner from Cleveland, an editor for the *Plain Dealer*, and a community organizer. The host asked his panelists, in regard to the photography of children, "Do we have the common sense to draw the line between cute and obscene?"

The community organizer worried that "we have common sense, but we don't use it."

The commissioner's concern was the intent of the photographer: "Was she going to put them on the Internet? Was she intending to make money off of her daughter? Most people believe the pornography laws relate to what is being *done* with the photographs. Where does the *crime* occur? Now, I don't have any reason to believe the prosecutor is out to make political mileage, but that's always the fear when the prosecuting arm of the government gets involved this closely in the life of a family."

The editor stepped in quickly: "I *want* Big Brother keeping an eye on the kids. If that was a mother who was having her eight-year-old walk down the street without clothes on, you'd *want* Social Services to get over there." She felt the legal system could be trusted to do the right thing: "We have a prosecutor—a tough guy, but I think a man of integrity—and he makes his call. And then, thank goodness we have a jury system, and they can make their call. It's a little nerve-racking that your family pictures could have you before a jury, but, on the other hand, how nerve-racking was it for the eight-year-old having pictures of herself in the shower?"

The host worried that he himself could be hauled into court for a favorite photograph of his two-year-old twins in the bathtub. But the editor made a distinction between photographs of two-year-olds and photographs of eight-year-olds. "That's where common sense comes in," she insisted.

"So you're in favor of the system of these photomats flagging these things down, turning them over to the law—even if there's nothing else on the record of the mother who shot the pictures?" the host asked.

"Yes," the editor said emphatically. "Spend five minutes on the Internet, and I think you'll agree."

Cynthia had spent almost no time on the Internet. She was not interested in learning how to use a computer or how to navigate the World Wide Web. She hadn't watched television since her childhood, when her father had allowed the family a total of three shared viewing hours per week. As an adult, Cynthia had gotten her news from the *New York Times* and *The Nation*. But since Nora's birth, she had been happily tuning out the newsworthy world.

And that detachment from the world outside her domestic cocoon, Amy believed, had magnified Cynthia's natural tendency to believe the best about everybody. Amy considered Cynthia equally naive about the legal and the criminal worlds: she assumed everyone in the legal system was devoted to discovering the truth, just as she had assumed her fellow arrestee was as innocent as she was.

Amy knew that the worldviews of police, prosecutors, defense attorneys, and social workers were usually skewed in the opposite direction. Jonathan Rosenbaum was her prime example. As a longtime prosecutor, Rosenbaum had routinely dealt with people who had done terrible things to other people, and as a result, she believed he had lost his ability to see innocence. He could see Cynthia's pictures only through the eyes of the perverts he prosecuted.

And that explained, she thought, why the prosecutors had added the provocative second charge of "photographing a child in a sexual performance." That charge required a great deal of interpretation of the photographs, if not a huge leap of the imagination. But perhaps it helped Rosenbaum and White to believe a wicked mother had posed her daughter masturbating in order to sell pictures to sickos? Otherwise, they would be prosecuting an innocent woman. And how, Amy wondered, would they be able to go to sleep at night knowing that?

7

Everything on Their Side

Oberlin is unlike any other community in Lorain County. Its college is one of the best in the nation, with a superb art museum and a world-class conservatory. The town and college wear their progressive history and liberal politics on their sleeves. The town's racially diverse population (a legacy of its abolitionist days) votes ten-to-one Democratic. Its most prominent church welcomes and affirms lesbians and gays. The college attracts intellectually engaged students who, according to *The Fiske Guide to Colleges*, are "more likely to discuss local poverty than the quality of cereal choices in the dining halls." For a number of years, the cover of the slick promotional brochure sent from the college's admissions office to prospective students showed a photograph of Earth against the black background of space. Hovering above the blue, cloud-swaddled planet were the words: "Think one person can change the world? So do we."

The rest of Lorain County is, in varying degrees, more conservative than Oberlin. The city of Lorain, fifteen miles north on the Lake Erie coast, boasts one of the highest per capita populations of Puerto Ricans outside Puerto Rico. Lorain's working-class communities have been hard-hit as the steel, automobile, and shipping industries have laid off workers and closed plants. Elyria, the county seat, is home to a hodgepodge of lawyers, county government employees, and factory workers. The northeastern part of the county is wealthy, white, and populated with professionals who commute over the county line into Cleveland. Also very white but less wealthy, the southern part of the county consists of small towns surrounded by orchards, dairies, and family farms where corn, wheat, and soybeans are grown.

Some people in Lorain County appreciate Oberlin as an oasis for art, music, opera, theater, and ideas. Others dismiss the place as a Midwestern Sodom and Gomorrah.

In 1999, most people in Oberlin who knew Cynthia were shocked by her arrest. Most of us were also uneasy and bewildered about if and how to help. When a friend and I first talked in my backyard about the prosecution, I noticed how our voices dropped, even though no one was around but our sons kicking a soccer ball in the distance. Imagining Cynthia exploiting Nora not only went against our instincts, but against everything we knew about her. Once the accusation had been made, though, once the prosecutor had claimed her pictures depicted a child masturbating, our imaginations couldn't help but go to work, imagining the worst. And so we vacillated between outrage toward a prosecutor we did not know and wariness toward a mother we had always admired. We also wondered what pictures of our own might have landed *us* in jail. And we wondered if Cynthia had, indeed, gone too far, gone over some line we ourselves would never cross. We felt disloyal to Cynthia for thinking such thoughts and resentful toward the prosecutor for putting repellent images in our minds. We swung between feeling too eager to believe the best and too able to believe the worst.

We also realized that we had no idea how a prosecution worked. Our experiences with police, lawyers, and courts had been confined to paying parking tickets, drawing up wills, and watching *Perry Mason* on television as children. We had no idea how to help Cynthia, even if we wanted to.

I brooded for several days about what I should do. I felt responsible to help a fellow parent who, most probably, had been wrongly accused. But mostly I felt responsible to my son. Nora and Jesse were good friends. What lesson would I be teaching him if I did not try to help his good friend's mom?

Not that I was looking for a cause to pour my time into. I was working two part-time jobs: teaching writing at a university an hour's commute away and working as poet-in-residence at the K-2 school across the street. My husband was recuperating from serious surgery and teaching physics and astronomy at Oberlin College. Our children, in third and seventh grades, had their own busy schedules with piano, violin, and art lessons, choir rehearsals, and soccer games. My life was already overly full. And because I had not seen the pictures, I felt reluctant to proclaim Cynthia's innocence too loudly.

A week or so after the arrest, I was sitting at the lunch table in the teachers' lounge at the elementary school. The teachers were concerned about what might happen to Nora. One teacher was married to a political science professor, and he had suggested that someone start a legal defense fund for Cynthia since high legal fees plus the loss of a job could bankrupt a family.

By the end of lunch, I had pledged to start the legal defense fund, and every teacher in the room had promised to write a check. It might have looked to those teachers as if I were taking initiative spontaneously and generously. But my actual motive was more calculated: I wanted to grab a good job when I could get it. If I could collect and deposit checks for Cynthia and David's family, then I would feel exempt from having to put myself on the line in any other way. I could collect money, while others took more public stands, if necessary.

I phoned Cynthia to tell her of the defense fund idea, and she was grateful. She and David were just about to write a $10,000 check to Amy—the flat fee Amy was charging for handling the criminal case—and that check would almost wipe out their savings. "All we had was $13,000 saved up to fix our wet basement," Cynthia told me, "and when that's gone, I don't know what we'll do."

Cynthia suggested our mutual friend Rebecca Cross as co-chair of the fund. Rebecca was the mother of two children, an English teacher at the middle school, and a fabric artist. Her daughter was a year younger than Nora, and when the girls had been preschoolers, Rebecca and Cynthia had often put them on the backs of their bikes and cycled out to orchards to pick apples and berries. Rebecca had been calling Cynthia almost daily since the arrest, asking what she could do to help.

The next day, Rebecca and I rented a P.O. box and opened an account for the Cynthia Stewart Legal Defense Fund at the local credit union. By the end of October, by word-of-mouth, we had collected more than $6,000, with donations as large as the check for $2,000 sent by Cynthia's college boyfriend (the young man on the cover of *Life*) and as small as the $25 a seven-year-old friend of Nora's had withdrawn from his savings account. Financial help also came to the family in the form of interim employment for Cynthia. A young Oberlin graduate who had recently opened an organic food market in town offered Cynthia a job, and Cynthia began working at the store most weekdays, with flexible hours for lawyer dates.

Offers of other kinds of help for the family began to pour in, too. A professor wanted to be a character witness and promised to shave off his beard if that would make him more presentable. A lawyer offered to be on a $10 retainer in case the family needed an attorney specifically for Nora. A sculptor made the family a talisman of stone and strips of willow. Nora's violin teacher stopped charging for lessons. Cynthia's landlady at 82 stopped charging rent. A retiree at the upscale retirement community in town sent a newspaper published by the American Association for Nude Recreation: he wanted Cynthia's lawyer to see photographs of nude young people that were sent regularly through the U.S. mail. One photo showed a pubescent girl with her grandfather, both naked, at a lakeside outing.

Churchgoers began to bring Cynthia and David's family up for prayer. A school secretary told Cynthia they had prayed for her at the Catholic church. The Quakers were holding her in the light. A member of First Congregational Church—the church where Charles Finney preached and Mark Twain flopped—convened an interdenominational prayer group for the family.

Advice was pouring in from faraway friends, too, along with sympathy, money, and even wardrobe makeovers. Amy had told Cynthia that for court appearances she was going to need new clothes, and she was going to need to buy and wear a bra. Cynthia didn't have money for a new wardrobe, but she thought of someone who might be able to help. An old boyfriend of hers—the one who had given her his Nikon—had ended up marrying Eileen Fisher, a young, independent clothes designer who, at the time, was completely unknown. Eileen Fisher, of course, had gone on to become a huge success in the New York fashion world. Cynthia called the old boyfriend, who talked with Eileen, who went to her own closet, picked out clothes she hadn't worn in the past year, and shipped them to Campeloupe. She enclosed a note written on handmade paper with a wildflower pressed into it: "I'm thinking of you in this difficult time. . . . All the best. Love, Eileen."

At first Cynthia drafted personal notes to thank friends for their gifts and contributions. "Dear Rob," she wrote her college boyfriend, "Thank you for the money. We used it to keep the wolf from the door (which phrase has gained new meaning in our household)." Soon, though, Rebecca and I began keeping a database of contributors' names and addresses on my laptop so that, when the case was over, everyone could be thanked at once. Cynthia also kept lists of the help and gestures of support people were giving her each day. One evening she added, "Perrotta says: we accept prayers, postures, vibrations, poems, votes of confidence."

But not everyone in Oberlin was sending prayers, poems, and good vibes. No one in the community had seen the pictures, and almost no one had read the law or understood how it had been subsequently constrained by the Ohio and U.S. Supreme Courts. People who didn't know Cynthia tended to be judgmental and suspicious, and there were plenty of conversations in which even her supporters wondered if she had shown bad judgment and should have known better. Arguments turned on whether it was ever appropriate for a mother to take pictures of a naked eight-year-old. Yet even people who argued "Never!" almost always backed down when asked if Cynthia should spend sixteen years in jail.

Anxiety also permeated conversations about acceptable levels of nudity in the home. If it wasn't appropriate to take photographs of your naked children, was it appropriate to *see* them naked? Was there something intrinsically wrong with being in the bathroom with your bathing eight-year-old child? And, if not, why was it wrong to take pictures of something that was not wrong in and of itself?

Because my name was linked to the defense fund, people struck up conversations with me everywhere. A nurse told me that she didn't think twice about being naked in front of her teenage sons. A father wondered whether he and his family were breaking the law since everyone in their household walked to their bedrooms nude after taking their showers. One mother hadn't seen her children naked since they were in first grade—and they had *never* seen her naked. Several parents said bedroom and bathroom doors started closing when their children hit puberty. One mother explained that she read to her ten-year-old son as he took his bath each night, that her son felt free to walk into the bathroom if she were bathing, too, and that she found that all natural and healthy. Her husband, though, was uncomfortable with the relaxed arrangement. He had never seen his own mother naked, except when he had peeked in the bathroom window from outside the house when he was twelve—something he felt guilty about for years. Which is exactly my point, countered his wife.

All these local conversations were spilling over into a flood of advice for Cynthia and David, particularly in regard to their legal counsel. Many friends worried that Amy was too young and inexperienced to handle a potentially explosive and consequential case. Some wanted Cynthia and David to hire a seasoned Lorain County criminal law attorney who could face the county prosecutor as an equal. Others wanted them to find a prominent East Coast attorney whose specialty was civil liberties and who might even do the work *pro bono*. A psychologist who worked with sex offenders urged Cynthia to get a sex crimes lawyer ASAP. One friend told David bluntly: "You need a *monster* for a lawyer."

Cynthia, however, trusted Amy and felt that they had developed a good rapport. She rejected the idea of hiring a sex crimes lawyer since she knew she hadn't committed a sex crime. And she distrusted the effect that bringing in a high-powered East Coast lawyer might have on a Lorain County jury. Cynthia countered all arguments against Amy with a story about two of her friends who years before had been busted for marijuana while crossing the border from Mexico to Texas: the friend who hired a local Texas lawyer served six months; the friend whose father brought in a big-name lawyer from New York to bully the locals served three years.

But Amy herself was already feeling overwhelmed by the case. She had fifty active clients and only a tiny staff. Her personal life was stretched, too: she had a young son and a busy physician husband, and her mother was ill with cancer. She was driving a couple of hours each way to Toledo twice a week to spend time with her parents.

Amy decided she needed help, and she suggested to Cynthia and David the idea of adding Kreig Brusnahan as co-counsel. An attorney who knew his way around Lorain County politics, Kreig had been practicing law for twenty years and had handled several media-intensive cases. Although Kreig Brusnahan and Greg White were active in opposing political parties, Kreig seemed to have good rapport with the prosecutor—which, Amy acknowledged, as a woman and a younger attorney she did not.

At their first meeting in his spacious, well-appointed office, Kreig reminded Cynthia of a suave bulldog. He was gregarious and sturdy, with a flushed face and thick dark hair swept back from his forehead. He had seen the photocopies of Cynthia's pictures, and he believed the case against her was absurd. Cynthia liked how adamant Kreig was that she had committed no crime, that she should take no plea deal, and that he would fight for her complete exoneration.

Among Kreig's former clients was the family of Clayton Hartwig, the young sailor accused by the Navy of detonating a lethal explosion on the USS *Iowa* in the late 1980s. Kreig had led the successful effort to clear Hartwig's name. He was proud of "making the Navy apologize for basically calling Hartwig a mass murderer." Cynthia liked how Kreig didn't mince words. She had been opposed to hiring a male lawyer who was part of the good ol' boy network, but now she was inspired by Kreig's florid confidence.

More enthusiastic about hiring a second lawyer all along, David appreciated what Kreig's criminal law experience and professional standing in the county would add to Amy's knowledge of family law. He and Cynthia agreed to hire Kreig as Amy's co-counsel for the criminal case and wrote him a check for $5,000.

David liked Amy—he liked her commitment to their family, and he liked how, in spite of her conservative suits and prim pumps, she could curse like a sailor. He found it amusing and comforting when Amy blurted out things like, "The police are goddamn liars!" But David was skeptical that even Amy and Kreig working together would be able to defend Cynthia effectively.

His colleagues at The Nation were skeptical, too. Victor Navasky, The Nation's publisher, called his contacts at the American Civil Liberties Union, and soon afterward, the president of the national ACLU called the executive director of the Ohio ACLU and encouraged her to file a brief on Cynthia's behalf. Navasky also put David in touch with Floyd Abrams, one of the nation's foremost authorities on the First Amendment and a co-counsel in the Pentagon papers case. Abrams spoke with David at length by phone and even offered to read, pro bono, Amy and Kreig's briefs.

Even with all these offers of high-level help, David had a grim view of what lay ahead for his family—a view shared by a friend who sent, along with money for the defense fund, a reality check:

> The best you can hope for in this situation is to throw massive amounts of money at lawyers and hope they can make the prosecution go away. You will be $30,000 or $50,000 poorer, and that will be a good ending. There is no possible way you will ever get any restitution. Your rights as a citizen start changing drastically once you're under suspicion and indicted, and your job is to spend as much money as you possibly can on legal assistance and hope that, if you prevail, the police and prosecutors will not bother you any more. They'll never apologize, they'll never compensate you for your time, and they'll never reimburse your expenses.

When David had worked at the New York office of *The Nation*, staff writer Katha Pollitt had often knocked on his door, seeking help with her computer problems. Now she told David she would like to write a piece on Cynthia's prosecution for her column "Subject to Debate." David gratefully faxed her ten pages of press clippings and background, but he felt conflicted about his family's privileged access to the publicity.

"You don't have to be guilty to have your life trashed," David moaned to Pollitt. "But what about the poor guys who didn't go to an Ivy League school and don't have Victor Navasky for a pal?"

"Your case will help *them*," she assured him.

David was not in the spotlight of the case, but he was under enormous strain. He was struggling to stay on top of his work for *The Nation*, while devoting long hours to working on Cynthia's defense. Several of the family's friends made supporting him their top priority, and since David was the main cook in the house, being supportive often involved food. One friend regularly brought over homemade biscotti, and another baked him bread each week. Another friend brought homemade pies as an excuse to stay for a cup of coffee and talk. Tom Theado would turn up sometimes in the evenings with a bottle of wine and say to David, "We're going to share this bottle of wine right here, right now." Tom thought nothing made a man feel lonelier than a woman's support group, and all of Oberlin suddenly seemed like Cynthia's support group.

Tom Theado also became a steady legal advisor to the family, taking them out to dinner at the one chic restaurant in town where, over pad thai and curried tiger shrimp, they talked through the realities of a Lorain County prosecution. Tom tried to give Cynthia a realistic view of what she was up against: she might *expect* the legal system to seek truth and deliver justice, but actually the system was not particularly interested in the truth. The law's primary purpose, he explained, was to maintain a balance between the right of the body politic to be protected from harm and the right of the individual to be left alone. And because the legal system was adversarial, its method of resolving conflicts was a lot like climbing up on two eighteen-hand steeds, wearing three hundred pounds of armor, and racing with thirty-two-foot lances toward each other at a gallop. Whoever was alive at the end was right.

Self-righteousness was the occupational hazard of the system. Tom acknowledged that whenever he represented an injured party in a civil suit, he easily convinced himself that his opposing counsels were agents of evil and deserved to be defeated. Prosecutors needed some of that self-righteous zeal, too, to keep them energized for a tough job. But when prosecutors began to see themselves as infallible—as he feared White and Rosenbaum now did—then they became a danger to the citizens they had pledged to protect.

Life at Campeloupe had changed dramatically in the weeks since Cynthia's arrest. The phone never stopped ringing. The family couldn't have an uninterrupted conversation at dinner. David and Cynthia quarreled about how much information to give to friends and family over the phone—Cynthia wanted to be as open as possible with everyone, but David was paranoid the police might be listening. He thought it was entirely possible that the prosecutors had wiretapped their phone and were monitoring his e-mail.

"But what do we have to hide?" Cynthia protested. David said he had no idea what else the prosecutors might take out of context and twist and turn against them.

Nora found her parents distracted, edgy, and not as playful as they used to be. David and Cynthia tried, as honestly as they could, to reassure Nora that they would be able to fight the charges successfully and that life would return to normal, but Nora was not easily reassured. One evening after speaking for a long time on the phone, Cynthia hung up and started crying. "I can't take this anymore!" she sobbed. Nora felt that was a signal to start worrying. Big time.

At school, Nora's friends were quietly and awkwardly empathetic. Other classmates seemed oblivious to what was going on. One day, though, as she was sitting on the playground swings, two girls teased her about being photographed "buck naked" and laughed that her "bad mother" was going to jail. Nora sought help from her teachers, and afterward the principal implemented a school-wide plan: if any child asked Nora anything about the case, she was to go straight to any teacher for help.

Nora was trying in her own ways to defuse her anxiety, too, and to think of ways to defend her mother. Nora kept reminding Cynthia to tell the judge that it had been *her* idea to take pictures in the bathroom that day. Other times, Nora tried to make her mother laugh. One night she called Cynthia into the bathroom for her rinsing game, and, as she was spraying off, Nora put her hand in front of her pubis, aimed the shower sprayer at her hand, and joked, "See, this is my fig leaf!"

Rebecca and I encouraged Cynthia to see a therapist to help her manage the stress, but she was resistant to the idea. Her attitude was both ideological—"I'm not broken; I don't need to be fixed!"—and pragmatic—"If there's nothing wrong with these photographs, but I go into counseling, what does that look like?" But when Cynthia and David asked Nora if she would like to see a counselor, she surprised them by saying yes. Several people recommended Pat Chmura, a therapist in Elyria who specialized in working with children. Rebecca and I encouraged Cynthia to use defense funds to pay for the sessions. Cynthia made an appointment for Nora with Pat right away.

Pat Chmura was a petite, middle-aged woman whose loose, curly gray hair made her look vibrant rather than aging. She dressed stylishly, and, when they met, Nora thought Pat looked a bit magical, like she lived up in a tower with a crystal ball. After her first meeting with Pat, Nora came back into the waiting room flashing her mother a private thumbs-up sign hidden behind her other hand.

Nora began to meet with Pat every few weeks. Pat would encourage Nora to talk about her fears, and she would coach Nora in how to manage those fears. When Pat asked Nora to put all her worries in a bottle and store them in a cabinet in her mind, Nora imagined placing a bottle of bright fuchsia liquid in her toy chest. When those worries "leaked," Pat and Nora joked about hiring her cats as a clean-up crew. Nora carried her stuffed cat Hannah with her to therapy sessions. If she and Pat talked about something upsetting, she would hold Hannah tightly.

On Pat's office walls were drawings other children had made. Nora would gaze at the drawings and wonder about those children's problems and feelings. In one picture, a girl had drawn herself between her mother and her father, with each parent pulling one of her arms. Nora always felt sad for the girl in the middle.

Pat asked Nora to draw pictures of her life before her mother's case, her life during the case, and her hopes for after. For before, Nora drew herself playing on the school playground with a couple of friends. For during, she drew a gigantic telephone beside a dragon with big teeth and claws labeled "Greg White." For after, Nora drew herself flying, with wings and a big bouquet of flowers. Nora had always told her parents she wanted wings. Seeing the drawings later, David kidded her, "Well, don't blame *us* if you don't grow wings after the case is over!"

Even from a distance, it was easy to observe rapid changes in Nora. Normally a confident, outgoing child, she had begun clinging to her mother and had become reluctant to be away from Cynthia for even short periods. After she and my son performed in a violin recital on an October Sunday afternoon, I was struck by the sight of Nora, tall and leggy for her age, crawling into Cynthia's lap and staying there while all the other children crowded around the cookies and punch. On another day, when Cynthia dropped her off at our house to play, Nora told her mother to "Be careful" more than a dozen times before she would allow her to leave. She wanted to know exactly where Cynthia would be every minute they would be apart and exactly when Cynthia would be back. It was hard for Nora to concentrate on playing; she kept checking the clock and asking me if I thought her mother was safe. That night, Cynthia wrote in her notes:

> *Ever-growing conviction as I see the inroads in Nora's peace of mind that something must be done so that this doesn't happen*

to someone else. I spend long stretches of time holding her like a baby, and it's not enough. And I have <u>everything</u> on my side: good lawyers, some money, amazingly supportive community, good relationship, strong family, strong aware daughter, national connections. What if? What if <u>any</u> of those weren't so?

PART TWO

We do not see things as they are. We see things as we are.

—The Talmud

8

The Sleeping Dragon Stirs

The silence from Children Services puzzled Amy. In August, she had expected Cynthia's pictures to trigger inquiries from Children Services. Instead, the prosecutor had bypassed that agency, taken the pictures to a grand jury, and criminally indicted Cynthia. But any child-pornography prosecution inevitably raised questions about the well-being of the child. And since the prosecutors for Children Services served directly under Greg White, Amy was worried that he or Rosenbaum might now put pressure on the agency to take action. A Children Services case could bolster the criminal case against Cynthia and provide an opportunity to fish for evidence against David, too. Amy warned Cynthia and David that social workers could still show up to question Nora. And there was a worse possibility: officers could swoop in with a warrant, take Nora away from home, and put her in foster care—a court-ordered removal to Emergency Temporary Custody during which the agency would have ninety days to determine if it was safe for her to return home.

Cynthia and David talked to Nora again about what to do if a social worker questioned her: give short, true answers. They worried that if she talked at length or used big words, a social worker might think she'd been coached on what to say. They also told Nora she might be taken to live with another family for just a little while. Nora vowed to run away and hitchhike home if Children Services tried to put her in somebody else's family. But her parents impressed upon her that she should not under any circumstances try to run away or hitchhike. If she were taken from Campeloupe, it would be temporary, and they would work every minute to get her moved to Gramma Gerry's or back home.

The eerie quiet from Children Services through August, September, and now half of October made Cynthia and David nervously joke to each other about "The Sleeping Dragon."

On the morning of October 20, the school principal called Nora from her classroom. As Nora walked down the hall, she could barely hold back tears. She guessed that Children Services had arrived, and she was scared of saying something that would make her mother look guilty. Beneath her large fear, however, Nora was aware of small countercurrents of feeling: she was proud of her French braids, which her mother had re-braided that morning, and she was annoyed to be missing a cursive lesson.

The principal led Nora into a conference room where the investigating social worker for Children Services, Teresa Thornhill, was waiting with a caseworker and a policewoman. Amy had asked the school to call her if Children Services showed up, and she had asked them to record any interviews. The principal had already called Amy, and now she turned on the video camera and sat down next to Nora.

Nora sat with her shoulders slumped. Teresa Thornhill asked if Nora knew where she and her co-worker were from, and Nora answered in a tentative voice, "A place where you take care of children." Thornhill asked if her mother had told her that someone from Children Services might come see her, and Nora replied, "She thought you might come see me about the case."

"What do you know about the case?" asked Thornhill.

Nora continued carefully, "Some people thought that a picture my mom took of me in the bathtub was something she shouldn't have done." Then she straightened up and said more forthrightly, "But I think it was just me cleaning."

Speaking more like a therapist than an inquisitor, Thornhill asked in a mildly curious way how many pictures Nora's mother had taken of her; how she felt when her mother took the pictures ("Fine!");

and what kind, size, and quantity of cameras her mother used.

"I saw some of the pictures, and some of them look like you were posing. Were you kind of posing in some of the pictures?" Thornhill asked.

"One of them—I saw this picture at a photo thing, and I decided I wanted to re-create it," Nora explained.

"Okay, yeah, I was wondering, because sometimes kids look at magazines or see things in catalogs—"

"No," Nora said. "It was a photo exhibit. My mom and I were there, and I wanted to re-create it."

"Is your mom a photographer?"

"She's not a professional, but she really likes taking pictures."

Thornhill pulled out some small charts and said, "You're eight years old. Do you think you know all these colors? Point and show me." Nora obediently named the blocks of color. Thornhill showed her a chart of animals, and Nora rattled off "Dog, frog, cat, rabbit, butterfly, bear." She asked Nora to name the colors in the butterfly's wings and the color of the dog, which Nora did.

Thornhill pulled out a different chart. "Here's a picture of a little girl. Do you think you know your body parts?"

"I think so," Nora said.

Thornhill pointed. "What's this stuff?"

"Hair," Nora replied.

"What are these?"

"Her eyes, her mouth."

"What's this?"

"Her chest."

"What are these?

"Her arms, her hands."

"What's this?"

"Her belly."

"What do you call that part?"

"Her vagina."

"What about these?"

"Her legs, toes, and feet."

"What's this?"

"Her bottom."

"Do you know which parts on this drawing are private parts?"

"The bottom and the vagina."

"There's one other private part on a girl," observed Thornhill.

"Her chest," Nora added.

"Has anyone ever touched you or hurt you on any of your private parts?"

"No."

"What if somebody did?"

"I would tell my parents."

"What if your parents weren't around?" Thornhill wondered.

"I could tell the police. Or my principal or my teacher."

Thornhill asked in a confidential tone, "What do you feel about all this stuff going on with these pictures?"

"I know my mom is innocent," Nora answered, in a voice that had grown more direct and confident.

"Innocent of what?" Thornhill probed.

"She would never try to hurt me with the pictures she took of me."

"Did it bother you at all that you are eight years old? That Dad saw?"

"No," Nora said firmly. "I feel like I *want* my life to be recorded so I can see what I looked like when I was a child."

"Basically, why I'm here is to see if you're feeling comfortable and safe."

Nora nodded, "I do."

"Do you have any concerns?"

"No."

"Do you still feel nervous?"

Nora shook her head.

"Think real hard—do you have any questions at all?" Thornhill asked.

"Not really."

Thornhill emphasized that if Nora had questions or concerns, she could talk to her anytime. Then Nora was allowed to go back to class, and everyone else sat tight-lipped in the room for a few long minutes until they could figure out how to turn the video camera off.

Amy arrived at the school just as Thornhill and her companions were driving away. She knew that the outcome of interviews with children depended on the ethics of the interviewers. By asking leading questions or making suggestions, interviewers could elicit misleading testimony or introduce "memories" into children's minds. Amy knew those manipulations were not always intentional—if interrogators believed a child had been abused, they might interpret a child's reticence as an attempt to protect a perpetrator and then feel justified putting words into the child's mouth. Video cameras made interviewers think twice about their tactics and helped keep their ethics high. Whether the video eye had helped keep this interview professional, Amy didn't know. But watching the tape, she felt relieved.

That afternoon, Amy called Teresa Thornhill. Thornhill did not want to take Nora into Emergency Temporary Custody. But she was concerned that Cynthia had taken "inappropriate" pictures and did not have proper boundaries in regard to her daughter's nudity. Thornhill wanted Nora to attend counseling to make sure she was healthy and "able to protect herself," she wanted Cynthia to attend counseling and perhaps parenting classes, and she wanted a caseworker to visit the family's home once a month. When Amy pointed out that Nora was already in counseling with Pat Chmura, Thornhill was pleased. Pat was one of their favorite counselors, she said.

Amy told Thornhill that her clients could comply with the agency's requests if the case was handled unofficially. Since most Children Services cases began with an effort to resolve a family's problems out of court, Amy saw nothing unusual in her request. Certainly an official case—with charges, court filings, sworn testimonies, and court hearings—would make it impossible for Cynthia and David to cooperate fully since anything they said in an official case could be used against them in criminal court.

Thornhill seemed amenable to an unofficial case. She said she would check with her supervisor and get back to Amy.

But Thornhill's answer the next day was "No." She said she had been instructed by her superiors that an unofficial case was impossible; official charges would be filed against both parents. When Amy protested, Thornhill referred her to Lisa Locke Graves, the assistant prosecutor who served as the head of the Children Services division in the county prosecutor's office.

Amy called Locke Graves and complained that the social worker who had met with and assessed the child was being overruled. Locke Graves said that if she had gotten *her* way, Children Services would have taken Emergency Temporary Custody. But Thornhill had insisted that ETC was not in the child's best interest.

Hours after Amy's call to Locke Graves, Children Services filed a complaint against Cynthia and David in court. The complaint asserted that two of Cynthia's photographs depicted a child "having sexual contact" with a running showerhead, it alleged that Nora was a "dependent/abused child," and it asked that Children Services be granted protective supervision or temporary custody of Nora.

Amy called Cynthia and David and asked them to come to her office immediately. When they arrived, she handed them photocopies of the relevant statutes from the Ohio Revised Code. A *dependent* child, they read, was a homeless, destitute, or neglected child or, as in Nora's case, a child whose "condition or environment is such as to warrant the state, in the interest of the child, in assuming his guardianship." Cynthia and David were surprised at such an amorphous, catchall category. Amy agreed the category was vague. But usually, she said, it was obvious when a child's environment was unstable or harmful enough to warrant the state's intervention, and usually intervention by Children Services was incremental. For example, if the parents were out of work, the agency might give them one month's rent, enroll them in budgeting classes, work with the gas company to keep their heat turned on, and help them find employment. If then the parents couldn't keep their new jobs, were about to be evicted from their house, and had no warm place to go, the agency might file an official complaint of dependency and ask for Emergency Temporary Custody. The children would be placed with relatives or in foster care until the home situation stabilized.

An *abused* child was a child who had been victimized under child endangerment laws, which forbade any person to abuse or torture a child or to "entice, coerce, permit, encourage, compel, hire, employ, use, or allow the child to act, model, . . . or be photographed for, the production, presentation, dissemination, or advertisement of any material or performance that the offender knows or reasonably should know is obscene." Obscenity had been notoriously difficult to define, as evidenced by Supreme Court Justice Potter Stewart's famous remark in a 1964 opinion (regarding another Ohio case): "I know it when I see it." Case law had tried to do better. In 1957, in *Roth v. United States*, the Supreme Court affirmed that obscenity was to be judged by "whether to the average person, applying contemporary community standards, the dominant theme of the material, taken as a whole, appeals to prurient interest." The definition the Court used for "prurient" was "having a tendency to excite lustful thoughts" or "a shameful or morbid interest in nudity, sex, or excretion, [which] goes substantially beyond customary limits of candor."

Amy explained the sequence of the family's upcoming Children Services hearings. The pre-trial would be a brief meeting to share preliminary findings and set dates for the other hearings. The adjudicatory hearing would determine whether or not Nora was a dependent and/or an abused child. A dispensational hearing, which would be held only if Nora had been ruled dependent or abused, would determine whether Children Services would be given protective supervision or temporary custody of Nora. Protective supervision would permit Nora to remain with her parents while the family was monitored by Children Services. Temporary custody would remove Nora from her home until the court decided if and when it was safe for her to return.

A magistrate would conduct the hearings, but a judge would have an opportunity to review the case and alter the magistrate's rulings. In the county in which Amy had previously worked, magistrates wore black robes; in Lorain County, magistrates wore suits. Amy believed that Lorain County judges reserved robes for themselves as a way of exhibiting their status and reminding everyone that any decision made by a magistrate could be reviewed and changed by the presiding judge. But Amy warned Cynthia and David not to get the wrong idea. Children Services proceedings, even if presided over by magistrates in street clothes, were real trials. Cynthia and David would be pitted against the state. This would not be kindergarten court.

Amy didn't yet know which judge and magistrate pair would be assigned to their case. But she characterized each possible pair—their personal and political backgrounds, their links to the prosecutor's office, and her own forecast of how the case would fare under them. One of those pairs was Judge Debra Boros and Magistrate Michele Arredondo. Boros was a brand-new judge who had built her career as an assistant prosecutor in Greg White's office. Arredondo, who had been her assistant in White's office, was now her magistrate. Amy feared that, as fellow Republicans and former subordinates of White's, Boros and Arredondo would be subject to pressure from their former boss and co-workers. She also feared that both women still looked at the world through a prosecutor's eyes and would likely see deviance everywhere they looked.

At the end of his notes, David drew three silver dollar–sized circles. Inside each circle he wrote the names of a different judge and magistrate pair whom Amy had described. Beneath the first circle, David wrote: "they'll throw it out." Beneath the second circle, David wrote "coin toss." Under the third circle, with the names Boros and Arredondo inside, David wrote: "we lose."

Before they headed home, Cynthia and David signed another contract and wrote another check to Amy—this time a flat $3,500 to handle the Children Services case. Kreig Brusnahan would serve as co-counsel for the criminal defense, but Amy would handle the Children Services case alone.

~~~

Nora was about to receive her own personal *pro bono* advocate: a guardian ad litem. Literally a "guardian for the litigation," a GAL was a court-appointed volunteer who, for the duration of the legal proceedings, was responsible to neither the defense nor the prosecution, the parents nor the caseworker, but only to the child. In Lorain County, the nonprofit Voices for Children trained and assigned each GAL, whose responsibilities included fact-finding for the judge, speaking for the child in the courtroom, acting as a "watchdog" for the child, and ensuring that the case was brought "to a swift and appropriate conclusion." Amy knew that GALs wielded enormous influence on the outcome of Children Services cases, so she was holding her breath, hoping for a good one.

When Amy received word that a woman named Virginia Behner had just been appointed Nora's GAL, the name didn't ring a bell. But Cynthia immediately heard unsettling news about the woman from a friend who was a social worker: Virginia was a fundamentalist Christian, a self-appointed zealot against child porn, and a woman who had a tendency to read perversion into benign situations. Cynthia despaired, but her friend counseled her, "Just be yourself around Virginia. Don't pretend to be something you're not. Honesty and openness in the way you've raised Nora were the start of this whole thing—maybe they can be the cure."

When Virginia Behner appeared the next day at Amy's office and launched into a tirade against child pornography, Amy groaned to herself, *Oh, man, we're cooked.* She was worried enough to call Lillian Leach, the director of Voices for Children.

Lillian told Amy, "I don't know if you know the history of this woman, but she's gone head-to-head with Greg White—she actually got a man off criminal charges. But, yes, she is very passionate against child pornography."

Amy kept trying to register her concern: "Lillian, I'm really nervous. My initial report about her is that she's a born-again."

Lillian was firm. "She's an up-and-up person. She'll be fine."

~~~

Virginia Behner was a short, plump, talkative woman who lived alone in a trailer park near Elyria. She had a thin ponytail, big glasses, and strong opinions. Virginia worked as a nurse, and she worshipped at Ernest Angley's Grace Cathedral, the Akron megachurch of a televangelist faith healer. She routinely drove a vanload of ailing folks to Angley's Friday-night healing services.

As a GAL, Virginia made it her mission to ferret out the truth. In her last assignment, she had taken an unexpected stand in defense of a father accused of molesting his son. From Virginia's point of view, the prosecution's case rested on the accusations of an unreliable person with an ax to grind. She was disgusted that "*nobody* investigated—not ten seconds of investigation!" Virginia *did* investigate, and she amassed a tall stack of medical documents that she thought proved scientifically that the father could not possibly have molested his child. Her gadfly persistence eventually resulted in the criminal case being declared *nolle prosequi* ("we shall no longer prosecute"). *Nolle* cases were almost unheard of in Lorain County, so Virginia was proud she had "forced Greg White to eat a crow."

In the process, though, Virginia believed that she had antagonized the assistant prosecutor assigned to the case and that as soon as he perceived her as an obstacle to his prosecution, he dropped hints at the courthouse that he was going to have her removed from the case or even prosecuted and sent to jail. Virginia hid $300 for emergency bail money in her shoe, but she didn't flinch.

After the case was over, Virginia went to her prayer group with a request: "I can't divulge the details, but there's this assistant prosecutor, and I am *sick* of the things he does. I wish God would expose him!" So everyone prayed for God's intervention. A few weeks later, the assistant prosecutor was removed from his job. Virginia heard from a judge that he had exposed himself to a woman in a courthouse stairwell. "Boy, did we get our prayer answered!" Virginia exulted to her fellow prayer warriors. She was delighted that God had such a good sense of humor.

Virginia's dogged defense of the wrongly accused father was remarkable considering her rabid opinions about the proper fate of child abusers. Hanging child rapists in front of the courthouse seemed like just punishment to Virginia. "Chopping their genitals off like they do in Saudi Arabia" was another reasonable option, she told anyone who would listen.

Virginia's rage was almost equally fierce toward people who abused the justice system, whether as plaintiffs who lied or as prosecutors who trumped up charges and manipulated evidence. She had developed an especially jaded view of the Lorain County legal system, perceiving its prosecutors, magistrates, judges, and Children Services personnel as too indebted politically and personally to Greg White, and to each other, to make independent judgments. "It's not about who's right and wrong," Virginia would complain. "Some people have a scorecard. They just think about their careers."

False charges of sexual abuse were, in Virginia's opinion, the number-one enemy of children who were actually molested. She had particular venom on that account for Jonathan Rosenbaum. She had never had dealings with him personally, but she had followed his 1994 prosecution of Nancy Smith, a mother and Lorain Head Start school bus driver. Smith was convicted of driving several children, instead of to school, to the home of a man who allegedly abused them sexually. Sentenced to thirty to ninety years in prison, she had been in jail now for five of those years. But Smith had always maintained her innocence, and many people in Lorain County believed her conviction to be an appalling miscarriage of justice. Investigative articles in the *Chronicle-Telegram* argued that the case against Smith had been built from contradictory testimony from young children and that evidence of Smith's innocence had been suppressed by the prosecutors. For Virginia, Nancy Smith's incarceration was the worst of what happens when hysteria rather than facts fuels a prosecution. She blamed Jonathan Rosenbaum and his "talent for making black seem white and white seem black."

After her *nolle* case, Lillian Leach had told Virginia that she would not be effective again as a GAL until feelings about her quieted down at the prosecutor's office and Children Services. "You're too controversial right now," Lillian had explained, easing her into retirement. So Virginia had turned her zeal toward the problem of child pornography. She read books, subscribed to activist newsletters, and monitored what was happening with the passage of new laws. Occasionally she would call Lillian to blow off steam. "Oh, I hate these pornographers!" she would exclaim. "I hope the earth opens up and takes 'em!" When Children Services requested a GAL for Nora, Lillian decided to bring Virginia out of retirement. Virginia thanked Lillian for the chance "to nail a real pornographer."

Virginia hoped, in fact, to nail a whole network of pornographers. Being a pornographer, she believed, was "like being a carpenter. You don't pick up a saw and start doing it; you have to learn it from somebody. You don't just get dirty pictures and put them on the Internet. You have to learn the trade." Virginia speculated that Cynthia could lead her to the child-porn underground in Ohio and beyond. "Child molesters are like mice," she reasoned. "If you see one, there's probably ten others."

Virginia rushed to Oberlin hoping to catch Cynthia "in the act." Instead, she found David reading on Campeloupe's front porch. David was polite but tight-lipped, saying only that Cynthia had taken Nora to a counseling appointment.

The next time Virginia popped up at Campeloupe, she only caught Cynthia in the act of sorting her duplicate prints into white envelopes to give to friends. Cynthia found the GAL quiet and distant, but Virginia's calculated coolness masked fiery thoughts: *Oh, these pornographers are sneaky! He's got a computer and works out of the home!* She wrote down everything Cynthia said but didn't believe a word of it.

When Virginia had read in the court filing that the child was masturbating in the pictures, she had found herself rooting for her old adversary Greg White. *Ooooh,* she had thought, *I hope the prosecutor gets 'em!* Now she decided to speed up her investigation by viewing the photographs herself.

At the police station, an officer eagerly produced Cynthia's pictures. "You've got to see these!" he said, leaning over and watching as Virginia shuffled through the roll.

But flipping back and forth through the prints, she grew agitated. "Which one? Which one?" she asked. "Where is it? Where is it?"

The policeman jabbed his finger at the picture in her hand and said, "There it is! Look at that! You know that ain't right!"

Virginia stopped and stared. "Oh, it's *that* one?" she asked in a deflated voice.

9

Consultations

Virginia didn't trust gut instinct, even her own. She wanted evidence, and lots of it.

Cynthia had prepared a list of references for Children Services and the GAL to interview: Nora's preschool, Montessori kindergarten, first-, second-, and third-grade teachers; her soccer coach; her summer arts program director; her Scottish dance teacher; her children's choir director; her violin teacher; Cynthia's landlady at 82 for twenty-seven years; Tom Theado, Cynthia's friend for thirty years; nine different sets of parents of Nora's friends; and Cynthia's mother, father, and seven siblings. A high percentage of Nora's friends' parents were college professors, but they also included a nurse, a ceramic artist and cabinetmaker, a middle school teacher, a few social workers, a building inspector, and a couple of writers. Virginia called everyone on the list; then she called people who weren't on the list. When she met Oberlinians outside Oberlin, she would say offhandedly, never mentioning that she was the guardian ad litem, "Oh, by the way, what do you think of that child-pornography case in your town?"

As it turned out, the pastor of Virginia's former church in Elyria had known Cynthia years ago when he was a teacher in the Oberlin schools. He wrote Virginia a letter praising Cynthia as "a loving mother so needed in today's society" and as "a warm, caring person who knows the difference between right and wrong, good and evil." That was the kind of language—*her* kind of language—Virginia was hearing from plenty of people.

But other conversations were introducing Virginia to jarring ideas. Ann Cooper Albright was a professor of dance and the mother of Nora's best friend, Isabel. When their girls had been small, the two mothers had vowed, as ardent feminists, to raise strong, confident, independent daughters. Nora was not embarrassed to be seen—or photographed—naked by her parents, Ann explained to Virginia, because Cynthia had taught her daughter that every part of her body was natural and good. Shame would never help a girl make good decisions about her body; pride and self-confidence would. Virginia didn't exactly know what a "feminist" was, but Ann's attitudes about nudity unsettled and intrigued her.

When Virginia met again with Amy, she was cagey about her findings, but her tone had changed. "I really don't think there's anything going on here," she acknowledged. "I don't exactly understand why the police are involved."

Before Amy headed into the Children Services pre-trial hearing on November 4, she shared mixed news with Cynthia and David. The good news was that the guardian ad litem seemed to be growing skeptical about the charges against them. The bad news was that Judge Boros and Magistrate Arredondo had been assigned to adjudicate their case—the duo Amy had dreaded.

The family was not allowed inside the pre-trial hearing, so they watched from the lobby as Amy disappeared into the hearing room. When she reemerged less than an hour later, she flashed them a big smile. The only other person who approached the family was a young woman named Tracy who had just been assigned as Nora's caseworker. Tracy introduced herself to Cynthia and David and gave Nora a friendly hello. Nora returned the greeting warily, uncertain of what to make of a young woman with long polished nails and makeup like a movie star's.

Amy led the family into a consultation room, shut the door, and cheered, "Yes!" She described how Locke Graves, the chief prosecutor for Children Services, had made clear at the beginning of the session that she would be personally prosecuting this case. But then Virginia Behner had argued that Children Services should *dismiss* the charges! The GAL had seen the photographs, visited the home, and spoken with the child's therapist, who had said that Nora was *not* abused but only traumatized by her mother's prosecution. Virginia had talked to dozens more people, too, all of whom had testified to the integrity of the family—including, as she put it, a "feminologist."

Locke Graves had listened but shown no willingness to recon-sider the charges. At the end of the meeting, however, she suddenly realized she was busy on the date they were considering for the adju-dicatory hearing and gave the case to her assistant, Faye List. "Once Locke Graves heard Virginia's report and realized the case was no longer fat and juicy, she wanted out," Amy told Cynthia and David. "Their case is *shit*, and she knows it."

Cynthia and David's refrigerator had acquired, through accretion, the look of a giant scrapbook turned inside out. The door was shaggy with layers of art and memorabilia, including Nora's school pictures, a postcard painting of *Black Hawk and His Son Whirling Thunder*, a snapshot of David reading to Nora and her classmates, photos of new babies, a Halloween card with cats in outlandish headdresses, and myriad newspaper clippings of Bob Dylan (including the unlikely photo of Dylan talking to Charlton Heston and Lauren Bacall).

Back when they had expected their first visit from Virginia, Cynthia and David had scoured the house for anything that might offend her. One thing their eyes had fallen on was a postcard taped up on the fridge—a gauzy painting of a woman wearing thigh-high boots and nothing else. She was holding a serving tray with apples right un-der her breasts so that they lined up apple, apple, breast, apple, breast, apple, apple, apple. On his own first visit to Campeloupe, my son Jesse had been mesmerized by the postcard, and Cynthia had watched him gaze at it for a long time. Finally he had said thoughtfully, "Nice boots."

But fearing a different reaction from Virginia, Cynthia and Da-vid had buried the postcard beneath other layers of fridge stuff. As it turned out, Virginia was offended by something on the fridge it hadn't dawned on them to hide: a postcard of a young and goofily beaming Bill and Hillary Clinton that David had bought at Drug Mart. David, who had a well-honed critique of the Clintons from the left, had hung up the postcard because he found it amusing. But Virginia, who had a well-honed critique of the Clintons from the right, assumed the postcard was hanging there as homage. Because she hated the Clintons, she had to tell herself, "Politics is not my job. My job is this little girl, and it doesn't matter what their politics are."

Virginia now phoned Cynthia and David and leveled with them. She didn't approve of Cynthia's taking photographs of Nora naked— "I'm not of your same thinking. I can't even *think* like that," she told them—but she had also seen real child pornography, and she was *very* confident that Cynthia's photographs were not pornographic: "No might be. No doubt in my mind." Virginia couldn't see the good in the photographs, but she couldn't see the harm in them, either. She impressed upon Cynthia, "If those pictures had been of a little girl masturbating, it wouldn't have mattered to me if you had the whole town plus Mother Teresa saying you were a nice person—they could hang you for all I cared! If that child was doing what they said she was doing in the pictures, what would it have mattered to me what anybody said? But she wasn't."

Virginia said that most attorneys feared Greg White because he went after anyone who opposed him. But she had stood up to White before, and she aimed to do it again. She would fight for dismissal of the case. Virginia made clear, however, that she would not give Cynthia and David every piece of information she had. She had boundaries in her mind between what she had the duty or liberty to share, and what she did not. When David asked Virginia which police officer had shown her the photographs, it was one of many times Virginia acted as if she hadn't heard his question.

And she kept repeating to Cynthia and David, "Me and you have *nothing* in common." For one thing, she believed that routine nudity in a family was a red flag for sexual abuse. She was convinced that adults who abuse children first undermine the natural shyness between the sexes by walking around naked and by cultivating a perception that nudity in the home is normal. Even walking naked from the shower to the bedroom was dangerous since "just like marijuana is the doorway to crack, nudity is the doorway to incest." A normal family would teach a child at the age of two to cover up as soon as she got out of the bathtub to prevent somebody from seeing her naked, like, for example, her father.

Over the following weeks, though, Virginia's talks with Cynthia and David grew less critical. She began to see their family as the exception to her rule. She became interested in the ways they sought to enrich Nora's life, and she wondered how to provide some of those opportunities—choir or violin, maybe—for her own granddaughter.

Virginia also began to provide Cynthia and David with more of the information she was gleaning from Children Services and the police. She learned, for example, that the police and prosecutors viewed with suspicion Cynthia's decision to hire an attorney. More surprising was their interpretation of the picture album Cynthia had submitted with her affidavit. Since the only nude pictures in the album were pictures of Nora as a toddler, and since Cynthia had added at the back of the album a handful of recent photographs of Nora fully clothed and posed among flowers, the police and prosecutors and even Teresa Thornhill, the investigating social worker, had leapt to the conclusion that Cynthia had taken no nude pictures of Nora since she was two years old—until the fateful June day in the bathtub with the shower sprayer. They saw a "big gap" in the supposed record Cynthia was keeping of Nora's life.

"Why didn't Cynthia 'document her growth' in between those years?" a policeman had asked Virginia sarcastically. Yet, to confirm their theory, the police and prosecutors had never asked to see any of the 35,000 other photographs Cynthia had taken since Nora's birth.

Soon after her arrest, Cynthia decided to contact Sally Mann, the well-known photographer whose book *Immediate Family* had created a firestorm of controversy in the early 1990s. *Immediate Family* was a collection of black-and-white photographs of Mann's three children, who were, by turns, petulant, dreamy, affectionate, bored, defiant, damaged by bee stings and cuts, flouncy in dress-up clothes, filthy with mud, and backlit by the elements. Sometimes they were naked, in a nakedness that seemed at ease with itself and with the lush muck of nature.

The nude images had unnerved more than a few viewers. Mann had never been prosecuted for her photographs, but she had been both vilified and praised for her work. Admirers thought Mann had captured the complexity of childhood without the distortions of sentimentality. Critics, especially from the religious right, had organized boycotts of her books and picketed stores that sold them.

Cynthia hoped to get Mann's guidance about her own troubles. Perhaps she would even agree to be an expert witness in the event of a trial. Cynthia wrote Mann a letter on October 6:

Dear Sally Mann,

I have taken pictures of my daughter since she was born—even before I knew about you and your work. I regard you as an artist. I regard myself as someone who maybe someday will be an artist but who is at present a journalist in the Boswellian sense. I don't mean to be obsequious here, but rather to set the perspective. I make my living by driving a school bus.

I have been arrested for some pictures I took of my daughter nude in the bathtub which have been misinterpreted by the local police. I am writing because I know that you have had troubles of this sort, and I am wondering, hoping that maybe you know of legal precedent, similar court cases, or could point my attorney toward case law that might be relevant to my situation.

I also think we may use your work in my trial as an example of documented artistic worth in work that, though the vision is much more clearly realized and skillfully articulated, has some similarities with the pictures I take. I would feel better doing this with your permission.

All this is a lot to ask, and, as my partner and I are breaking the bank to pay for legal representation, I cannot offer you anything in return.

Except my heartfelt thanks.

Cynthia Stewart

P.S. I am sending you the two sections of law that contain the counts with which I am charged (marked on each), and two pictures of my daughter.

Knowing only that Sally was married to a lawyer and lived near Lexington, Virginia, Cynthia wrote to Larry Mann in care of their county courthouse. She sent a package of newspaper clippings and wrote across the envelope, "Please give these to your wife." When Sally received the package, she promptly e-mailed Cynthia at David's address. The subject line read "Unreal":

I can't believe that this is still happening.

It never happened to me, however, but I think I can be of help to you.

Not infrequently I have had requests like yours for assistance and with distressing regularity I found the charges, if not justified, then at least understandable. I feel partially responsible for all those weirdo guys who felt that *Immediate Family* gave them permission to cajole the clothes off their little suburban step-daughters and begin shooting-- in some cases--borderline photographs.

So, if you wouldn't mind, I would appreciate seeing the images that have gotten you in trouble; the statute they are prosecuting under is hair-raising and vague.

I don't know how you want to proceed with this. When Larry gets off the tractor and puts his lawyer hat back on he said he'd be happy to write you and your lawyer. You have a lot of resources available

to you and, although it's been a long time since
I've riffled through that particular, unsavory file,
I think I can pass on a few to you.
  Boswellian. I love it.

SM

In November, Cynthia e-mailed Sally back:

Dear Sally Mann,

Thank you for your kind and prompt reply. Forgive me
for not writing back right away.
  My case has received so much local publicity that
the district attorney removed the garden-variety
prosecutor who originally had the case and assigned
his chief of criminal prosecution to it. This guy
is prosecuting the case much more actively, and his
first move to put pressure on us was to involve
Children Services. So we've been overwhelmed trying
to keep our daughter out of the maw. She's still at
home, but there's a lot to do.
  My attorney is talking about making you some kind
of expert witness so that you can see the pictures.
She'll be in touch with you. In the meantime,
thanks.

Cynthia Stewart

Despite Rosenbaum's threat to indict her for pandering, Amy
still planned to show Cynthia's photographs to defense witnesses. But
she planned to show those pictures—or photocopies of the pictures,
if that's all she ever got from the prosecutor's office—only to *subpoe-naed* witnesses in the privacy of her own office. If Sally Mann were

willing to travel to Elyria, Amy would be delighted to subpoena her and show her the pictures. In the meantime, Amy was not going to put photocopies in the U.S. mail and risk indictment for interstate trafficking in child porn.

So Cynthia described her photographs over the phone to Sally. They talked about their cameras, their daughters, their rural childhoods, their eccentric families. At the end of their long conversation, Cynthia could tell she had passed Sally's test. It helped that their backgrounds had been so similar: growing up wild on a farm with parents who bucked convention.

10

Rorschach

Faye List, the assistant prosecutor now in charge of the Children Services case, called Amy right away with a deal: if Cynthia and David pleaded guilty to the dependency charge and accepted protective supervision, then Children Services would drop the abuse charge and forgo any attempt to take custody of Nora. List was sure the family would do just fine under protective supervision. She urged Amy to take the deal and get it all over with quickly.

Amy was not receptive. Her clients did not believe they had done anything wrong, and, quite frankly, she agreed with them.

List pointed out that the *magistrate* would decide if the parents had done anything wrong. Everything rested on the magistrate's gut reaction to the pictures.

Amy argued that more than a gut reaction was needed to prove that a child was dependent or abused.

List disagreed and warned that she was giving Amy and her clients a way out.

When Amy stood her ground, List offered to change the wording of the Children Services complaint to read that Nora was a dependent child *because* of the stress of the criminal case. But when Amy presented that offer to Cynthia and David, they turned it down. They certainly agreed that Nora was stressed by the criminal prosecution, but they did not believe a ruling of dependency would alleviate that stress—or assign proper blame for the existence of the criminal case to begin with. If they agreed to the deal, List could turn around and claim that the criminal case and, thus, Nora's stress were Cynthia's fault since she took the pictures to begin with. Cynthia and David were not going to fall into that catch-22.

Amy knew that Cynthia and David's decision to refuse List's deal was made easier by the fact that Nora had not been taken into Emergency Temporary Custody. Having a child in ETC sapped the fight out of parents. By the time the adjudicatory hearing rolled around, parents seemed willing to give their right arm to get their children back.

The family's adjudicatory hearing was scheduled for late November, and Cynthia's criminal pre-trial was scheduled for December. But in mid-November, Amy gave Cynthia and David bad news of her own: her mother was dying. Amy was increasingly torn between her work and her need to be with her mother. She had felt unfocused and unprepared in court recently with another client, and she didn't want that to happen again. She offered to seek continuances—postponements—of both the Children Services and criminal proceedings so that she and Kreig would have more time to prepare. She also offered to bow out as Cynthia's lawyer altogether.

But Cynthia was adamant about keeping Amy. She encouraged her to seek continuances and then wrote a note for Amy to pass along to her mother:

> *Dear Amy's mother,*
>
> *We haven't met. I'm sorry our first communication is happening in such circumstances. But I want to thank you for raising such a compassionate, smart, funny, wise, and fearless daughter. In my present circumstances I can't imagine being without her. . . .*

When Amy visited her mother that week, they had a heart-to-heart talk about her work. It was painful and poignant for them to speak about Cynthia and Nora. Amy's mother, who had been a public librarian for years and an advocate for civil liberties, felt strongly that

Amy needed to do everything she could to protect this family. If Amy failed, then a mother and child might be torn apart. For Amy and her own mother, that future was devastatingly real.

Amy applied for the continuances. When both were granted, Cynthia wrote in her notes: "Everything is on for January 3rd: criminal pretrial at 8:15, and Children Services hearing the same day." Then she noted Amy's sad caveat: "Sometime in the next month, Amy's mother is going to die, which will throw everything off."

Contributions were trickling in to the Cynthia Stewart Legal Defense Fund, all solicited by word of mouth. But word of mouth was going to be a slow way to get the family the financial help they increasingly needed. Rebecca Cross and I decided it was time to officially announce the creation of the fund with letters to the editors of area newspapers. We had qualms about how to phrase such a letter since we hadn't seen the photographs, and we had anxiety about how Lorain County beyond Oberlin would respond. So we decided to test the waters by sending our letter first to the weekly *Oberlin News-Tribune*. We described Cynthia as an exemplary mother and an avid photographer, we accused the county prosecutor of "a grave error in judgment," and we appealed for monetary help, noting that "not many of us have $30,000 on hand just in case we are indicted for a crime we did not commit."

In the late afternoon of the day our letter appeared, I received a phone call from a woman I knew slightly. Her husband was a prominent professional in the county. She wanted to know if I had sent that letter anywhere besides the *Oberlin News-Tribune*. When I told her no but that we planned to send it to the two county newspapers and the *Plain Dealer*, she warned me not to. She asked if I had followed the trial of Nancy Smith, the Lorain Head Start school bus driver who had been convicted of child sexual molestation a few years before and had been sentenced to decades in prison. I told her no, I had never paid attention to Lorain County politics and scandals—until very recently, that is. She was clearly exasperated by my detachment from events outside Oberlin. She believed that Nancy Smith was innocent and had been framed by Rosenbaum and White. She mistrusted the prosecutors and feared Cynthia could end up in prison just as Nancy Smith had. She also believed I had jeopardized myself by publishing the letter, and she urged me to be careful with every move I made from then on—one slight infraction of the law, and I could wind up in very big trouble indeed.

"The prosecutors don't like criticism," she told me, "and they get even. Don't run a red light. Don't break the speed limit. You don't want to end up in court for *anything* right now." If my criticism of Cynthia's case stayed confined to the Oberlin press, the prosecutors would probably write it off as business-as-usual in left-leaning Oberlin. "But don't make this a cause célèbre outside Oberlin," she cautioned. "It will only backfire, and people will get hurt."

She wanted to contribute anonymously to Cynthia's fund; she did not want her name to wind up on some database of contributors. "Please don't tell anyone I called you, and please be careful," she said as we were hanging up.

I placed the phone back in its cradle, stood alone in our darkening family room, and knew, with a surge of shame, I would not send that letter out to any more newspapers. I would keep my voice confined to Oberlin, where it could stay camouflaged in a crowd of other voices like it.

Just hours after the Children Services pre-trial on November 4, Amy called the agency to set up a time for Tracy, the new caseworker, to visit Nora and her family in their home. Amy also faxed Tracy the list of references Cynthia had provided the GAL. Children Services kept an activity log for each of its cases. The log recorded visits, consultations, even short phone calls made or received by the caseworker in connection to that case. The log recorded Amy's call on November 4 and receipt of the reference list.

Amy was eager to get Tracy into Campeloupe so that Children Services could see that Cynthia and David had nothing to hide. But as Cynthia's legal counsel, Amy wanted to be present to make sure Tracy did not probe for information that could be used against her client in the criminal trial. Amy and Tracy scheduled a home visit, but, at the last minute, Amy had to cancel it because of an emergency with her mother's illness. Tracy's supervisor recorded in the log that the cancellation was "due to Amy's scheduling and not to the parents avoiding the Agency." The log also noted that Amy had given permission for Nora to be interviewed at school by anyone at Children Services *without* Amy's presence: "It is okay for us to see the child at school as long as teacher, principal, or Guardian Ad Litem is present."

One week later, Tracy arranged a school visit with Nora. She reported on that brief meeting in the log, referring to herself as "the worker":

> 11/18/99 20 minutes. School Visit. People involved: Cynthia, Nora, principal, and the G.A.L. While worker was walking into the school, she caught Nora's mother, Cynthia. Worker asked if she would like to be there when this worker speaks with Nora. Mother stated all okay. Worker met with Nora and mother. Nora seems alright although [mother] states that Nora appears to be regressing, wanting to be held a lot. Worker stated to both mother and Nora that she would not visit the school since this tends to upset Nora. She feels different than the other kids. Nora stated that she and her mother are getting kittens tomorrow. Mother thought that this would be good therapy for them. Mother was leaving so worker asked if she would like a school representative to sit in on the rest of the visit. Mother stated, No. Worker stated that she just wants to abide by their lawyer. Amy Wirtz is attorney. Mother stated that she believes that Amy trusts me (the worker), and Mother does not see it to be a problem if I meet alone with Nora. Nora and this worker only met by ourselves for approximately 2–3 minutes. This worker felt that it was important for Nora to get back to class.

~~~

Cynthia called Nora's daily visits to see her new kitten "Kitty Therapy," and she was thrilled every time Nora let go of her hand and ran over to cuddle her new pet. Midway through the cat visiting, Cynthia decided Kitty Therapy might do her some good, too. So she picked out the firstborn male of the litter and named him Primo. On November 19, the family brought Jennie and Primo home. Cynthia held Primo in her lap while David drove, and Nora zipped Jennie into her jacket. With the warm kitten nestled against her, Nora felt happy for the first time in a long while.

During her visits to Campeloupe, the GAL had been working to gain Nora's trust by focusing on their mutual love of cats. Using bribes of luncheon meat, Virginia had taught her own cat Petey to jump through an embroidery hoop. Now Virginia suggested that Jennie and Primo could learn that trick, too, and Nora might even travel the world someday with her performing cats. Virginia and Nora named the new little circus troupe "The Catapults."

On a late November visit to Campeloupe, Virginia gave Nora an embroidery hoop, a pair of tutus she had made out of a pair of socks, and tiny matching hats she had embroidered with the letter C. While Nora was trying to coax her tutu-clad kittens through their hoop, Virginia pulled Cynthia aside. "Sometimes these things resolve to the best interest of the child, and sometimes politics wins," Virginia confided. "But I'm gonna do my best to deliver a knockout blow."

Amy subpoenaed about thirty people to serve as witnesses at the upcoming adjudicatory hearing—essentially everyone on Cynthia's list of references, including me. Amy scheduled interviews with each of us in December to ascertain what kind of testimony we could contribute and to show us the photographs Cynthia had been indicted for.

Female attorneys were not abundant in Lorain County, so Amy and Faye List had naturally become professional comrades. They didn't socialize much but were friendly in the courthouse and occasionally lunched together. After Amy's subpoenas went out, List hinted that Amy needed to be careful with those pictures. She said she hoped Amy wouldn't put the prosecutor's office in the position of having to prosecute *her*, too.

Faye's comments angered Amy and stiffened her resolve. She seethed to the other women in her office, "What? They're going to prosecute Cynthia for photographs nobody's allowed to see?"

In fact, Amy knew several people who had already seen the photographs without subpoenas: people in the court clerk's office, people on the judge's staff, people in the prosecutor's office other than the prosecutors. From the small world of the Lorain County legal community, with its grapevine of clerks, bailiffs, deputies, and secretaries, she had learned more than the prosecutors imagined. Rosenbaum and List might be trying to intimidate her, but Amy believed they would never follow through with prosecuting her. For one thing, she had a legal right to show the evidence of her client's alleged crime to defense witnesses. For another, if White and Rosenbaum decided to prosecute her, then Amy could turn around and subpoena people who had seen the photographs thanks to *them*.

When I arrived for my appointment at her office, Amy briskly introduced herself, led me to her conference room, and shut the door. I gave her the stack of photographs Cynthia had given me through the years. They were mostly of my son: Jesse in his blue-and-silver Jack Frost costume, Jesse playing the violin, Jesse diving for a soccer ball with oversize goalie gloves. But there were also pictures of me cheering on the soccer sidelines, pictures of my daughter Anna-Claire sporting her new braces and metallic smile, and the only pictures we had of my husband's bald head after his surgery for a brain tumor. At the time, it hadn't dawned on us that we would want to remember what his head had looked like bearing a raw, ragged incision. But Cynthia had seen Dan at a soccer game during his early convalescence and had wanted to photograph his shorn and stitched-up head. Once his hair had bristled back in and all the danger was behind us, we were grateful for Cynthia's insatiable camera and her double prints.

I had also brought a few pictures I had taken of my own children naked: three-year-old Anna-Claire grinning and wearing nothing but the squiggles she had drawn on herself with watercolors, and three-year-old Jesse wearing nothing but his sister's pink fairy wings.

Scribbling notes as I talked, Amy quizzed me about my perceptions of Cynthia, David, and Nora. Then she asked if I would be willing to give my honest reactions to Cynthia's bathroom pictures. I told her I would. But I was nervous about seeing them. What if, after starting a defense fund and publishing a letter of support in the local newspaper, I now found the pictures objectionable? Would I still be able to believe in Cynthia's innocence if I objected to her judgment?

Amy opened a manila folder and handed me several sheets of paper. Each photocopied sheet had four photographs, reduced to half-size and clustered in a lower quadrant of the page. The black-and-white images were highly contrasted, with splotches of white where the flash had made something shiny in the original color prints.

I glanced through the pages thinking, Amy must be warming me up with these—mild ones first, then she'll bring out the zingers. I glanced at them again and asked, "Is this it? Are there others?" Amy assured me she had given me all the nude pictures. I felt a surge of relief. "These are so much tamer than I imagined!" I burst out cheerily, instantly embarrassed that I had betrayed my lingering doubts.

Then, one by one, I looked carefully at the photographs and tried to fix them in my memory. There were four shots of Nora rinsing herself with the shower sprayer, and they appeared to be a sequence. All of them showed Nora's whole body, with her legs closed, and a wide view of the bathroom with its rubber ducks, shampoos, and mildew on the walls. The first two photographs showed the shower sprayer touching her neck, with water falling down on her neck and chest. The third photograph showed the sprayer aimed at her pubic area, which was hidden by the water's spray. The sprayer itself was not touching her body. The fourth photograph showed the sprayer's water aimed at her buttocks, but, again, the sprayer was not touching her body. The expression on Nora's face in all four pictures looked matter-of-fact—as if she were rinsing off in a routine way.

I knew I would not have taken those photographs of my own

daughter at eight years old; nevertheless, I did not feel alarmed by them. My daughter had grown modest by that age, not locking me out of the bathroom during her bath, but clearly feeling more private about my presence than she had at younger ages. But Nora's matter-of-fact expressions, I thought, suggested a familiarity with and nonchalance about the presence of her mother and her mother's camera.

Many of the other photographs were waist-up or chest-up portraits of Nora with a towel wrapped, turban-like, around her head. Some were brightly lit and some darker, depending on whether a flash had been used. These seemed unremarkable to me, too, except in the number of them: about a half-dozen. In each of these, Nora was gazing straight into the camera, and she was not smiling, which made the photographs look artistic and posed rather than offhand and candid. More like suburban Vermeer than point-and-shoot Kodak.

The four photographs I found most striking were a sequence of Nora lying in the bathtub. In three of the photographs, Nora was mostly submerged in bathwater and propped up on her elbows, with only her head, shoulders, and chest lifted above the water. In two of these, Nora was looking up directly into the camera; in the other, Nora's eyes were closed, and her head was thrown back, with her long hair swirling behind her in the water's thin froth—the aftermath, evidently, of large bubbles. In the fourth photograph, the bathwater had drained out, and Nora was lying against the tub with her arms stretched out beside her, palms turned up. Her wet hair was sleeked back, her skin glistened, and, although she was not smiling, her look was open and unguarded. With her large eyes, she appeared to look straight up into the eyes of a viewer above.

This image startled me. It gave me the sensation of looking down at a gorgeous child who was consciously offering herself to my gaze. I imagined Cynthia in the bathroom looking down at her daughter through her camera, and Nora looking up into and trusting her mother's lens. It was a riveting photograph—a private homage, I thought, to the glistening beauty of a daughter's body and to the pleasure a mother takes in the miracle of her own child.

And then my mind lurched, and I imagined a stranger looking at that photograph: a film developer, a policeman, a prosecutor—someone trained to look for the sordid beneath the guise of innocence—or, worse, a pedophile who might feel a dark thrill looking down at the glistening child. For a sickening moment, the image in my hands distorted into a sexual invitation.

Amy interrupted my thoughts: "Would you have taken those photographs?"

"No," I told her, "I would not." I explained that my daughter at age eight would have been much too modest to allow me to photograph her naked. On the other hand, my son at age eight was an exuberant, outgoing child who was not at all protective of his privacy. He liked talking to me while he took a bath, he wasn't embarrassed for his older sister to see him naked, and I doubted that he would mind if I took pictures of him nude.

But, I pointed out, as a writer, I had recorded my children's development—their witticisms, their routines, their imaginative play—more in my poems and journal entries than in photographs. Cameras were not usually sitting around my house ready to shoot, and when they were hauled out, everyone tended toward a "Cheese!" mentality. No one noticed, though, when I went into my study and recorded family moments in my journal with my inconspicuous pen.

I had brought Amy several photocopied pages from a handwritten journal I had kept when my children were younger. Sometimes in my journal entries I had written about my children's nakedness. But what if I were a photographer instead of a poet? Would these little anecdotes, which seemed benign in words, have looked sinister through the wordless lens of a camera? Could the same family moment appear chaste in one medium but pornographic in another?

I handed Amy the copied pages. In the first entry, my son was two-and-a-half years old and just learning his colors, and my daughter was six:

> Jesse plunges in—always walking right in, chattering away.
> He talks a lot, and he often talks very loudly, as if everything

*he says is an exciting pronouncement. "Mommy, I pupple, I
pupple!" he said getting out of the tub & examining the head of
his penis the other night. After he was dried off, he ran naked
into the kitchen to give Anna-Claire and Dan an opportunity
to share in this revelation: "Daddy! I pupple! I pupple!" He
was so pleased.*

In the second entry, Jesse was three years old:

*Tonight we were eating supper in the backyard. Jesse was
naked from washing the yellow car (& pretending he was
Captain Hook. He'd walk the "plank"—a step stool—and
"splash into the sea"—a bucket of water that he could just
fold up into. He made me be Wendy & walk the plank, too.)
Anyway, at supper he was still naked, standing on the picnic
bench, smeared here & there with pesto & a stray squiggle of
capellini. He scooted close to me to eat &, out of the blue,
slung his naked little arm around my shoulder, leaned his little
naked body against me, & said with satisfaction, "Sure is a
good family!"*

Amy slipped my journal entries into a file folder with my name
on it. She thanked me and said she would be back in touch about
testifying.

When Katha Pollitt's column—"Prosecuting Innocence"— appeared
in *The Nation* in December, it was the first mention of Cynthia's prosecution in the national press. Pollitt described David's relationship to
The Nation, the events leading up to Cynthia's arrest, the coverage in
the local media, the Ohio laws, and then she continued:

I've spent days talking to legal experts, and I still don't understand what is supposed to be pornographic about taking
a picture of your naked child. Depending on the child, it
might be a bad idea—or a good idea—but unless you be-

lieve nakedness itself is obscene, what makes it porn? It
can't be the use to which the picture is put. The state is
not arguing that Cynthia was planning to do any of the
things people do with porn: publish it, sell it, trade it, use
it for personal sexual gratification, like those home videos
people make of themselves having sex. What makes the
photos of Nora porn seems to be that they struck a handful of total strangers as "over the line," in the words of
the Oberlin cop who first investigated the photo lab re-
ferral. Such a judgment call raises the question of whose
judgment is being called upon. In one photo Nora's facial
expression appears to the prosecutor as "provocative";
to Cynthia's lawyer Amy Wirtz it looks "sarcastic." The
showerhead Cynthia's accusers apparently see as a mastur-
batory aid looks to others who have seen the photos like,
well, a showerhead.

The column concluded with the address of the defense fund.

Immediately, *The Nation* began receiving e-mails to the editor.
Pollitt forwarded those e-mails to David, including one from a man
in Colorado:

Dear Nation:

Katha Pollitt's article about Cynthia Stewart, the
woman ridiculously charged with child pornography,
reminded me of a joke. A man (probably, I now
realize, a district attorney) is taking a Rorschach
test. He has a lewd interpretation for every slide
the therapist presents to him. Finally, in shock,
the therapist exclaims, "You have the dirtiest
mind I have ever encountered." "What do you mean?"
replies the patient. "You are the one showing the
dirty pictures."
  These days, this joke is more telling than funny.

My check to the Stewart Defense Fund follows by
ordinary mail.

Once or twice a week, Rebecca or I had been checking the mailbox
we had rented at the Oberlin post office. In early December, we had
collected another $2,000 for the fund—mostly local money donated
in response to our letter in the *Oberlin News-Tribune*. But after Pollitt's editorial appeared, the tiny mailbox was crammed daily with
letters of support from all over the country, accompanied by checks
ranging from $5 to $500.

"A 70-year-old woman who has <u>always</u> hated injustice" sent
$20 from San Francisco. A woman from Gary, Indiana, sent $20 and
wrote: "We used to love to take snapshots of our little grandchildren
in the tub, but no more. What happened to you could happen to
any of us." A "Wellwisher from England" sent $20 and a note full of
exclamation points: "The world is going mad!! What next? Are we
going to be banned from changing our babies' nappys!?" A man from
Independence, Missouri, sent $20 and a bit of cynicism: "We're not
really that far removed from the epoch of the Inquisition and the
witch hunts. Justice being a commodity in our society, I can only
hope this helps you buy some."

Some letters invoked God's help ("I just read *The Nation* article & May God give you strength!"), some letters vented anger ("A
Bloody Outrage!"), and some letters did both ("God's speed, and
don't let the bastards get you down!"). A man from Oregon sent $25
and a "satiric verse" he had composed titled "Justice":

> The mother's photos show her little girl nude.
> The DA saw clearly that they were lewd.
> They'd caused him erections again and again.
> For those offenses she must go to the pen. . . .

The writer acknowledged, "Perhaps I take undue liberties with the
character of the DA, but he must have a salacious imagination to

do what he is doing." A ninety-year-old man from California, who had worked as a locomotive fireman in Toledo in the 1940s, sent $25 in "Honor & in Praise of Buckeye Bravery!!!" A man from Palo Alto sent $20 and one question: "Where is the ACLU when they are needed?"

Some people asked to be kept informed about Cynthia's case, while others made clear they didn't want to be thanked. A man from Atlanta sent a check for $50 with the note: "Cash it, good luck, and please don't put my name on any mailing list or database. I get enough junk in the mail as it is."

A number of lawyers wrote with advice and moral support. An attorney from a rural Ohio county sent $50 with the explanation: "This Oberlin graduate (class of '46) and small-town lawyer knows that dealing with that puritanical zealot, Greg White, requires far more than a sympathy card." A judge in Missouri, who described himself as an "official gatekeeper against small-town prosecutorial excess," ended his letter with a wry pun:

> In concord against jurisprudery, I am
> Yours truly,

One man described a similar incident in the D.C. suburbs. "The bottom line," he wrote, "was that the authorities—police, child protective services, and, at first blush, the court—were certain their inquisitional methods were doing God's work."

And a dozen women on the staff of a Midwestern abortion clinic sent the story of a trial six years before. The clinic director's wife had taken pictures of their young daughter playing dress-up. For those pictures, the wife had been indicted by a grand jury, tried for contributing to the delinquency of a minor, and placed on probation. The motive for the prosecution seemed political to many people since the state's attorney general had been outspoken in his opposition to abortion. The staff's Christmas gift to their director this year was to send $100 to the Cynthia Stewart Legal Defense Fund.

Katha Pollitt forwarded a check for $100 she had received from her former college English professor at Harvard—and the letter he had typed on an actual typewriter:

> *I promise you that writing you letters is not going to become a weekly habit, but your column in the December 13 number struck home, literally. I grew up in Oberlin and remember it as a stuffy place in its way—teetotal, e.g., to the great regret of the Yorkshire-born pressman at the printing shop where I worked, who missed his beer. But I don't remember it as given over to zeal-of-the-land, busy invasions of ordinary privacy, of the kind you now report.*
>
> *You might like to know that besides sending a check to the Stewart Defense Fund, I've written to the minister of the First Church, to which I once belonged and which has a long tradition of outreach to those in need, near and far, urging the church to give its support to Cynthia Stewart and her family.*
>
> *So you see your pen, or word processor, or whatever you use, retains its power.*

Within a few weeks of Pollitt's column appearing in *The Nation*, the defense fund had received more than two hundred letters from across the country, and we had deposited $18,301 more into the bank.

11

New Year's Dread

To get to her boxes of photographs stored in the basement of Amy's office, Cynthia had to go into a storage room, pull up a brass ring fastened to the floor, heave open a trapdoor, and ease herself down a steep flight of wooden steps while trying not to hit her head on the basement ceiling. Soon after the arrest, Amy had asked Cynthia to comb through her pictures and find every nude shot she had ever taken of Nora. She wanted to gather the context that would make Cynthia's bathtub shots explicable to a judge or jury. With a card table and a few lamps from home, Amy had improvised a workspace for Cynthia in the cavernous, cement-floored basement, whose shelves were piled with legal records and now her client's "Boswellian" archives.

For Cynthia, the assignment was a gift. She was grateful to be contributing something positive to her own defense, and she loved working with her pictures. Because it made her nervous, though, to separate original prints from their dated and annotated envelopes, she meticulously documented her work. She placed each nude print into its own white envelope on which she noted the print's negative, roll, and box numbers, its developing date, a brief description of its subject ("Nora standing in tub with toothbrush in ear," "Nora sitting in tub with mutton chop bubbles on face," "Nora with bee sting getting bath at Bash with Gramma"), and the phrase "Marked on Bag" once she had recorded the print's negative number on its original package. It was a complicated, cumbersome process—which is why Cynthia had been spending part of several days each week in Amy's basement.

Through November and December, Amy and Kreig had been very busy, too, researching, drafting, and filing various motions. In the Children Services case, Amy filed a motion urging the magistrate to conduct an *in camera* interview—a private interview in her personal chambers—with Nora as soon as possible. Amy thought Nora herself was the most persuasive evidence that she was not an abused child. But Amy did not want to traumatize Nora by making her testify at the hearing; indeed, children were almost never required to take the witness stand in a Children Services case. An *in camera* interview was the more humane and common practice.

The prosecutor's office filed a response—signed by Faye List and Greg White—opposing the *in camera* interview. They argued that anything the child said would be "irrelevant" since Children Services only had to show that she was a minor and had been the subject of obscene material to prove she was an abused child. If the magistrate perceived the pictures as obscene, nothing the child might say could change that.

In the criminal case, Kreig and Amy filed a motion asking the prosecution to identify which of the photographs on Cynthia's roll of film had incurred the indictments. White and Rosenbaum responded:

> Now comes the State of Ohio and submits that there are nineteen (19) photographs depicting the victim of this case in the state of nudity.
>
> Nine (9) of these photographs have the juvenile victim assuming adult-like postures or expressions which are inappropriate and beyond her years. Two (2) of these photographs have a hand-held shower orifice held and utilized in a both provocative and adult-like manner which is inconsistent with normal photographs of a child of tender years and certainly inappropriate. The State alleges that all of these photographs, particularly the two mentioned above, violate the laws charged in the indictment.

Kreig and Amy submitted another motion asking Judge Zaleski to conduct an *in camera* inspection of the testimony presented to the grand jury. In Ohio, the presiding judge must rule that a defendant has a "particularized need" for a grand jury transcript to be inspected before that judge can see it. Kreig and Amy argued that if the prosecutor informed the grand jury only of the original law but not of the subsequent constraints placed upon that law, then the indictment would be "defective." And since the usual justifications for keeping grand jury testimony secret (flight of the suspect; protection of victims and witnesses) were irrelevant in this case, the only reason for secrecy here was to protect misleading behavior by the prosecutor. "Simply, what is at issue," they argued, "is the probability of prosecutorial misconduct during the grand jury stage in order to secure the indictment of an individual who is innocent."

Judge Zaleski ruled that Cynthia did show a particularized need to have the grand jury transcript reviewed, and he ordered White and Rosenbaum to submit the transcript for his *in camera* inspection. Instead of complying with Zaleski's order, however, the prosecutors returned to the grand jury and came back with new indictments on the same charges. These indictments were identical to the previous ones except for the addition of one sentence: "The Grand Jury further finds that the photographs in question constitute a lewd exhibition in that they show or intend to excite lust or sexual desire."

Again, Kreig and Amy filed a motion requesting an *in camera* inspection of the grand jury transcript. Rosenbaum filed a response bristling with indignation. He wrote that it was "ridiculous" for the defendant to suggest that the state would "obtain indictments in cases that the State could never win at trial." And he rebuked the defendant's "efforts to cast aspersions upon the prosecutor's office and to make false claims in an affidavit exonerating herself," although he did not specify which of the statements in Cynthia's August affidavit he considered false claims.

Another defense motion—to obtain copies of Cynthia's color prints—also made sparks fly. Kreig and Amy argued that since the photographs formed the basis of the charges against Cynthia, the color prints were critical to the preparation of her defense. If the judge did not compel the prosecution to provide those prints to the defense, then the prosecution should be barred from introducing the photographs as evidence.

Rosenbaum filed a response in which he refused, absent a court order, to give Amy and Kreig anything more than the black-and-white photocopies they already had. He argued that expert witnesses would not be allowed to testify at the trial since only the trier of fact (the judge or jury) had the power to determine if the photographs were lewd. Expert opinions were irrelevant.

Although the prosecutors had in their possession both sets of Cynthia's prints and could have given one set to Amy, Rosenbaum couched his response as a refusal to *reproduce* porn: "The State of Ohio is not in the business of reproducing child pornography in violation of the [law]. . . . Clearly the fewer copies of such prohibited materials that are in existence will make the task of destroying them and removing them from the face of this planet much more easy."

The editorial page of the *Chronicle-Telegram* had a history of challenging the prosecutor's office, but the Elyria newspaper had not yet weighed in on Cynthia's prosecution. After Rosenbaum's refusal to provide the color prints, however, they published a blunt and skeptical editorial with the headline: "Obscenity Case Smells of Something More."

Echoing the prosecutors' own language, the editors accused White and Rosenbaum of acting in "a provocative and inappropriate manner." And they savaged Rosenbaum for claiming to withhold prints from the defense because it would make the task of "removing them from the face of this planet much more easy":

> Whew! What zeal! Wish we could believe he meant it and nothing more. But it has the odor of grandstanding, and it suggests to us that something other than justice is on the agenda of the Lorain County prosecutor's office.
>
> Why not just supply the reproductions? If the photos

are as objectionable as the prosecutor's office says they are, they might encourage the defense to cop a plea. . . .

This isn't the first time Rosenbaum has been involved in a child sex case during the run-up to an election, nor the first time the defense has complained about access to information. The infamous Head Start case, which went to trial during White's unsuccessful run for Congress in 1994, bristled with similar issues.

The pitiful thing about Rosenbaum's refusal is that it doesn't make any sense. Even though he says the state is unwilling to reproduce pornography, it already has reproduced the photos, in photocopy form.

So what's he saying? That the state will reproduce low-quality porn but not high-quality porn? That Ohio is Larry Flynt, not Hugh Hefner?

Cynthia, David, and Nora were spending the holiday at the Stewart family's Christmas Bash. Like the summer Bash, this gathering had its own rituals, including the Christmas Program in which everyone in the extended family performed music, a skit, or a bit of guerrilla theater.

This year for the Christmas Program, Nora had decided she wanted to perform a solo act with her kittens. Before the show, Nora wrote "STLUPATAC" in thick red letters across her forehead with a tube of lipstick. She'd tried to write "CATAPULTS," but she'd done it by looking in a mirror, so the word had ended up backward.

When her act was announced, Nora placed her costumed kittens on a piano bench, and then, flourishing chipped ham, beckoned them to jump through her embroidery hoop. The kittens did not jump through the hoop, and they showed absolutely no interest in the chipped ham. Instead, they jumped off the bench and slipped into the audience in their tutus and caps. Everyone laughed, but Nora was pleased. The Catapults hadn't exactly cooperated, but it had been her first Christmas Program performance without either of her parents, and that made her feel grown-up and proud.

The family needed to come home before New Year's to ready themselves for the Children Services hearing scheduled for Monday, January 3. When they arrived in the wee hours of December 30, they found their answering machine flashing "Full." Several friends had called, excited about the *Chronicle-Telegram* editorial; Virginia had left two urgent messages; and Amy had let them know that Nora's caseworker Tracy had finally called to arrange her first home visit. Amy had agreed to meet Tracy at their house on Thursday, which now meant *today*.

Cynthia and David woke early so they would have time to clean the house before Tracy arrived. But first they returned Virginia's and Amy's calls. Virginia had finished her GAL report for Children Services and had written the strongest report she could—so strong that the secretary typing up her first draft had added the word "Duh!" after Virginia's wry observation: "I've never heard of pornographers taking their film to Drug Mart!"

Virginia had given Amy and Faye List each the opportunity to read her report. The two women had both arrived at the Voices for Children office just as Virginia was proofreading the document page by page as it came out of the printer. The meeting had started off testily—List and Amy had evidently had heated words earlier in the day—but ended with List bemoaning Virginia's positive assessment of the family. "Maybe we can get the charges reduced to growing fungus on the bathroom wall," she had complained. "According to this report, that's the only thing I can convict them of."

Virginia also wanted to tell Cynthia and David her new theory about Rosenbaum: that he didn't want to provide the defense with color prints because he knew they were weak as evidence. Amy had shown Virginia the photocopies, and Virginia had thought the black-and-whites looked moodier, more artsy, posed, and sinister than the color snapshots, which looked more like normal life.

From Amy, the news was terrible. She had just learned that List was issuing a last-minute subpoena for Nora to testify for the prosecution on Monday. Amy was furious, especially since List and White had opposed an *in camera* interview with Nora as "irrelevant." She guessed that List wanted a dramatic way of establishing in the courtroom that Cynthia had taken the pictures of Nora. Instead of submitting as evidence the affidavit, in which Cynthia had freely acknowledged she was the photographer, List preferred to put Nora on the stand and ask questions without context: "Is this a picture of you?" *Yes.* "Who took these pictures of you?" *My mother.*

Amy's personal news was worse: her father had just called, and her mother was failing quickly. She would come to Campeloupe for Tracy's visit but would leave immediately afterward for her parents' home. She couldn't predict what the next few days would bring.

That afternoon, minutes after Amy arrived, Tracy knocked on the door, right on time. When Cynthia welcomed her, Tracy apologized—she had someone waiting in the car and could only stay a few minutes. In less than half an hour, both Tracy and Amy had come and gone.

Late that afternoon, a sheriff's car pulled into Campeloupe's driveway. Nora, who was playing in her room with two friends, saw its flashing lights. Too scared to move, she watched two deputies walk to the house, disappear onto the front porch, then walk back to their car and drive away.

Nora raced into the living room and clung to her mother, who was reading a piece of paper. She assured Nora that no one was being taken away. "It's okay," she hugged Nora. "It's just a subpoena. I'll explain it to you later." Relieved, Nora went back and told her friends, "It's okay, it's just a subpoena." Although none of the children knew what a subpoena was, Nora believed that, at least compared to being taken away in a police car, a piece of paper never hurt anybody.

But that evening, when her parents explained that the subpoena was for her, Nora worried that the deputies would come back in the night and take her away. Cynthia and David assured her that would absolutely *not* happen. Like Amy, they were angry, but they tried not to show that anger to Nora. They explained that she would be questioned at Monday's hearing by three women: one woman she didn't know named Faye List, and two women she did know, Amy and Virginia. All she had to do was give short, true answers.

At bedtime, Nora always said goodnight to all the fish in her aquarium and all the cats in the house. Through David's repertoire of voices, each fish and cat would wish her goodnight and sometimes add a special message. The night before a violin recital, a goldfish might tell Nora to "Break a fin!" If Nora was feeling blue at bedtime, Horatio, the bristle-nosed plecostomus, might encourage her, in a cultured British accent, to "Keep your bristles up!" After all the fish and feline goodnights, Cynthia and David would tuck Nora in with their family's invented blessing: "Nigh nigh nigh tucka roo roo roo." Lately, though, the goodnight ritual had not been enough to settle Nora. That night, like many others recently, Cynthia had to lie down among her daughter's lumpy menagerie for a long time before Nora drifted off to sleep.

The next morning—the morning of New Year's Eve—Nora burst into her parents' room early. Cynthia feared something was wrong with Jennie and Primo because Nora always carried the kittens up to their room as soon as she woke up. "What's happened?" her parents asked, alarmed, as Nora tore into the bed, burrowed between them, and began to sob. Haltingly, she described a nightmare she had just had. After they cuddled and calmed her, Cynthia asked Nora if she would repeat the dream into their tape recorder. Nora agreed and retold her dream in the stuffy-nosed voice of a child who, though now sanguine, has recently been crying.

The dream began with a normal day at school, except that there was a huge volcano outside on the playground. At first, no one was especially concerned about the volcano. Then the classroom floor started opening up beneath them. Nora and her classmates ran outside and found themselves in a stone maze of streets. "I found our house," Nora told her parents, "and the three of us scooped up the kittens, and the cats, and the fish in a bucket, and kept running."

Soon everyone else disappeared, and Nora found herself alone in the maze with a giant who was threatening to dump out a huge bottle of poisoned blood. "Then the giant poured the blood, and it sort of became a river," she continued, "and the splash was so big that it started to rain. And I got on top of this big structure because I could fly—I had big purple wings just like I always wanted to have. And I was sort of taunting him with the fact that I was up high and he was down low and there was nothing he could do about it. But I had to get down, or he would climb up.

"So I flew down. But the giant filled up the door so I couldn't get out. The giant and some of his knights said they wanted to take away my senses. And obviously they weren't *just* going to take away my senses because there were tools and scissors."

So Nora woke herself up. "I woke up panting from my dream," she remembered, "but I didn't really want to wake up because I didn't really know if it *was* a dream! I felt like the giant could be standing in front of me! I glanced around and saw the kittens, and I ran upstairs. I was too scared to do anything else."

On Sunday morning, January 2, Amy called Cynthia and David on her cell phone. In a small shaken voice she said that hospice had been brought in and that she was driving to Toledo again to be at her mother's side. The Children Services hearing scheduled for the next day would have to be postponed. Could Cynthia and David call the witnesses and let them know?

Cynthia felt terrible for Amy. But she also confessed in her notes that night a private sense of relief that the hearing would be delayed—"like the fleeting relief someone on a raft in the middle of the ocean feels when a cloud briefly covers the blazing sun."

12

Motions, Briefs, Schemes,
and Case Plans

Virginia was outraged. She had never heard of a child being sub-poenaed to testify in a Children Services hearing, no matter what awful thing that child's parents had allegedly done. Virginia believed *in camera* interviews were the only acceptable way to get testimony from a child, and, as Nora's guardian ad litem, she was go-ing to protest the subpoena loud and strong.

On New Year's Day, Virginia left a long message on Campeloupe's answering machine letting Cynthia and David know that she had called the executive director of Children Services at home and "reamed him out over this subpoena thing." On Monday, she was go-ing to request that Nora be appointed an attorney of her own. "Even if they're only going to ask one question, Nora needs an attorney," Virginia declared. "And she needs an attorney because I'm going to suggest that she turn around and *sue* Children Services. Out of the thousand or more cases that Lillian has been involved in, not once have they ever subpoenaed the child to juvenile court! This is just an abuse of power. And, listen, you know that bus driver, the one—I hope you're not lettin' Nora listen to this—that bus driver for Head Start? She didn't do *anything* ahead of time. You need to wage all-out war *now* because afterwards it's too late!"

Early Monday morning, Virginia made several calls to Children Services, then phoned Cynthia and David and complained, "Tracy didn't know about the subpoena, and she's Nora's caseworker!" Tracy's supervisor hadn't known, either. "What do you *mean*, a sub-poena?" she had asked Virginia. All this proved to Virginia that the caseworkers were pawns for the county prosecutor and that decisions about Nora were being made from the top down and for the wrong reasons.

In the Children Services log, Tracy detailed these conversations with Virginia, including a last tense exchange in which Tracy advised Virginia to call Faye List directly. Virginia shot back, "Don't *you* tell the prosecutor what to do? Or are they just doing what they want?"

Virginia did call List, who insisted, over the GAL's objections, that the subpoena was "necessary to get complete information."

Virginia wanted to challenge Tracy's professional social worker's license because she was taking orders from the prosecutor rather than standing up for Nora's needs. But Lillian at Voices for Children calmed her down, suggesting that Tracy was young and perhaps felt put on the spot by her superiors. Plus, Lillian thought that the Children Services case was inherently weak. She told Virginia of a conversation she'd had with Tracy's supervisor, who had admitted they hadn't yet figured out what to put in the Children Services case plan.

Amy's mother died on January 3, the day Amy had been scheduled to defend Nora's family. When she returned to work a week later, Amy learned that the subpoena for Nora was not going to be reissued. List had ended up meeting with Lillian Leach at the Voices for Children office, and the upshot of their conversation was that Nora would not be needed at the rescheduled hearing—now set for January 20. As long as the GAL agreed to testify that Nora was the child in the pictures and that the pictures were taken in the family's bathroom, the child would not be re-subpoenaed.

Amy was grateful to Virginia for making List back down. She herself was exhausted and raw with grief. But Amy was determined to do everything in her power to make sure Nora Stewart did not lose her mother, too.

As executive director of the Ohio ACLU, Christine Link had been flooded with e-mails from people urging her to defend Cynthia Stewart. At meetings, members pulled her aside and asked, "What are you going to do about that terrible prosecution in Oberlin?" And because people at *The Nation* had talked to people at the national ACLU office, she was getting calls from the highest ranks of constitutional scholars asking, "What the hell is going on in Ohio?"

But the ACLU almost always joined in a criminal case *after* a conviction, and only when there was justification for an appeal on constitutional grounds. For one thing, the ACLU didn't have the resources to hire investigators to find out what the real facts were in a criminal case. In charges of child abuse, Link's usual position was "to stay about ten miles away." And because the ACLU's lawyers were experts on constitutional law and spent their days in libraries not courtrooms, defense attorneys like Amy Wirtz and Kreig Brusnahan provided better representation at the criminal trial stage than ACLU attorneys. A tough woman with a sly rumble of a laugh, Link liked to explain it with a malpractice analogy: "It's like when you go to have your gallbladder out. You want the doctor who routinely does gallbladders—not the doctor who specializes in hysterectomies."

Cynthia Stewart, however, had "good facts," and her case raised immediate constitutional issues. Plus Link and her board had come to view this case as a *political* prosecution—that is, one of those cases "when you need as many guns as you can get to face down a prosecutor who is abusing his power." For all those reasons, they had decided to submit an amicus brief in support of the motion to dismiss that Kreig and Amy were preparing. Even filing an amicus brief so early in a criminal case was unusual for the ACLU—it was only the second or third time in Link's ten years with the Ohio affiliate that they had weighed in before a criminal case had come to trial.

The ACLU's amicus brief embraced the premise that no citizen should ever be prosecuted for breaking a law that can't be clearly defined. The brief noted that the Ohio Supreme Court had itself objected to vague laws because they "fail to provide fair notice of what conduct is prohibited"; they "allow or encourage arbitrary and unequal enforcement"; and they "often proscribe conduct that is not morally culpable." The ACLU praised the Ohio law for trying to protect children from exploitation but criticized its unconstitutionally vague language, which made parents "necessarily speculate as to the meaning of the statute and whether taking snapshots of their children will subject them to a lengthy prison sentence."

Along with the ACLU's amicus brief, Kreig had filed a motion to dismiss the criminal case in Judge Zaleski's court on January 3. In that motion, Kreig and Amy argued that Cynthia's photographs were legal since the documentation of family events and milestones in a child's growth and development fell under the law's "other proper purposes" category of acceptable reasons to photograph a naked child. They also argued that the statute, even as constrained by the Ohio and U.S. Supreme Courts, was unconstitutionally vague and unconstitutionally overbroad. "The 'other proper purposes' language," they wrote, "does not save this defendant from having to go through the anxiety, expense, and torture of a criminal indictment and trial in order to show that she has 'proper purposes.'"

The following week, Jonathan Rosenbaum filed a response arguing that the law *was* constitutional, "despite the lofty claims of the American Civil Liberties Union" and that "the government has a right to protect children from abuse and to prohibit the creation and possession of some photographs or literary works even if it stifles someone's creativeness." He also reiterated the argument that only the trier of fact could determine if the photographs were lewd, and, therefore, a determination could be made without reference to the context of the photographs or the intentions of the photographer. The only "fact" upon which guilt or innocence should be determined was the judge's or jury's perception of the photographs.

Rosenbaum also accused Cynthia of lying to the police. His allegation was based on assumptions he had made after viewing the photo album she had submitted with her affidavit. Rosenbaum wrote:

> Examination of that binder clearly shows that the taking of photographs while the child is in the state of nudity stopped at the age of two or less. Only six of the sixty-six photographs submitted show the child in the state of nudity and she is at an age of two or less where such conduct is

totally acceptable and appropriate as dictated by the norms of our society. . . .

Therefore, it appears that the affidavit upon which the defendant so heavily relies in an effort to extricate herself from her activities with the police and in her motion to dismiss, is false and misleading. . . . As a result, such an affidavit is probably a further criminal violation as it is false since the photographs submitted do not bear out her claim that she has taken similar photographs as a chronicle of her child's growth and development.

Cynthia and David were appalled by what they called Rosenbaum's "wait-until-she's-ripe-to-photograph-her-nude theory," even though they knew his theory would take only a few minutes to refute in court. Combing through her pictures in Amy's basement, Cynthia had already accumulated a shoe box full of nude shots of Nora. Cynthia also had the film processing envelopes, with their dates and her jottings, to prove that virtually all of those photographs had been developed at public labs, mostly through the Oberlin Drug Mart. Among the pictures were a naked three-year-old Nora being tossed high into the air by David; a naked seven-year-old Nora walking on the banister of her front porch, pretending it was a tightrope; a naked eight-year-old Nora climbing a tree with her naked best friend, Isabel, both pretending to be monkeys; and naked bathtub pictures at all ages: Nora in bubble baths alone, Nora in bubble baths with her cousins, Nora in bubble baths with her cat, Nora in the bathtub with sticker-animals stuck to her, and even Nora, at ages three and five, rinsing herself off with the shower sprayer from top to bottom. Those two sets of pictures were more dramatic than the rinsing shots Cynthia had been indicted for. In the younger versions, Nora was hamming up her Power Ranger stance, brandishing the spray nozzle and making ferocious faces.

Cynthia could choose to be tried by a judge or a jury. Either way, Amy had concerns. So far, she had been pleased with Judge Zaleski's rulings in this case. He had recently ruled that Rosenbaum did have to provide the defense with Cynthia's color prints or forfeit the right to use her pictures as evidence. And he had just ruled in favor of Kreig and Amy's request of an *in camera* inspection of the second grand jury's transcript.

But Zaleski had not yet seen Cynthia's photographs himself. And if those pictures struck him the wrong way, Amy didn't know what he would do. She kept reminding Cynthia and David that Judge Zaleski was a Catholic man with a passion for protecting children.

But she was even more nervous about Lorain County jurors, who tended to be gray-haired people from more conservative parts of the county. Amy didn't know what they would think of a woman from Oberlin who didn't shave her legs and had never felt the need to marry her child's father.

On January 11, a front-page story in the *Chronicle-Telegram* gave Cynthia and David a fleeting moment of glee and a reason to think they might forgo a jury trial and take their chances with the judge: Democrat Zaleski and Republican White were having an election-year spat. Beneath the headline "Judge Alleges Scheme in Primary," the article reported that an attorney representing the prosecutor had approached the judge with a private deal: if Zaleski persuaded Democrats not to field a candidate against White in the 2000 prosecutor's race, then White would guarantee that no Republican ran against Zaleski for judge. According to the article, the judge rebuked White's offer:

> Who decides to run for an office and who doesn't is "none
> of my business," Zaleski said. . . .

White responded defensively:

> White would neither confirm nor deny that such an offer
> was made. But he contends Zaleski is misrepresenting the
> circumstances.
> "Ed Zaleski is being disingenuous with his position

here. . . . Ed needs to get out more. He needs to get a life," White said. "He raised nothing prior to the filing deadline. What does that tell you?"

When the Ohio Secretary of State's office was questioned about the legality of the offer, a spokesman said that no state law addressed this sort of situation. "I would encourage you to contact your county prosecutor to see if there are any applicable criminal statutes," he suggested, presumably without irony.

Soon after he had filed the motion to dismiss, Kreig Brusnahan called Greg White. He decided to bypass Rosenbaum because, over the years, Kreig had watched the chief assistant prosecutor take "one too many, or maybe one *hundred* too many, cheap shots." After a while, Rosenbaum's credibility had been compromised, at least in Kreig's eyes.

On the other hand, Kreig respected White. They shared a mutual friend who had, on occasion, brought them together for golf. Kreig believed that it was to his benefit—and to his clients' benefit—if he cultivated an open line of communication with the county prosecutor, and so he had.

White agreed to meet with Kreig and Amy to discuss the Stewart case. At the meeting, White listened and was courteous but said little. Kreig detailed the legal reasons to dismiss the charges, but he also tried to put Cynthia's family and photographs in context, explaining that Cynthia was "an old hippie" with a lifestyle that differed from their own. Kreig acknowledged that neither he nor White would have taken those pictures, but he insisted that Cynthia had intended no harm to her child, and, indeed, no harm had been done until the child's mother had been arrested.

Amy felt ignored by the two men during the meeting. At one point, she broke in and urged White, "Nora truly *is* a healthy child, and you are destroying a mother-child bond that can never be replaced—." But tears filled her eyes and caught her off-guard.

Though courteous, White seemed unconvinced by Kreig's arguments and unmoved by Amy's plea. He thanked them for the meeting, but expressed no interest in altering the course of either the criminal or Children Services prosecutions.

At the end of a therapy session in early January, Nora's therapist asked to speak privately with Cynthia. Nora rocked in a rocking chair in the waiting room while Cynthia went into Pat Chmura's office. Nora liked the waiting room because sometimes the ambient music circled around to the soundtrack from *Titanic*. If David were in the waiting room when that Hollywood music came on, he would get irritable and go outside for fresh air. But Nora always listened for "My Heart Will Go On," and sang earnestly along.

Pat had not seen Cynthia's photographs until recently. She told Cynthia that she remained unequivocally positive about Nora's psychological health. But about the taking of the pictures, she asked, "What was in your head? You must be incredibly naive!"

Cynthia explained that she was making a photo journal of Nora's life and that "we don't censor our family life, so I haven't censored my pictures."

"But she's eight years old!" Pat said. "You can't just send these photographs out in the world because *this* is what can happen!"

Between January 3 and January 20, Tracy initiated phone conversations with five people to discuss Nora Stewart. In the Children Services log, she recorded rave comments about Nora and her family from the first four, all from Cynthia's list of references. The last person Tracy spoke with, on January 19, the day before the rescheduled hearing, was Pat Chmura. It was her first talk with Nora's therapist.

Tracy submitted the Children Services case plan to the court just before the hearing began on January 20. The case plan acknowledged that Nora was intelligent, articulate, close to her parents, had appropriate friends and activities, and that Cynthia and David were very involved with Nora and her well-being. The concerns were 1) that Cynthia had taken nude pictures of Nora and had been charged in criminal court for those photographs, which was causing anxiety for

Nora; and 2) that Cynthia and David might not understand "the impact the pictures could have on Nora at some point."

To produce the desired changes in the family, Nora would need to continue in counseling, and Cynthia and David would need psychological testing, counseling, and parenting education. Tracy would monitor the family with home visits, school visits, ongoing access to Nora's therapist, and regular written reports from Cynthia and David's counselors and parenting educators. The family's progress would be reviewed monthly by Tracy and her supervisor, semi-annually by Children Services, and annually by the court.

To Cynthia and David, the case plan was both infuriating and ludicrous. The fact that Tracy—an inexperienced young woman with little knowledge of Nora or their family—would be monitoring and evaluating their family's "progress" struck them as laughable. They wondered how many abused children and desperate families would not receive the help they needed while their own family was being monitored, evaluated, written up, and reviewed.

Virginia submitted her guardian ad litem report to the court, too. She described her observations of the family, including various ways they were culturally different from the mainstream. She listed the forty-six people she had interviewed, quoted specifics from many of them, attached letters from some of them, and reported her findings in frequent boldface, capital letters, and underlinings:

> This case is different than any other this GAL has been involved with in that out of **ALL THE PEOPLE INTER-VIEWED (100%)** not one person had anything but praise for Cynthia Stewart (Mother) and David Perrotta (Father) and spoke in glowing terms about them as individuals and concerning their parenting skills.
>
> Also, **EVERYONE (100% OF THOSE INTER-VIEWED)** believes that Cynthia's nude photographs of Nora were **NOT** meant for harm. . . . In fact, they expressed anger at the system that brought harm into this child's life.

In her summary, Virginia blasted Lorain County Children Services:

> It was this GAL's understanding that the original intent of LCCS was to handle this case at the lowest level possible (in-home monitoring). How did the system go from the lowest level of intervention on the part of LCCS to the highest level possible (abuse)? What happened? Who lost perspective?

The database of defense fund contributors stored on my laptop was growing large. But Cynthia didn't have faith in my digital archives. She wanted more tangible data: a photocopy of every donated check. So after all the relevant information had been entered into my computer, I passed along stacks of checks to Cynthia to photocopy—a process that sometimes slowed down the depositing of money by weeks.

In mid-January, Cynthia had gone to the local copy shop with a fresh stash of checks. As she duplicated them a few at a time on a self-serve copier, Cynthia looked at the donors' names and thought about the many small and large sacrifices people were making to help her family. That night, she wrote a letter to the editor of the *Oberlin News-Tribune*, which David faxed to the newspaper:

To the Editor:

So there I am standing at the copy machine Xeroxing checks (because eventually I want to thank everyone individually), and I'm standing there with tears running down my face. I am simply overwhelmed with the support and generosity shown to me and my family by the people of Oberlin. Thank you all.

The letter was published on the eve of the Children Services hearing. That night Tom Theado left a message on Campeloupe's answering machine: "I'm not going to sing my message, but I will compliment Cynthia on a nice letter to the editor, which is what prompted this call. And the musing of what additional crimes has she admitted to as a consequence of photocopying checks? Interesting! Well, I'll talk to you later, goodbye!"

13

"I Know It When I See It"

Lorain County had outgrown its nineteenth-century stone court-house. Soon a seven-story, glass-sleek Justice Center would take its place, with enough courtrooms for all criminal, civil, and juvenile proceedings. In the meantime, Children Services hearings were being held in a converted office supply building—a low, gloomy, industrial-looking place that did not inspire meditations on the grandeur of the law.

Nora, though, was eager to go to that building with her parents on January 20, to be as close to them as possible during the Children Services hearing. Cynthia and David agreed to let Nora skip school if Cynthia's mother kept her company in the lobby. Gerry came along with a canvas bag full of books so the two of them could read together. Soon after they had settled into the lobby's hard chairs, though, Gerry realized Nora was too nervous for reading. So they watched people coming and going and began to tell each other stories about the strangers, imagining who they were, where they were going, and why.

The magistrate's office doubled as a cramped courtroom, with a large table filling much of the available space. The magistrate sat at one end of the table, with an empty chair beside her for witnesses and a tape recorder in front of her in lieu of a court stenographer. Amy, Cynthia, and David sat on one side of the table; Faye List and Tracy sat on the other side. Virginia sat at the table's far end. Whenever the door opened to let a witness in, Virginia had to scoot her chair out of the way.

Michele Arredondo, the magistrate, was Latina and fortyish.

Cynthia thought she looked stiff in her meticulous suit and nervously remote, as if she were waiting for a bomb to explode and would like to be as far away as possible when it happened. Cynthia tried to make eye contact with her but could never catch the magistrate's eye.

Faye List was a stout woman with a big voice. "Phlegmatic" was the word that floated into Cynthia's mind as she watched the prosecutor across the table. Cynthia worried that List might dominate Amy who was young, petite, and had a girlish voice—though she certainly knew Amy could become sharp-tongued when provoked.

Amy expected the hearing to take most of two afternoons. On this first day, List would call the prosecution's witnesses, with enough time left over for Amy to call the GAL and Nora's therapist to testify. Amy would finish up with witnesses from Cynthia's community on the second day.

Magistrate Arredondo opened the hearing by acknowledging that she still needed to rule on Amy's motion for an *in camera* inspection of Nora. Within seconds, it became clear the proceedings would be tense. The magistrate asked List if it were true that the prosecution had subpoenaed Nora to testify. List replied, "I did not subpoena her for this hearing, Your Honor. I had subpoenaed her for a previous hearing, subsequently discovered other ways of going about my case, and did not subpoena her for this hearing." When Virginia informed the magistrate that Nora had been traumatized by the deputies coming to her house, List bristled: "I just want the record to reflect the fact that I did not subpoena her for today."

Virginia wouldn't let it go. She said List had been "adamant, adamant" about bringing Nora to testify, even when informed of the distress the subpoena had caused her and even when this "would have been the first time in the forty-one-year history since 1959 from my research that a child has ever been subpoenaed to Domestic Relations Court. There has been children raped, burned, everything; this is the first time."

"Well, I certainly can remember situations in which children have been brought to court, at least for *in camera* interviews," Arredondo pointed out.

"*In camera*," Virginia agreed, "but not subpoenaed."

Arredondo tried to move the proceedings along: "Well, we are not here to place blame on anybody, okay? We are simply here to decide what's going to happen to the child." She said she would wait until later to rule on the *in camera* interview.

The prosecution's first witness was Detective Tom Anadiotis. Anadiotis described how, upon receiving the photographs from the Mansfield police, he had "managed to track down" the photographs to a Ms. Stewart and "eventually" been able to identify Nora as the subject of the photographs. Then, "as a result of my investigation," he said, "I obtained a secret indictment against the defendant." The officer's choice of words irritated Cynthia since they inflated the amount of sleuthing needed to pin those pictures on her.

During cross-examination, Amy established that Anadiotis had been a police officer for twelve years, had been working in Oberlin for only six months prior to this case, and had never received training in how to evaluate photographs for pornography. Amy asked Anadiotis if he had consulted members of the Oberlin community about what kind of mother Cynthia was before taking her pictures to the prosecutor, but List objected to the relevance of Amy's question, and the magistrate sustained the objection.

Amy's question and List's objection exemplified what would be their different tactics in the hearing. Amy would contend that Children Services needed to show harm had been done to Nora for her to be ruled abused. For List, all that mattered was whether the trier of fact—in this case, the magistrate—agreed with Anadiotis and the prosecutors that at least one of the photographs was obscene. If she did, then Nora was an abused child.

Yet any description of the photographs was quickly called into question—one side's "fact" becoming the other side's "interpretation." And even as List argued that intent was irrelevant, her own witnesses kept bringing up the issue. When List asked Teresa Thornhill, the investigating social worker, what her concerns had been when she first saw the pictures, Thornhill replied, "I had some questions about some of the photos that I would have wanted to talk to mom about, like what the intent of the photos were."

As guardian ad litem, Virginia was supposed to have the opportunity to cross-examine and to call her own witnesses. But Virginia was inexperienced in the courtroom and had not been well-briefed on rules and procedures. During cross-examination, Virginia accused Thornhill of misleading her early in her investigation by claiming that Cynthia had taken nude pictures of Nora as a toddler, had stopped taking nude pictures, and then had begun again when Nora was eight. Thornhill acknowledged that she had gotten that impression from the pictures Cynthia had submitted with her affidavit, but she denied presenting that impression to Virginia as an investigated fact.

"Well, I beg to differ," Virginia blurted out.

The magistrate chastised her: "You are not here to testify. You can't bring in your own statements. At this time, you can only ask questions."

Virginia apologized.

The prosecution's principal witness was Nora's caseworker. As Tracy took the seat next to the magistrate, Cynthia caught a whiff of her perfume and glanced at David. They had joked after Tracy's short home visit that her perfume had lingered longer at Campeloupe than she had.

List asked Tracy to describe the concerns that had motivated the Children Services case plan. Tracy said her first concern was "the poses in which Nora was standing" in the bathtub pictures. When List suggested that her second concern was that "Parents may have not understood the impact the pictures could have on Nora at some point," Tracy agreed.

"Why is that a concern for you?" List asked.

Tracy explained that Nora's parents may not have understood the impact being photographed nude could have on "Nora's own thoughts."

"Have you been able to work with the parents to explore where Nora is at on these issues or where the parents are at on these issues?" List asked.

"No."

"Have you made efforts in that regard?"

"Yes. Time permitting, yes, I have."

"And that has been difficult to get those things arranged?" List suggested.

"Due to time restrictions and due to, unfortunately, Amy's mom is ill, so, unfortunately, the first home visit I had to do was just almost a month ago," Tracy answered.

During cross-examination, Amy pushed Tracy on how many times she had spoken with Nora. Tracy said that she had briefly introduced herself to Nora at the pre-trial hearing. Then she listed the three other times they had spoken: "I spoke to her and had her mom present at school, just for a short period of time. I spoke to her at the home visit last month, and I said hello to her today."

"What specifically disturbs you or do you find inappropriate about these pictures?" Amy asked.

"The disturbing fact to me is that Nora was in a pose or a stance in a sexual position and her mother took a picture of it," replied Tracy.

Amy handed Tracy the photographs. "What about these pictures, to you, is a sexual stance?"

"The one in particular that concerns me is Nora standing in the bathtub with the showerhead up against or near her vagina."

"You can't tell if it's in her vagina or even touching her vagina, can you?"

"It's showing in front of her at least."

"In front of her," Amy repeated. "Isn't a reasonable or a plausible explanation that she is merely rinsing herself?"

"That is possible," Tracy acknowledged.

"And you don't know that that's not what is occurring, do you?"

"No, I don't know. I was not there."

"And you're using your own life experiences to interpret that picture, is that correct?" Amy asked pointedly. List objected, though Tracy didn't seem to catch the snide import of Amy's question.

Amy rephrased her question: "How did you come to the conclusion that that was a sexual picture?"

"I'm not saying whether or not anything was going on, I'm just saying there was a concern there, and that—."

Amy interrupted. "You can't even, other than just a guess, a pure guess, jump to the conclusion that that is sexual in nature, correct?" But List objected that Tracy had already answered the question, and Arredondo sustained her objection.

Amy quizzed Tracy about the reasons she had delayed her investigation of the family ("Just due to time schedules and things of that sort"), what she had learned about Nora from her teacher ("She said she was a great kid"), and how many people she had interviewed about the family ("I spoke to like five individuals, I think"). Tracy acknowledged that everyone had spoken of Cynthia as a photographer and devoted mother who had a strong, loving bond with her well-adjusted child.

"And you've had absolute access to Pat Chmura during this case. Is that correct?" Amy asked.

"Yes," said Tracy.

"And you have only spoken to her once?"

"Yes, I spoke to her yesterday."

"Yesterday?"

"Uh-huh."

"You didn't call her initially and make sure that Nora was going to counseling?"

"No. I took mom's word that she was going to counseling."

"Have mom and dad done what you have asked them to do thus far in this case?"

"I have not asked mom and dad to do anything."

"Except sign a release, correct?"

"Yes."

"And they did that?"

"Yes, thank you, yes."

"And it was communicated to me that you wished that Nora would continue that counseling. And then that has continued the whole time, correct?"

"Yes."

"And barring my schedule, they did make Nora available to you?"

"Yes."

"And didn't inhibit that, correct?"

"No, not at all."

"And so they have been very cooperative in this?"

"Yes, they have."

Several times during Tracy's examination, cross-examination, and re-examination, testy exchanges erupted between Amy and List. One of those exchanges occurred when Amy, in examining the case plan, asked Tracy questions about child development and the sexuality of children. List objected, "I don't think that this witness has been qualified as a psychologist on child sexuality."

"Well," Amy argued, "then I would ask that all of her previous testimony and relevance to the appropriateness of this case plan be stricken. If she doesn't understand sexual development and sexual relevance in regards to children, how can she write this case plan as it sits here today?"

List appealed to Arredondo: "Your Honor, the case plan . . . doesn't have anything to do with the child's sexuality or what the child feels about it. The case plan concerns are concerns about the parents, not concerns about the child."

"Allegedly, Children Services is here to protect Nora," Amy retorted. "If we are not here for that, then the agency should dismiss their complaint, and we should get out of here, and I'll go home."

Arredondo allowed Amy to continue with some of her questions but warned her not to go "too far afield" since Tracy had already "explained what her concerns are and why she has those concerns."

~~~

After Tracy's testimony, the prosecution had only two more witnesses to call: Cynthia and David. Amy had instructed both of them to take the Fifth Amendment because of the pending criminal trial. When List pointed out that there were "no criminal charges pending against Mr. Perrotta," Amy's response made tempers flare again.

"There are no *current* pending charges," Amy said. "However, through my investigation in this case, talking to Detective Anadiotis, it is my belief, and maybe a little paranoid, but, as an attorney, I have to instruct my client that there may be charges coming against him and may be investigation going on in that nature, and I believe that's why we are here today."

"Your Honor, that's about the fourth time Attorney Wirtz has made that particular reference," protested List. "In fact, I would encourage her, as she encouraged Lorain Children Services, to take a look at the welfare of this child and take a look at these photos and accept the fact that there is some responsibility here and this child may indeed be an abused child by virtue of the provisions of the Revised Code. I have allowed that to pass about four times, and I can't allow it again. It's inappropriate and out of line, and it doesn't belong in this proceeding."

Arredondo chastised Amy: "I would ask that you not bring that up again. You certainly made yourself heard." Then she allowed both Cynthia and David to assert their Fifth Amendment rights.

With no more witnesses to call, List moved to introduce the photographs as evidence. Amy objected. The photographs could not be admitted as evidence, she argued, until they had been shown to violate community standards for obscenity. And a violation could not be determined until community standards had been established. Amy contended that the magistrate could not establish those standards herself because she did not have authority to speak for the community. A diverse jury or an elected judge *might* be able to establish community standards without consultations, but as one individual appointed, not elected, to her position, Arredondo would need to consult widely with Cynthia's community in order to determine what the standards of her community were.

List countered that the magistrate, because she was the trier of fact, already *had* the legal authority to establish community standards. The magistrate agreed with List. She admitted the photographs as evidence.

Amy then made a motion to have the Children Services complaint dismissed, arguing that the prosecution had shown no evidence that the child was either dependent or abused. List argued against dismissal, contending that all that was necessary for a ruling of dependency was that the Court had some concern about the child. And List assured the magistrate that when she viewed Cynthia's photographs, she would be concerned.

List insisted that Nora was abused as well. For the first time in the hearing, she alluded to the part of the statute that prohibits the presentation and dissemination of obscene material. List argued that "these pictures have, in fact, been published. They have been published to the people at the film processing lab. Now we find they have been published to police officers. Furthermore, there was a reasonable chance even had those people not become involved, that these pictures could be published to some other individual."

Amy objected to the hypothetical charge. "There has been no evidence of that or even an insinuation of that," she argued hotly. But Arredondo overruled Amy's objection.

"Finally, Your Honor," List continued, "art only goes so far, until it can be shown to be violative of the obscenity laws. These pictures go beyond nudity. They show a child—. I won't go there. The Court can determine what they show, but they go beyond simple nudity, Your Honor."

Arredondo overruled Amy's motion to dismiss. "I haven't seen the photographs. I haven't made a judgment," she acknowledged. "But even a very good parent can do a wrong thing."

It was already after five o'clock. There was no time left for Amy to call witnesses. But she did have one last question for Arredondo: how could she make a ruling on the motion to dismiss before she had even viewed the photographs?

"I will review the pictures this evening and rule again, if you think that would be appropriate," Arredondo offered.

"I do, Your Honor," Amy replied.

As the hearing adjourned, Cynthia and David packed up their notepads and file folders and left to find Nora in the lobby. Nora quizzed her parents about the long afternoon, asking repeatedly if everything was going to turn out all right. Cynthia tried to reassure her, but Nora noticed how subdued her mother was, so she grew silent and worried herself. On the car drive home, however, David made Nora giggle by mimicking, in exaggerated voices, all the different ways the policeman's name—Anadiotis—had been mispronounced by the magistrate.

14

"The Average Person
with Average Sex Instincts"

David awoke the next morning with aches, chills, and a sore throat. The feverish discomfort of whatever flu bug he had caught seemed to David an appropriate response to the Kafka-esque experience he'd had the day before: sitting in a dull, cramped room and listening to lawyers argue about his family in the third person. He had had anxiety about how events would unfold from the moment the police had first come to Campeloupe's door. But he was still surprised by yesterday's proceeding, which he had found to be a bizarre debate bolstered by half-baked arguments and piecemeal appeals to legal precedents. As he and Cynthia packed up for their return trip to the makeshift courtroom, David added a box of tissues and a bottle of vitamin C to his briefcase.

David and Cynthia told Nora she had to return to school that morning. But they agreed she could come to the courthouse after school with her principal and teacher, who would be joining the group of witnesses Amy had subpoenaed.

The magistrate reopened the hearings by saying she had viewed the photographs and was again denying Amy's motion to dismiss. After reviewing case law, Arredondo disagreed with Amy's contention that a community standard for obscenity needed to be established before photographs could be admitted as evidence of abuse. And she concurred with List that it had not been necessary for the prosecution to present witnesses for the purpose of establishing a community standard. However, she did assure Amy, "I certainly will not prevent you from presenting any witnesses of that kind."

Amy's first witness was Nora's guardian ad litem. Amy established Virginia's credentials as an activist against child pornography, the timeline of her investigation, and her highly positive impressions of Nora's emotional well-being. But List objected frequently, citing irrelevance and complaining that Virginia was "wandering all over the place" in her responses. Arredondo upheld some of those objections, telling Virginia, "It isn't necessary to answer the question with every detail of every victim that you may have come across." When Virginia began to relate information from Nora's teachers, List objected to the testimony as hearsay. Arredondo sustained the objection.

Amy moved to a series of questions about Cynthia's photographs. She was hoping to establish—by the cumulative testimony of people who were not offended by the pictures—that Cynthia had not violated the obscenity standards for either the community of Oberlin or the greater community of Lorain County. Virginia was doing her best to give honest, helpful answers, but she became flustered by Amy's questions since her own community was quite different from the one she'd come to know through Cynthia. When Amy asked, "Do you believe that these pictures would offend the average person with average sex instincts?" Virginia acknowledged, "Maybe not offend, but I believe they would wonder why she was taking the picture of an eight-year-old."

Amy switched tactics and tried to establish that Nora's home environment was healthy and did not warrant a ruling of dependency. List objected several times that Virginia was merely repeating hearsay from those she had interviewed, and Virginia finally understood she was only allowed to give her firsthand impressions.

"Okay," Virginia said. "I observed that Nora is very close to both of her parents. I observed that she had these running jokes with her father all the time. She would go over and stand there like this and make a remark, like a comedy team. She would say something, and they would pick up the jokes. The jokes keep going. And with her mother, a very loving relationship. Very above average. More than most. I would say, I don't know what percentage, 80 or 90 percent of what people do for their child. They are on a real high level of parenting skills."

Virginia described how Nora had played the violin for her: "Well, I couldn't believe it. Like she should be in a symphony."

During cross-examination, List suggested that Virginia's perceptions had been too influenced by Cynthia's friends, and she questioned the relevance of many of Virginia's observations. She asked Virginia if Nora's intelligence, talents, or close and loving relationship with her parents would prevent her from being a victim of child pornography. Virginia acknowledged, "No. That wouldn't prevent her from being a victim."

"You talked about the word 'pornographic.' What makes a photo a pornographic photo?" List asked.

"I think a lot of it is intent," said Virginia. "How do they intend to use the photos."

"So," continued List, "you would agree with me that, perhaps, if these photos were taken not by the child's mother but by the man next door, they could be pornographic photos, in your definition?"

"Yes."

"So the content, just looking at the picture in and of itself, isn't what caused you to determine that that is or is not a pornographic picture?"

"In this case it was," Virginia insisted.

"Because you knew what the mother's intent was," said List.

"I didn't know," said Virginia. "When I saw the photos, I didn't think they were lewd. I didn't think they were sexual."

"Would you have concerns for your ward if these pictures were shown to the guy next door?" List asked.

"Well, yes. I don't think they should be shown around," said Virginia.

"Would you agree with me that one of the other components of pornography is whether or not it's acceptable to be shown in the community?"

"Actually, in their community of Oberlin College," Virginia said, haltingly. "I would say they actually teach this at Oberlin College. This is something you're supposed to do to raise your daughter in that context—."

"I'm talking about *your* community. This is *your* ward," interrupted List.

Amy objected that List was not allowing Virginia to finish her answers, and Arredondo sustained the objection.

List began again: "In your community of experience, is it appropriate to show these photos publicly?"

"In my community of experience, it's not appropriate to live together unmarried," Virginia pointed out.

When Amy re-examined Virginia, she circled back to Virginia's perceptions of her own community. Virginia explained that she was an evangelical Christian and "probably part of the most conservative-thinking community."

Amy then produced a book, *The Family of Children*, which had been checked out from a Lorain County public library and contained nude pictures. It had been her own mother who had encouraged Amy to submit library books as evidence when they had talked about Cynthia's case in the fall. A librarian herself, Amy's mother had urged, "Think about what a library is. It's a public building with public access. Librarians pull books off the shelf if they upset the community, and there are restrictions on what children can see. What a good place to see a community's standards reflected!"

As Amy flipped through the pages, List objected that the book was irrelevant. She complained, "All I saw was naked infants. I didn't see any naked eight-year-olds. I saw no child that looked older than toddler age."

Arredondo asked Amy if the photographs were limited to infants. "No," Amy said, showing the book to the magistrate, "there are different age children in here. There is one that looks like he's four or five. That's above toddler."

"And well below eight," snapped List.

Arredondo ruled that Amy could show Virginia the book for the purpose of pursuing the question of public viewing.

So Amy handed Virginia the book. "Would you please review

this book and look at all the tabbed pictures? Do you feel those are appropriate for public viewing?"

Virginia leafed through the pages and said, "Yeah. The kids were kind of cute."

Amy then handed Virginia the stack of Cynthia's photographs. "Did you feel that Nora was cute in these pictures?"

Virginia grew flustered again. "Cute, I think, that was, you know, when I had seen—the first couple I saw, I think that was my first impression."

"And do you believe that nude photos of children should be shown anywhere in the community?"

"Well, the book doesn't offend me. I see nude children. As a pediatric nurse—."

Arredondo interrupted, "Just answer the question, Ms. Behner."

"I'm not sure how to answer it. Would you state it again?" Virginia asked Amy.

"Do you believe that nude photos of the children, family nude photos of children, should be shown in the community at all, ever?" Amy asked again.

"It depends what context," Virginia replied.

"What's a correct context?"

"I can't even—I can't even come up with an answer. I think it would be individual."

"An individual choice?" Amy asked.

"Individual choice, if it doesn't harm the child."

When List resumed her cross-examination, she pointed out that Nora wasn't smiling or giggling in her mother's photographs. She implied that Nora was not happy and had been forced to pose for the photographs against her will. Then List said, "You indicated those pictures would not arouse an average person with average sex instincts, in your opinion."

"Not an average person," Virginia replied.

"Okay," List continued. "Do you know what a pedophile is?"

Amy objected: "Case law states it is not appropriate to base community standards on a pedophile's outlook. You have to use a reasonable person with average sex instincts."

When the magistrate sustained the objection, List began pursuing another argument that had surfaced from Rosenbaum and White—that the photographs were illegal because of what could have *potentially* happened to them.

"Do you think the child could suffer harm if these pictures fell into the hands of a pedophile?" List asked Virginia.

Amy objected again: "Inappropriate due to the fact there is no evidence that was intended, and there is not even a scintilla of evidence that that was to happen in this case."

"Your Honor," List argued, "they went to a public photo processing lab. Anybody could get a hold of them there."

Amy appealed to Arredondo: "Your Honor, there have been thousands and thousands of pictures developed at photo labs all over this country that no one has ever paid any attention to. Just a mere assumption that maybe someone would pick them up is so far-fetched from the field that it is inappropriate to bring it in this case."

Arredondo sustained Amy's objection. List had no more questions. Virginia was finished with her testimony.

Cynthia felt Amy had made a tactical error in her questioning of Virginia. Virginia thought so, too. Later she complained to David, "I don't know why Amy asked me if it was acceptable in my community to take pictures of children nude. We're still working on the graven image thing."

David had pinned his own hopes on the guardian ad litem: on her own testimony and her cross-examination of the prosecution's witnesses. He believed that Virginia had developed a surprisingly judicious assessment of their family and a rather sophisticated understanding of the issues. But once in court, he had cringed at Virginia's procedural mistakes. And now he despaired as Virginia's testimony came to an end and her main chance to help them was past. David feared that Arredondo and List dismissed Virginia as a country bumpkin who wasn't playing by the rules or observing the decorum they expected.

David, on the other hand, had come to admire Virginia. He found her to be an interesting kind of fundamentalist—one who was open-minded and had no patience for people who, for career purposes, wouldn't make trouble with their superiors. Virginia had extreme beliefs, David thought, but she didn't just mouth them in some sanctimonious way unconnected to the way she lived. She wouldn't stand by and say, "Well, evil things happen, and I've got this much capital to expend, and I can't use it all up in one place." Virginia was willing to go out on a limb to do what she believed was right. And, as different as they were in every other way, David had come to respect Virginia for that.

Amy's next witness was Nora's therapist. Cynthia watched nervously as Pat Chmura took her seat beside the magistrate. Cynthia didn't know whether Pat would emphasize her critique of Cynthia as naive or her praise of Nora as psychologically healthy, but she was certainly hoping for the latter.

Pat's testimony established that she was a therapist long-experienced in working with children. When Amy asked whether she had tested Nora for sexual abuse, Pat explained there were no tests for sexual abuse, but there were behavior checklists that indicated whether the child was depressed, anxious, or exhibiting "sexual acting-out behaviors." Nora "feels very close to her parents," Pat testified. "She feels supported by them. Loved by them. She quibbles with them and disagrees, as many kids do."

When Amy asked Pat if she believed Nora was an abused child, List objected. Abuse was something for the Court to determine, and Pat was "not qualified to make that legal determination," List claimed.

"Your Honor, I would respectfully disagree," Amy argued. "She is the treating therapist. She has training in abuse. She has done evaluations. She has talked to the child. She has viewed the child."

"However, Attorney Wirtz, I'm sure that Ms. Chmura's definition of abuse and how it is viewed in the statute are something different," said the magistrate. "Are you asking her for a clinical answer to that question versus what is in the statute?"

"The clinical answer," Amy replied.

Arredondo said she would allow the clinical answer, which Pat then gave: "She is not abused."

Amy handed Pat the shower sprayer pictures and asked, "Do you believe that those pictures, when viewed by an average person, one with average sex instincts, would become aroused or have prurient thoughts about those pictures?"

"No," Pat said.

During cross-examination, List pressed Pat about the pictures: "If you were presented with those photos, given your training and experience, would those photos cause you concern for the welfare of this child?"

"They would cause me concern," Pat replied.

"And is it not true," List continued, "that one of those photos appears to be depicting a child masturbating?"

"I don't see it that way," said Pat.

"Do you think that some people could see that picture as though the child were masturbating? An average person with average sexual instincts in our community, could they see that picture as depicting masturbation?"

"It's possible."

"What did you mean by that when you said she is not abused in a clinical sense?"

"What I meant," explained Pat, "was that, in talking with Nora and learning about her sense of privacy, her sense of boundaries, her sense of feeling intruded upon or violated, her sense of how she views words of force or secrecy, she demonstrated none of that. She demonstrated, in her view and by her description of her behavior and contacts with others, that she had a good sense of her own body. She had a good sense of what is private, what is not private. She had a good sense of what other families consider private and not private. She had a real healthy sense of limits, boundaries. Examples like, when she uses the restroom, the door is closed. When she is dressing, she is in her room."

"In this particular instance, however, with these photos, she was using the restroom and the door certainly wasn't closed. Isn't that true?"

"I don't know what the door was," replied Pat.

"It certainly appears to be she is in a restroom," List pointed out.

"Correct."

"And she is not alone?"

"Correct."

When Amy re-examined Pat, she asked what she saw in Cynthia's pictures. "I see Nora using a handheld shower, flexible hose, rinsing herself off in the pictures, both in terms of her front genitals, her buttocks, and using the hose under her chin. Knowing Nora, it looks playful to me," Pat replied.

"And is it possible that someone could view that—an average, reasonable person, Ms. List asked you—an average person with average sex instincts could view it as masturbation? And you said it's possible."

"Yes."

"Is it also possible they could view it as her rinsing herself or being aggressive? Fierce? Playful?"

"Yes."

When List returned for another round of cross-examination, she directed Pat's attention to the expression on Nora's face: "If I were to suggest the word 'sensual' or 'sultry,' would you agree or disagree with that characterization? Couldn't her facial expressions be construed as sultry or sensual, whether affected or not?"

"It's possible," Pat answered.

Amy asked that List's question be stricken from the record since it didn't specify *who* might see Nora's facial expression as sultry or sensual: "Are we talking about an average person with reasonable sex instincts, or are we talking about a pervert?"

Pat enlarged her answer: "I think the average person with average sexual instincts could project on a picture, they could project a sultry look. They could project a look of she is rinsing herself off. One could project a variety of expressions in that face."

The magistrate asked what concerns Pat would have had if she had been shown those photographs without knowing Nora.

"My concern is that it's a child who is prepubescent, and she is nude, and she has views of both genitals and buttocks," Pat replied. "I would want to know more about that and more from the child's perspective or the parents' perspective, how did these pictures get taken? What was the thinking? What is the context?"

But Pat had talked with Nora about the pictures, and those conversations, Pat said, "alleviated my concerns."

As Arredondo recessed the hearings for a break, Cynthia felt a small surge of optimism. She was pleased that Pat had been so positive and emphatic about Nora's psychological health. Her answers had been succinct and careful, but Cynthia felt they had been fair. She was relieved.

Still, being a silent spectator in the courtroom was excruciating for Cynthia. Nothing else in her life had required such a combination of action and inaction, of being on such a high adrenalin alert without the possibility of doing anything about it. The breaks in the hearings weren't much help since there was nowhere to go to unwind. At least she could relax her attention for a few minutes. And David could take a couple of vitamin Cs and down a bottle of juice.

Down the hall, in a room with bare walls and the purplish hum of fluorescent lights, I was waiting with Amy's two dozen other subpoenaed witnesses. With the exception of a young woman from Lorain, Nora's Scottish dance teacher, we were all from Oberlin. Amy had warned us not to share our perceptions of Cynthia's bathroom pictures with each other. Otherwise, she had done nothing to prep us for the hearing. The mood in the room was a mixture of excitement and foreboding—of being on holiday from work, but for the wrong reason. And chatting about everything *except* what was on our minds felt surreal, like making small talk in a hospital waiting room during a loved one's surgery.

Halfway through the afternoon, Nora arrived with her teacher and principal. She was thrilled to find so many people she admired all in the same room. Seeing the director of her drama camp sitting next to her choir director was like seeing George Washington and Abraham Lincoln side by side, she thought. And knowing that all these important people had come to help her family made Nora feel important, too.

The grown-ups greeted her warmly but soon turned back to their own fidgety conversations. So Nora sat down beside her teacher, and began to watch, and wait, and worry.

When the hearing reconvened, Amy called her first community witness, Kathy Plank—the poised and precise founder of the Oberlin Choristers, an organization that had grown to five children's choirs, one of which toured internationally. Kathy walked into the courtroom expecting to say, "I know Nora, and I know Cynthia, and here is my understanding of their relationship. I am a teacher and a mother, and I looked at those photos, and here's how I reacted to them." She expected to share her perceptions, be thanked, and be out quickly. It was how most of us were imagining our testimony.

Amy asked Kathy to give her perceptions of Nora ("happy, bright, confident, creative") and of her relationship with her mother ("wonderful, warm"). Then Amy handed her Cynthia's photographs and asked, "Do you believe that an average person with average sexual instincts would be sexually aroused by those pictures?"

List objected, arguing that the magistrate was the only "finder of fact" for community standards and the "few or a majority or any number of people that the Defense wishes to bring in here" were not relevant. List urged Arredondo to exclude Kathy's testimony: "Merely selecting a number of individuals who happen to be acquainted with Mother and be her friends to be the definite defining factor of the community is inappropriate, Your Honor."

The magistrate agreed that testimony from Cynthia's community was not required. Nevertheless, she said she would allow some of that testimony as long as Amy did not present "the same repetition of information. In other words, not ten friends coming in to testify." Amy pointed out that Kathy Plank was not a friend but an independent caregiver connected to Nora only through Choristers.

Arredondo reiterated, "I am certainly going to permit her testimony. I am just asking that we not have twenty more of the same."

List argued against the magistrate's decision: "I have no doubt Attorney Wirtz is competent enough to only call people who are going to say their community standards are not violated by these pictures. Any competent defense attorney would do the same. Oddly enough, all of these people are here supporting Mother. Acquaintances, social friends of Mother and Father. I intend to raise this objection at each turn, Your Honor." The magistrate assured List she could object to the witnesses, but that she was "not going to exclude all of these witnesses, because I think Mother has an absolute right to be able to bring in appropriate witnesses. But at some point," Arredondo warned Amy, "I don't think that we need to hear the same thing over and over and over again."

Amy asked Kathy what she saw as she looked through Cynthia's pictures, and Kathy replied, "I see a normal, happy girl taking a bath."

During cross-examination, List grilled Kathy on when, where, and why she had first been shown Cynthia's bathroom photographs. The implication was that Amy had inappropriately shown the photographs to witnesses. Amy objected to the questions as infringing on her right to prepare her client's case, but the magistrate permitted most of List's questions.

List asked if she had ever taken nude photographs of her own children, and Kathy said yes. But List tried to draw a distinction between Cynthia's photographs and any Kathy might have taken. List asked, "Did you ever take twenty nude photos of your child at a particular time?"

"No," Kathy replied.

"Did you ever take in excess of three nude photos of your children?"

"Yes. Yes."

"How many nude photos of your children did you take at one time?"

"I'm not sure I can answer that. I don't remember."

"But more than five?"

"Yes."

"You yourself took these photos?"

"Yes."

"And did you take them when your child was eight years old?"

"I don't think I have one at eight," Kathy acknowledged.

"Do you recall approximately how old your children were when you stopped taking nude photos of them?"

"Maybe six or seven."

"Why did you stop taking nude photos of your children at that point?"

"Probably because they started giving themselves their own baths, and I just didn't happen to be in the room."

"So, at some point in time," List suggested, "their privacy issues kicked in." Amy objected that List was answering the question for the witness, and Arredondo sustained the objection.

List handed the shower sprayer photographs to Kathy and asked, "Would it be appropriate for someone other than the child's mother to take a photo of this kind?"

Amy objected that List's question was irrelevant, but List argued that "the photos can't be interpreted with reference to the intent of the taker. The question is whether or not the photos are obscene, nudity material or sexually oriented material. Not who took them or why she took them."

Amy accused List of "trying to get in other information through the back door in the guise of your interpretation of the statute." The magistrate agreed that List's question seemed irrelevant "since that is not the situation that we're here about."

List continued to argue, "Well, it's relevant in that it presents a threat of harm to a child if she doesn't know not to let the next door neighbor take the same kind of pictures."

Amy objected again: "There has been no assertion she doesn't know that. That is not the assertion in the case." Arredondo sustained Amy's objection.

So List began to pepper Kathy with other questions, asking her to describe what was happening in the photograph ("She is rinsing herself") and to interpret Nora's facial expressions ("She looks like she is being silly"). Then List asked, "Do you also believe it's possible that an average individual in the community viewing that photo could conclude that she is masturbating?"

"No. I don't think they would conclude that," Kathy said.

"You don't think there is anybody in the community that could view that in that way?"

"Not in my opinion. Not in my opinion."

"And this community that you refer to, how do you define your community?" List asked.

"The community I'm defining is my friends, my family, the people I work with."

"The people that you are personally acquainted with?"

"Yes."

"So you're not defining your community as Lorain County?"

"I don't know all of Lorain County."

List shifted gears, "Well, the nude pictures that you have of your children, to whom do you display those?"

Amy objected that List's question was irrelevant, but the magistrate overruled her objection.

Kathy replied, "They are in the photo albums that the family sits around and shares when we get together."

"And these pictures should be in Nora's family photo album?" List asked.

"It wouldn't bother me if they were."

"And it would be appropriate to be shared with family?"

"Umm-hmm, yes."

"Would it be appropriate to be shared with friends?"

"If they were my friends, yes."

"And her school friends? Are they appropriate for sharing with her school friends?" pressed List.

Amy objected yet again: "There has been no evidence that these have been shared with school friends, or they were ever going to be shared with school friends. Ms. List is asserting facts that don't exist in this case in order to color the interpretation of the Court. There is no scintilla of evidence these were going to be displayed to school friends."

But Arredondo overruled Amy's objection. List continued, "Would it be okay of Nora to take her family photo album to school with those pictures in it?"

"I don't think I would send my daughter to school with this particular photo," Kathy acknowledged.

"Would you allow her to show it to the next door neighbor?"

"If the next door neighbor were in my home and they were friends, yes."

"Just a casual acquaintance, you would not allow them to see the pictures?"

"I'm not sure I can answer that," Kathy said. "I haven't been in that situation."

List tried again. "You indicated you have nude photos of your children."

"Yes, I do," agreed Kathy.

"Would you permit your children to exhibit those photos to casual acquaintances?"

"They have never asked me to do that, so I haven't had that experience."

List returned to Nora's expressions. When Kathy said that Nora looked happy and playful, List prodded her: "You're sure of that? Isn't it accurate that in virtually none of these photos this child is smiling? Would you like to look at them again?"

"I don't need to look at them again," Kathy replied. "I look at children's faces every day of my life singing songs, and there is a wide variety of expressions. The raised eyebrows and the big eyes and all of that, which is part of being happy and playful. You don't have to be smiling to be happy."

But List persisted, saying that she "would be curious as to what facial clues" indicated happiness to Kathy. When Kathy began to answer, "I have had the occasion to sing with Nora a lot of children's songs, like the 'Hokey Pokey' and all that kind of stuff—," List interrupted: "Objection, Your Honor. I would ask the witness to respond to my questions."

"I believe she is trying to respond," Arredondo pointed out.

Kathy went on. "What I'm going to say is, I have seen looks like this, eyebrows raised and playful, where there is not a smile on the face, but it's clear to me the child is happy."

"And that is based on your experience?" List asked.

"With lots of children, yes."

"And the conclusion that you draw from these pictures is this child is happy?"

"Yes."

Kathy had been gone from the waiting room for what seemed like a very long time. When she came back, she collapsed into a chair and gasped: "Faye List may be a very nice person, but she wasn't nice to me! I felt like I was on trial myself!" Kathy had tried to keep her voice controlled and her face calm in the courtroom. But now she was flushed and shaking.

I hoped I would not be called to testify next. Better yet, maybe Amy wouldn't need me at all. As I was calculating my chances, dividing the minutes left in the afternoon by the number of witnesses left waiting, Amy stuck her head inside the door and called for Molly Johnson, Nora's violin teacher. Molly had actually *asked* to testify next. But seeing Kathy Plank look so shaken, even Molly, who was known for her irrepressible enthusiasm and big, ready smile, was unnerved.

Kathy and Molly looked at each other for a long moment. Then Molly braced herself and headed down the hall.

During Amy's questioning, Molly detailed Nora's accomplishments in violin, praised the family, and described Cynthia's pictures as: "Bathing. Before, during, after." During cross-examination, List asked Molly if it would be appropriate to place the shower sprayer pictures in a family photo album or share them with friends. Molly thought either would be acceptable if it were okay with Nora, but that Nora should have "veto power."

"Should she also have a veto power as to whether or not they were taken in the first place?" List asked.

"She obviously didn't have any problem."

"Well, you weren't there," List pointed out. "You don't know the circumstances under which they were taken."

"That's true," Molly acknowledged.

"So you don't know whether—. Well, does Nora evidence a desire to please her mother?"

"Oh, sure."

"And do the things her mother wants her to do?" List added. Then she and Molly went round and round about whether Nora looked happy or unhappy in the pictures.

Finally Amy objected, "Ms. List is insinuating, over and over again, you can't take a picture of a child, or it's not appropriate to take a picture of your child clothed or unclothed unless that child is smiling. Just because a little girl doesn't have a happy smile on her face doesn't make these pictures inappropriate. I'm going to ask the Court to not allow her to keep doing that."

Before the magistrate could respond, List asked Molly, "You think those are normal poses for an eight-year-old girl?"

"No," Molly said. "They are normal poses for rinsing yourself."

Deciding that her next witness should be someone who could enlarge the definition of Cynthia's community, Amy called in Caroline Jackson-Smith, an African American woman who was a theater professor and the mother of one of Nora's classmates. Although Caroline herself was from an East Coast, Ivy League family, she had married into a large, working-class Lorain County family. Tall and commanding, Caroline had a way of talking that could be both down-to-earth and erudite, friendly and fiercely self-confident. As she squeezed past Virginia and took her seat at the table, she hoped to stay focused and composed since she knew she had a tendency to be "a soapbox kind of person."

List immediately objected to Caroline's testimony as redundant. But the magistrate said she would allow the questioning to go forward as long as "this woman has a broader background than some of the other witnesses." She asked Amy to keep the questions closely relevant to the issue at hand.

Amy asked about Nora, Cynthia's photographs, and Caroline's own daughters, who, Caroline said, "are very secure and happy about their bodies and who feel safe and secure in their home, as I believe Nora does."

But when Amy began to ask about African cultures that are comfortable with nudity and about the African American community in Lorain County, List objected that Amy was "constantly struggling to define and redefine this community as one that is going to make these pictures acceptable." List argued, "We can't select our community. The community is what the Court feels it is, and the Court is going to make that determination." Arredondo allowed the questioning to continue, but she urged Amy to keep it short.

During cross-examination, List asked Caroline if families could cross the line and go too far with photographs of their naked children. Caroline agreed they could. List, however, could not get Caroline to specify what that line was.

"But we agree somewhere there is a line that you don't take a picture of your child doing that," said List.

"I don't know if we all agree as to what that line is," replied Caroline.

"Right. That's what I'm saying. But there is a line. We all think there should be a line somewhere. There is that picture out there somewhere that we would all agree that shouldn't be taken by anybody."

"By anybody is a different question than by a family," Caroline pointed out.

"Even by the family," List insisted. "There is that picture out there we could all agree that shouldn't be taken even by the family."

"I don't know if we should all agree. I think it's important for society to make an effort to protect children, but I don't know if we all agree to what these lines are."

"Well, somewhere out there—What I'm saying, it's a continuum," List said. "Somewhere, way out on the far end, is a picture that we would all agree was so outrageous that the family shouldn't have taken that, or most of us would agree?"

"It's hard for me to answer that question," Caroline replied, "because there are people in our country who believe in total family nudity, and that's their belief system. They have a right to believe that and to live that way. I don't want to take that right away from them."

"And somewhere we might also have a line in a picture depicting a child masturbating. We might agree that picture of a child crosses the line," suggested List.

"But [it] would be subject to interpretation that that *is* the act," Caroline countered.

When List rephrased her questions, Caroline agreed that society had an interest in protecting children and that even a family member could photograph a child in a way that could be deemed obscene. But, she said to List, "what you define as obscene and what I define as obscene may be different."

When Caroline added that family laws could be vague and difficult to agree on, List said tartly, "Thank you for sharing that, but there is no question in front of you."

List changed tack: "Would you take nude photos of your eight-year-old daughter?"

"Certainly not since this has occurred," Caroline replied. "My husband just said he's scared to put his rolls of film in the shop because we can't remember what is on them."

List handed Caroline the stack of pictures: "Do you believe that the average person with average sexual instincts could determine that certain of those photos depict masturbation?"

"Most of the people I know personally would not conclude that," said Caroline. "However, obviously, someone concluded this who wrote up the charge. That must be some average person in our community whom I am not personally acquainted with."

List was finished with Caroline.

The magistrate asked if Virginia would like to cross-examine. Virginia was eager for Caroline to elucidate this new idea about raising girls: "Is this sort of common, in your circle of friends and Cynthia's circle? Is this sort of like a goal or something common, to raise your daughters to be comfortable with their bodies?"

List interrupted: "Objection. We're giving this long diatribe again."

Virginia continued, "To be comfortable with their bodies, is this common? And that includes nude and being comfortable?"

"Yes," Caroline said.

"It's like applauded that you're raising your daughters in your community to be comfortable with their body."

"To be without shame about their bodies, yes," Caroline agreed.

"In the community of all of Cynthia's friends that are sort of maybe connected to Oberlin College or elsewhere, this is like applauded as like a goal, maybe?" Virginia repeated.

List objected again, "Your Honor, 'applauded like a goal' is just a little bit inappropriate. We've been down the road. We've covered it." The magistrate agreed, thanked Caroline for her testimony, and adjourned the hearings until the next week.

Only three people from our room of two dozen had testified during the long afternoon. Amy popped in the door and said she wasn't sure how many of us she would ask to make the trip back the next week. She would let us know over the weekend.

As we all spilled out into the hallway, I saw that Nora had already found her parents and Virginia. Nora looked upset, but Virginia seized both of her hands and lifted them up as if in victory. Swaying their arms back and forth, Virginia began to dance and sing, "We're gonna win! We're gonna win!" until Nora was grinning and dancing, too.

There were no smiles, however, on Cynthia's and David's ashen faces.

15

Cogs and Wheels

Amy knew that the magistrate would not allow her to call many more witnesses. Still, she wanted to push as hard as she could to establish that Cynthia's community did not see her pictures as obscene. When the hearings reconvened the following Tuesday, January 25, Amy asked a half-dozen witnesses to return to the court's waiting room. The rest of us were on call. Since Nora had had enough of courthouses for a while, she came to my house to play with Jesse after school that day.

Amy's first witness was A.G. Miller, an African American man in his mid-forties with a round face, round gold-rimmed glasses, a thoughtful manner, and a full résumé: he had worked as a social worker, had earned a Ph.D. in religion from Princeton, and now taught at Oberlin College and pastored a small congregation. His youngest daughter was a classmate of Nora's. After A.G. had praised Cynthia as a mother, Amy handed him the shower sprayer pictures and asked, "Do you believe that a normal adult or average adult with average sexual intentions, male or female, would be turned on by these pictures or sexually aroused by these pictures?"

List objected. She had been conducting more research over the weekend and had discovered that "the actual language is whether or not the average person, applying contemporary community standards, would find that the work taken as a whole appeals to the *prurient interest*. Not whether that particular average individual would become *aroused* by the photos." A lengthy argument ensued, with both lawyers quoting case law and disputing the definition of "prurient." Eventually they agreed that prurient was "a shameful or morbid interest in nudity, sex, or excretion, which goes substantially beyond customary limits of candor." A.G. replied that, no, he did not find the pictures prurient.

During cross-examination, List spoke to A.G. as a former social worker: "Let's assume that you don't know Cynthia and you don't know Nora and those pictures came to you in the case file. If you were sitting at your desk with your social work background, would those pictures cause you concern for this child?"

"Well, I would ask the question, Why were they taken?" A.G. said.

"And that is a fair question that social workers ask, don't they?"

"Right. I have no problem with the investigation. I think that it would be only fair to ask the question, and the conclusion that I would draw is not necessarily one that would be negative toward Cynthia or Nora."

"When photographs like these are taken, where would be the appropriate place to exhibit these photographs?" List asked.

Amy objected: "It doesn't go to the test in the case, and there is no scintilla of evidence that she was going to exhibit them in some store window in Oberlin or sell them or anything like that."

"Your Honor, it's very easy for someone to sit and hear a dictionary definition of obscene," List argued. "It's much more difficult when confronting the real question that underlies obscene, and that is, Are you comfortable with the pictures? Should they be publicly displayed? and Should they be taken?"

"And I would object to, 'Are you comfortable with them?'" Amy argued. "That is *not* the legal standard. Just because the agency is uncomfortable with these pictures does not make them violative of the obscenity law." Arredondo overruled Amy's objection.

List asked A.G. what the child was doing in the pictures, and he responded, "It looks as though she is spraying her vagina area." When List asked if the pictures could be seen as masturbation, A.G. acknowledged it might be possible, but that was not what he saw: "All of the pictures, to me, are not focusing on the vagina area, but rather on the eyes of this individual, capturing the whole picture of the young person."

When Amy called her next witness—Nora's soccer coach—List wondered "at what point we stretch the bounds of relevance in this case with lay witnesses." Arredondo agreed and asked Amy to summarize what each of her remaining witnesses' testimony would be.

Amy said Nora's soccer coach would show a book titled *Family* that she had checked out from the Oberlin Public Library and that included nude photos of children: "They are nude girls at a beach; you can see their butts. There is also a picture in a swimming pool, and there is frontal nudity of both girls and boys that look like they are all the way up to the age of twelve. Some of them have pubic hair."

List objected and tried to turn Amy's own argument about intent and context against her: "The crux of this argument has been that because Nora Stewart is a wonderful child and her mother is a wonderful mother, you have to read these pictures within the context. Unfortunately, we have no context with regard to pictures in a book."

As Amy described twelve other witnesses, List objected frequently and complained, "This case could drag on ad infinitum if we were to go to having one person from every social economic group testifying for each side as to their particular opinion of the pictures. This is not a vote, we are not taking an opinion poll. It's up to the Court to decide what the community standards are." List even objected to Nora's schoolteachers on the grounds that their testimony would be relevant only at the dispensational hearing, when Nora's living situation would be decided. After a long sequence of List's objections, List surprised even the magistrate by *not* challenging Amy's last witness, the only one who did not live in Oberlin: Nora's Scottish dance teacher.

"With the exception of the Scottish dance, it sounds cumulative to me, Your Honor," List concluded.

"You do not believe that the Scottish dance teacher is cumulative?" Arredondo asked.

"No, I said, no. I just meant that Scottish dance is different than violin and school," List tried to explain. "I guess that I am getting a little giddy. I apologize."

The magistrate chastised the defense: "I would like you to know, Attorney Wirtz, Mrs. Stewart, and Mr. Perrotta, since the three of you have not seen fit to limit the number of witnesses, I will do that." She recessed the court for a short break, during which, she said, she would decide which of the remaining witnesses to allow to testify.

When Cynthia and David came back from the break, List was the only person in the courtroom. David considered Faye List the enemy, and he had no interest in fraternizing with the enemy. Cynthia, on the other hand, kept thinking that if the prosecutors just got to know her, they'd realize how ridiculous this prosecution was. She tried out a pleasantry on List. As they were edging their way into small talk, List suddenly declared: "I truly believe in our system of justice." Then she launched into what Cynthia heard as a little sermon, comparing the justice system to the cogs and wheels of a machine and explaining that if all the parts just worked together and did their jobs the best they could, then justice would be the result.

Astonished, Cynthia felt that List, in some odd, strident way, was trying to apologize for—or at least justify—her role in their family's ordeal. Before Cynthia could respond, however, the magistrate, Amy, and Virginia drifted back into the room. The strange, charged moment with List was over.

Arredondo wanted to hear from four witnesses: a friend of David's, two of Nora's teachers, and an Oberlin College librarian. The first three gave glowing reports of Nora and her relationships with her parents. Nora's current teacher described Nora as a "mature, really solid, down-to-earth, healthy kid" who had been able "to maintain an even keel" at school throughout her mother's prosecution.

Amy's follow-up to the teacher's assessment resulted in a snide exchange. When Amy asked, "You feel it's because she has a good base that she is able to get through this?" List objected that what a witness "feels" is irrelevant.

"You just hate that word," Amy snapped.

"I am a very feeling person," List replied.

"I don't know about that," Amy shot back. "Strike that, sorry. I have no further questions."

The college librarian brought six photography books from the Oberlin College Library for Amy to proffer as evidence, including *Immediate Family* by Sally Mann. Arredondo agreed to look through the books, but she emphasized that she would only consider a photograph relevant if it were of a child about Nora's age in a similar position, preferably in the bathroom.

Arredondo, Amy, and List began looking through *Immediate Family*. List turned to a photograph early in the book in which Mann's three children were lounging on a bed, reading the comics from a Sunday newspaper. The two girls were nude. The younger girl was lying on her stomach; the older girl was lying on her side facing the camera, but her pubic area was concealed by shadow. The boy, the oldest, was wearing shorts. Their ages seemed to be about five, ten, and twelve.

"For the record," Amy said, "this book is Sally Mann's *Immediate Family* and we are on page—"

"No page number," Arredondo noticed.

"No page numbers, that is wonderful," Amy moaned. "We are going to have to go from the descriptions of the pictures."

Flipping through the pages, Arredondo said, "I don't see that any of these photographs fit the category that I am looking for. I admit that I am restricting this a great deal, but I don't see bath pictures, I don't see similar poses, and I see most of these children as being younger." She turned another page and stopped. "No, this child is probably not younger."

The magistrate had turned to two photographs titled "Hayhook, 1989" and "Emmett, Jessie, and Virginia, 1990." In the latter photograph, Mann's three children were standing outside, at night, in still water, with the water just covering their genitals. They were not smiling. The children looked to be the same ages as in the Sunday comics photograph. In "Hayhook," on the outdoor deck of a cabin, the older girl was holding onto a black hook, with her naked body hanging straight down and completely exposed to the camera. She looked prepubescent, but just barely. The younger girl was also naked and standing nearby, blowing on a snorkel.

"Your Honor," Amy pointed out, "the ages of the children in the lake have got to be older than Nora or exactly the same size, the same age. The boy looks like he's fourteen and the girl looks like she is twelve, and the third one looks like she is about Nora's age. The one with the girl hanging from the hook in the barn is a teenager."

Arredondo agreed that the children were older in these photographs but said that she didn't find them "to be in any way similar" to Cynthia's photographs.

"Your Honor," Amy argued, "I believe that the pictures are relevant, also, because of the expression on the children's faces. The agency repeatedly questioned the witnesses as to the child's expression and that she is not smiling, that she is not happy. How could she be playing, how could she be bathing if she is not happy, and I believe that these pictures are relevant in that nature, as well."

But Arredondo agreed with List that the photographs had to be "almost directly on point with the pictures in question" before they would be relevant as evidence on community standards.

Amy protested: "Your Honor, so you are saying unless it's a bathtub picture with a kid holding a shower nozzle around her buttocks or vagina, it's totally irrelevant, is that what you are saying?"

The magistrate agreed that was essentially true.

List also objected to the relevance of *Immediate Family* because it "contains lots of pictures of lots of people, including clothed children" in addition to the nude photographs. Amy countered that the same could be said for Cynthia's roll of film, in which almost half of the photographs were not shot in the bathroom and contained no nudity.

But Arredondo did not allow *Immediate Family*—or any of the other books Amy proffered—to be admitted as evidence.

With no other witnesses allowed, Amy renewed her motion to dismiss. She argued that the State had failed to prove the pictures were obscene, failed to show harm to the child, and failed to show that the child's environment warranted intervention. Arredondo denied Amy's motion to dismiss and asked Amy to present her closing argument.

In her closing, Amy emphasized the relevance of context in interpreting and evaluating Cynthia's pictures—the context of the rest of the roll, the context of Cynthia's photographic habits, the context of Nora's home life, the context of their community. "That is what family court is about," Amy declared. "We are here for the best interest of the kids, and we are here to look at the context of the family." To follow the prosecution's interpretation of the law is illogical, Amy insisted—"totally illogical in a family court setting. This is a picture of a child as seen through a mother's adoring eyes, and I don't think that the Court can ignore that or should ignore that."

Amy also criticized the lack of investigation by Children Services: "We had an investigator on the stand who just because of the pictures and one ten-minute conversation with the child determined that this is a case that needed to be filed and followed through. And then we had the ongoing social worker who did not call any of the witnesses that were given to her until after the third of January. She was given the witness list long before Thanksgiving. That is an insult to Nora, that is an insult to her family, and I think an insult to this Court, that they would pursue this case with so little investigation, Your Honor, and just on the hopes that you would be offended by these pictures, and then they will win because your initial reaction would be offense. That is what this case is about. They brought this case in hopes that you would be offended."

List objected: "Your Honor, I understand Attorney Wirtz has to be zealous in the defense of her client, and, again, I am allowing her to go very far afield in shaming the Agency, but I think that has just gone about far enough at this point."

Arredondo overruled List's objection. "I would ask that you address that in your closing, Attorney List. They *are* closing arguments."

Soon List began her own closing argument: "Your Honor, the issue before the Court is whether the child fits the definition of abused child as that term is defined in 2151.031. We are not here to talk about the greater good or the broader purposes of determining what is best for this child, or what kind of family is this, is she a wonderful child, are these wonderful parents. 2151.031 defines abused child as one who is in danger, as that term is defined in the criminal statute.

"It does not require that you prove each and every element of the criminal case. Our society has deemed it fit to determine that somewhere there is a line, and that line defines what pictures we will take of our children and what pictures we will not take of our children.

"We cannot judge the picture with reference to the intent of the person taking it. Either the pictures are or they are not obscene, nudity oriented, or sexually oriented material. That is something that the Court must decide. It's interesting to note that the individual that viewed the photos without context, that is without knowing the family, without interviewing the mother, without interviewing the child, that is three police officers and two social workers, all concluded the pictures were obscene, and they caused them concern. And that they were inappropriate."

Amy interrupted. "I am going to object to the use of obscene. The questions with the definition of obscene were never asked of the State's witnesses. They all said that they felt they were inappropriate, which means that the State did not ask crucial questions about community standards. And, therefore, their testimony shouldn't be used for community standards. 'Inappropriate' is not the definition of community standards."

"Your Honor, the Court can decide community standards," List countered.

The magistrate agreed, first with List and then with Amy. "The Court will decide community standards, although we are again in closing, and I would like everyone to now cease with the objections, if possible. But with respect to that testimony, I don't recall questions to the caseworkers with respect to whether or not they viewed the pictures as being obscene."

List went on, arguing that "Children Services desperately wanted to conduct an investigation," but, she complained, the Agency had not been permitted to interview the parents about the photographs and "the Agency was not permitted to access the child to any great extent, Your Honor."

List alluded to the dispensational hearing, when the decision about Nora's living arrangements would be made. She said that "many, many, many of the arguments set forth by Attorney Wirtz in her closing relate not to whether or not the child should be adjudicated abused, but what is the appropriate disposition." List acknowledged that a child *could* be ruled abused and still returned to the legal custody of her parents, but she also made clear that was not the solution she was advocating: "You can have a finding of abuse and disposition of custody to the parent. Now at this point, I am not willing to advocate that; Children Services is advocating a different disposition."

A shiver of terror went through Cynthia and David.

When List concluded, Arredondo realized she had not given the GAL an opportunity to make closing remarks. She apologized and gave Virginia an opportunity to speak. Virginia began talking about what she would have liked to have asked the dance professor Ann Cooper Albright, one of Amy's witnesses who had not been allowed to testify. List objected, but the magistrate then realized she had also never given the GAL a chance to call witnesses of her own, as she was legally allowed. Arredondo apologized to Virginia again and allowed her to describe the testimony she would like to have elicited from Ann. Virginia described Ann's theory of raising daughters who were proud of their bodies, and how photographs of naked children were part of that, "and when you start talking to her, you get a grasp of just how many people believe that this is all right, and acceptable, and, in fact, this is the proper way that you should raise a daughter."

Arredondo asked Virginia to summarize her position in this case. Virginia described her own investigation and criticized Children Services and Tracy for not interviewing anyone until the last minute. "Nora wasn't their focus," Virginia insisted, but as she elaborated, she kept being stopped by the magistrate who seemed increasingly exasperated with her.

Virginia urged Children Services "to exit the case and let the child be at peace. This would give her peace, believe me, and let the child have peace. I would be glad to turn in a report and make sure that Mother is taking counseling, and I would even get letters from the therapist."

"Your Honor," List objected, "the guardian is stating a position on adjudication. She apparently doesn't want the child adjudicated. I don't think that we need to keep going."

The magistrate turned to Virginia, "Ms. Behner, you need to understand that pursuant to the statute, it's not possible for you to remain involved in the case if Lorain County Children Services is dismissed. It's simply not the way it happens. The statute would indicate if Children Services is out of the case, you, too, are out of the case. I am sorry that your questions were excluded, but you need to rely on the court procedure just like the attorneys must."

Virginia tried again. "In other cases that I have been involved in, Children Services exited and basically because—"

List objected: "I don't really want to know about the other cases, Your Honor, and it's getting—it is almost six o'clock, Your Honor." Arredondo agreed and cut Virginia off. She asked Virginia if it was correct that she wanted the Children Services case dismissed. Virginia said yes.

The magistrate then said she would carefully consider the evidence and would "certainly write up" her decision "so everyone is clear on what my position is." She thanked everyone, adjourned the proceedings, and told Amy to expect a ruling within ten days—by February 4, the Friday of the following week.

All afternoon, as Nora played with Jesse, she ran frequently to the living room window to check for her parents' car in the driveway. I tried to convince her that it was good news her parents were late— the magistrate had probably let more witnesses testify than Amy had expected.

When I started cooking supper, Nora slipped into the kitchen. She wondered if I had heard yet from her mother. Not yet, I told her. I asked if she and Jesse would like to help me cook. After I laid out the ingredients for cornbread and gave them my recipe, they stayed busy for a long time making a floury mess of the kitchen and themselves.

When Cynthia and David finally arrived around seven o'clock, Nora raced into their arms. My family gathered around, eager to hear what had happened in the courtroom. Cynthia told us, halfheartedly it seemed to me, that their witnesses had done a good job, that Nora's teachers had said wonderful things about her, and that Amy had wrapped things up very well. But she and David agreed they were "just blotto, worn out, completely drained." I asked if they'd like to stay for supper. Nora begged them to taste her cornbread, and they said they were happy to sit down to hot food in a house without a ringing phone.

While the children were at the table, we chatted about Nora and Jesse's school day, the painting my daughter had made in her after-school art class, the secret ingredient in the kids' cornbread. After the children left the table, Cynthia and David became more candid about the hearings. "List cut the supports out from under us one by one until even community standards didn't matter," Cynthia despaired. She felt her family's fate was now in the hands of "one conservative, Latina, Republican woman who is outside every community I am a part of."

David was exhausted but furious. He said that the philosophy major part of his brain had tried, through the feverish haze of his flu, to follow the hearing's legal arguments. But soon his head had started spinning from the fast-and-loose rhetoric, unsupported assertions, and assumptions whose implications were never acknowledged or examined—like the unspoken idea that *doing* something might not be bad in and of itself, but taking a picture of it *was*. He pointed out that nobody was saying, "We need to have a law against parents running around the house naked with their kid" or "We need to have a law against eight-year-old girls rinsing themselves." But taking pictures of those actions had somehow been elevated to a different legal status.

The debate about intention had also exasperated David. List had argued that pictures could be obscene even though Cynthia had not intended them to be obscene. "But if there's no *intention* for a picture to be obscene, what makes it obscene? The context in which it is viewed? Well, those pictures were intended to be viewed at home, infrequently, like all the other photos we have," he said with an ironic laugh that turned quickly into a coughing fit.

When Cynthia, David, and Nora returned home that evening, they found a loaf of homemade bread and a homemade pie on Campeloupe's front porch. The voices of many friends—some singing, some not—were waiting on their full and flashing answering machine. Tom Theado's upbeat voice declared, "The *only* song in my repertoire is 'Happy Days are Here Again.' But I'm not going to sing it until I know whether there's any reason for believing it. Let me know!"

Virginia had called twice. "Oh, hi," she said in a quiet, discouraged voice in her first message. "Just wondering how you're doing, if you're okay. . . ."

But in her second message, Virginia was forming a new plan. If Nora were ruled abused, then Cynthia and David should sue Children Services for not acting in good faith. She had already spoken with the agency's ombudsman to alert him that she, the guardian ad litem, certainly did not feel the agency was acting in good faith. She had also spoken with a First Amendment lawyer at Case Western Reserve University who believed Cynthia and David had grounds to sue.

"So, anyhow, that's it, goodbye!" Virginia signed off, this time more cheerily.

PART THREE

A piece of paper blown by the wind into the law court may only be drawn out again by two oxen.

—Chinese proverb

16

The Politburo

"Child May Be Taken From Mom" was the headline of the *Chronicle-Telegram* the next morning, Wednesday, January 26. The large words stopped me as I walked downtown for coffee. I bought the newspaper from the street dispenser and stood in the cold scanning it. Executive director of Children Services Gary Crow had said that if his agency gained temporary custody of Stewart's daughter, she could be placed in a foster home for up to fifteen months; after fifteen months, "Children Services would be required to seek permanent custody."

I rushed to the Java Zone, where I showed the article to my friend Carter, whose son was Nora's and Jesse's friend. Carter and I both felt the need to do *something*. But what? After brainstorming various dramatic actions, we settled on more modest ones: Carter would call the prosecutor's office; I would write another letter to the editor.

That night I wrote a fiery letter that concluded with a pitch for the defense fund and an unspecified call to arms: "The only obscenity in this case is the relentless persecution of Cynthia Stewart and her family. . . . That our government is spending its resources on traumatizing a healthy, nurturing family is an outrage. It is time that we as a community let our outrage be heard." The next day, I felt brave as I mailed copies not only to the Oberlin newspaper, but to the two county newspapers as well.

Carter phoned the prosecutor's office the next day and expressed his concerns to the secretary. Within minutes, Greg White called back. He asked if Carter had seen the photographs. Carter said no,

but they had been described to him by his friend Lynn Powell, who
had said they were not pornographic. White assured him that they
were. If you saw the photographs *yourself*, White insisted, you would
change your mind. White told Carter that no one else had called him
about the Stewart case.

That afternoon, I received a call from a woman I knew slightly. She
wanted to meet privately with Rebecca Cross and me since we were
the co-chairs of Cynthia's defense fund. She was leaving work soon
and would drive straight to Rebecca's house, but she made a point of
saying that she would park in a nearby school parking lot so that no
one would recognize her car in Rebecca's driveway. She begged me to
tell no one about our meeting. I had always admired this woman for
her poise and easy elegance. That she didn't want to be seen talking
to us made me feel alarmed.

By the time I arrived, she and Rebecca were sitting in a cozy room
with large windows and art quilts brightening the walls. But the mood
in the room was not bright. The woman looked tense, and she was
choosing her words carefully. Cynthia was in grave trouble, she said,
and Nora would be ruled an abused child by the end of next week if
Cynthia's community did not stop it from happening. Maybe Cynthia
felt awash in community support, but that support was invisible to
Greg White. And Greg White had more influence over the outcome
in the Children Services courtroom than we might imagine.

She declined to tell us who had given her this information, but
she did tell us where it came from: inside the courthouse. "You've got
to make some noise, and you've got to do it *now*," she urged us.

She encouraged a quick flood of letters, both to the editors of
newspapers and to the prosecutor. "Don't alienate White," she advised. "Don't tie up his phones. But *do* write strong letters and in-
undate his office with them." If Nora were ruled abused, she warned,
Cynthia and David would be in danger of losing custody of Nora,
Cynthia would never drive a school bus again, and a criminal conviction would become more likely.

Rebecca and I were stunned. This woman was an extremely

credible person, not given to hyperbole and not known for political activism. As soon as she left, we phoned a half-dozen friends. We asked them to come to my house on Saturday morning, and we encouraged them to pass the word.

That Saturday morning, January 29, I dragged my children's old Fisher-Price easel from the garage into our living room, clipped some large sheets of art paper to it, and wrote a brief agenda in Magic Marker. I carried in extra chairs and put water on for tea. At eleven o'clock, people started pouring through my front door. Soon, more than thirty people were squeezed into my living room—people I expected to be there, people I hadn't thought of inviting, and people I had never met. I abandoned the cups of tea, pulled up more chairs, and threw some pillows onto the hardwood floor.

We were, on the whole, a forty-something crowd: mostly parents of children around Nora's age, with a few college students, Unitarians, and politics professors sprinkled in. Many of us had been involved in political causes in the past, though our political skills hadn't been exercised much in the years of building careers, paying mortgages, and raising kids. But the headline in Wednesday's *Chronicle-Telegram* had frightened everyone, and one couple had already taken action. Stan Mathews, an architect, and his wife Pat, an art professor, had drawn up a petition calling for Greg White to "cease and desist prosecution" in *Ohio v. Stewart* and declaring that the undersigned were "outraged by the Lorain County Prosecutor's relentless pursuit of unwarranted felony obscenity charges against Ms. Stewart." Everyone agreed the petition was a good idea. We passed around a sign-up sheet for distributing it around town.

But other issues were harder to agree on. Should we hold some sort of protest at the county courthouse? Rebecca and I said we had been advised by an anonymous source not to antagonize Greg White, and a protest sounded antagonistic. Others argued a protest was the only way to get media attention. Maybe it could be a candlelight vigil, someone suggested. I left the living room to call Amy for advice. Amy didn't think a demonstration was a bad idea as long as it was peaceful, we got permits from the city, we didn't block traffic, and

there were at least fifteen people there to make a good showing. "Fifteen people!" I said. "There would be a lot more than fifteen people.
I've got thirty people right here in my living room!"

When I came back into the room, two politics professors were
arguing about how to deal with the most powerful political figure
in our county. Marc Blecher (who taught courses in Chinese politics and Marxist theory) was advocating an aggressive stance toward
the prosecutor. Marc didn't like small-town, right-wing, conservative
Republicans, and he had come to the meeting fired up that we were
going to turn Greg White out of office in the 2000 elections. In fact,
the evening before, Marc had sent an e-mail to Greg White, with cc's
to the Ohio attorney general and to our U.S. congressman:

Mr. White,

Kafka's THE TRIAL begins something like this:
"Someone was telling lies about Joseph K., because,
without having done anything wrong, he found himself
under arrest one fine day." You risk making yourself
into an object of historical opprobrium just like
Kafka's inhuman, amoral bureaucrats if you continue
with this prosecution. Eventually, you also risk
becoming a laughingstock; for there is potent
political opposition building against you as a
result of this prosecution.
    . . . Would that you had taken the time and care
to look into Ms. Stewart's situation before plunging
headlong into an invidious prosecution that is
motivated by sheer politics and is bound to fail--as
a prosecution and as a political maneuver. . . .

But Ben Schiff (who taught courses in international relations, arms
control, and international law) argued that we had to separate par-
tisan, electoral politics from Cynthia's case. He urged us not to back

the prosecutor into a corner, but to work the back channels and give White an honorable way out.

Ben and Marc's argument led to a discussion among the whole group about how to speak publicly about Cynthia's prosecution and on what grounds to defend her. Some people in the group were very comfortable with political rhetoric; others flinched at language and arguments that sounded too ideological or too left-wing. Was this a First Amendment issue? A censorship of art issue? A family privacy issue? A men-trying-to-control-women's-bodies issue? A liberal Oberlin versus a conservative Lorain County skirmish in the cultural wars? A political misuse of a well-intentioned law? The persecution of a good but unconventional mother?

Cynthia's close friend Ann Cooper Albright bridled at the "good mother defense." She had been complaining to Cynthia for weeks about the defense many of us had been making on her behalf: that she couldn't possibly be guilty of abuse because she was a devoted mother of a gifted daughter. Ann had a high-powered career as a professor, dancer, and scholar of dance history, and she traveled often to give lectures and performances that could be edgy and provocative. Her husband, a Russian professor, was the more nurturing and more present parent. Ann had been telling Cynthia, "If you're the *good* mom, I'm the *bad* mom. Think how screwed I would be if I had taken those pictures of Isabel! No one would be putting up the good mother defense for me!" Ann thought the issue needed to be argued on larger feminist principles.

I listened to Ann with anxiety. I had been raised in a Southern Baptist home in East Tennessee—five hundred miles from Oberlin and light years away politically. As a nine-year-old, I had shaken the hand of Richard Nixon as he had campaigned for Barry Goldwater in Chattanooga. I was now more ideologically at home in Oberlin than in my hometown. But with my Southern, evangelical, Republican roots, I had strong opinions about which arguments would persuade the average American and which would fall on rocky ground. I argued that to be effective in *this* county with *this* prosecutor we had to defend Cynthia pragmatically, and not take stands that were principled yet incendiary outside the Oberlin bubble.

After an hour of debate, we did reach some agreement on how to proceed. We would flood Greg White's office with letters, but not phone calls. We would write letters to the editors of all the county newspapers and solicit more letters by e-mailing friends. We would publicize a fundraiser the Unitarians were holding in February. We would circulate petitions and return them to Stan and Pat by March 1. If the magistrate handed down a ruling of abuse in the Children Services case, we would hold a protest or vigil the night before the dispensational hearing about Nora's custody. Stan would begin contacting the area media about our activities. I would contact Cindy Leise, the reporter at the *Chronicle-Telegram* who had been covering Cynthia's case so well.

Marc Blecher, the politics professor who had argued earlier in the meeting for something like a coup d'état, had been persuaded by his colleague's argument for diplomacy. Now Marc wondered if we might make some kind of personal overture to White. He suggested we put together a small delegation of conservative but concerned citizens to approach White privately. We began brainstorming who might be part of that delegation.

Connie Grube spoke up: "I'd be happy to be part of the group, and it might help that I'm a registered Republican." A few jaws dropped, and for a moment the room fell uncharacteristically silent. No one had imagined we had a real, live Republican in our midst.

Connie was a mother of four and a soccer coach of many of our children. She looked more like an Oberlin liberal with her long hair and habitual jeans. She had grown up in a foreign service family in the Middle East and always said that she "had majored in political activism" at Oberlin College in the 1970s. Now she was an active parishioner in the Catholic church and a pro-life advocate. Connie, like Marc, had known Cynthia for more than twenty years—the three of them had been part of the same social circle back when Marc was a young professor and Cynthia and Connie were young townies who had stayed on in Oberlin after their college days. Their social lives hadn't overlapped for years, but the roots of those relationships went very deep. Connie said she would go to the mat for Cynthia's family. She and Marc agreed to confer on who else to recruit for the delegation.

As the meeting broke up, I felt grateful to have escaped without too many new responsibilities. The Cynthia Stewart Legal Defense Fund was suddenly becoming a diverse group of people taking action—not just two of us picking up checks from a post office box. But that made me uneasy, too. Oberlin folks were famous for standing on principle. It just wasn't clear which principle we were all going to be standing on.

The letter to the editor I had sent to several newspapers before Saturday's meeting appeared on the following Tuesday, February 1. At least one Oberlin resident, Melissa Ballard, read the letter and took to heart my vague call to action ("It is time that we let our outrage be heard!"). On Wednesday morning, she called Greg White.

Melissa Ballard was a spunky woman who knew civic responsibility from both sides. She had been a gadfly to the Oberlin School Board for many years before being elected to the School Board herself—a position in which she suddenly had to deal with other gadflies.

Like Carter, Melissa left a brief message with the prosecutor's secretary, and White soon called her back. Melissa spoke emotionally of Cynthia's family. White said he understood that this was an emotional case and that "artistic types" were concerned about censorship. Melissa clarified that her concern was not censorship; her concern was that a good family was being traumatized by an unjust prosecution. White countered that *he* had seen the pictures, and she hadn't. If *she* had seen them, she would agree there was a criminal case.

"Don't assume that," Melissa objected. "Unless, of course, the pictures were horrific, or being sold or posted on the Internet, or unless the child was being harmed."

White pointed out that some people thought having sex with children didn't harm them.

Melissa was offended that White was lumping her with pedophiles, and she told him so.

White said this case wasn't about what Greg White thought or wanted. It was about what a jury thought.

"But who decided to take this case to the grand jury in the first place?" Melissa asked.

White acknowledged it had been his office's decision.

When Melissa expressed concern that a healthy child could be sent to foster care and her mother sentenced to thirty years in prison, White complained that the *Chronicle-Telegram* had gotten the facts all wrong. He said he was going to have to spend a half-day writing that newspaper to correct all their inaccurate information. Children Services had only asked for protective supervision, he insisted, and Cynthia was being charged with second-degree felonies, each of which had a minimum sentence of probation and a maximum sentence of eight years.

"Eight years is still ridiculous!" Melissa exclaimed. "And even if she got probation, she wouldn't be able to work again for the schools." She pressed him: "Many, many people are upset about this prosecution."

White pointed out that she was only the second person to call him.

"Well, I would suggest that's because the perception is: 'Don't mess with the prosecutor's office. They're vindictive,'" she replied.

White expressed surprise and asked why people thought of his office as vindictive.

"I don't know," said Melissa, "but I've been a public official, and I know if someone has that perception, whether or not you think it is accurate, you need to know so that you can change that perception." Then she asked, "Do you want to hear from other people?"

White said that he did.

"Good. Then I will tell people to call you." Melissa thanked White, hung up, typed up two pages of notes, and called me. I called Cynthia and David. We agreed that since White had now invited calls, he couldn't view it as antagonistic if we encouraged those calls. I sent out an urgent message to our growing e-mail list with the prosecutor's phone number.

A more cheery e-mail went out Wednesday evening announcing the Unitarians' benefit concert for the defense fund. Someone forwarded the message to a local environmental group whose members included a woman prominent in the county Republican Party. She didn't live in Oberlin, she didn't know Cynthia Stewart, and she hadn't spoken with anyone who knew Cynthia. But based on what she had read and what she had heard from people she knew at the courthouse, she believed Cynthia was innocent and being framed. She fired several e-mails back to the entire group. "You may say amen to a fundraiser for Cynthia Stewart, but unless something is done by tomorrow night she will be labeled as an abuser on Friday morning," she warned. "Nothing can take that back." She claimed Cynthia's case had already been decided and was "what we refer to in the county as a done deal." Her friends inside the courthouse were surprised no one had protested on Cynthia's behalf, and they advised bombarding the media "before it is too late."

A neighbor of Cynthia and David's printed out a hard copy of the message and rushed it over to Campeloupe. "Who *is* she?" they asked after reading the dire warnings. The neighbor said that she had a reputation as a fighter; that some people respected her while others found her too extreme; that she had had both impressive successes and failures in her political ventures. Now, he said, she was their very own "Deep Throat."

Soon the phone at Campeloupe was ringing with calls from people ready to take action, including Stan Mathews, the architect who had drawn up the petition. But Cynthia and David were torn about how to proceed. Finally, they asked Stan to send out a 10:30 P.M. message to calm their supporters. Stan's message asked people to "FLOOD THE SWITCHBOARD!" at the prosecutor's office, but to hold off on protests until a ruling had been made by the magistrate and "we know exactly what we are protesting."

One of my part-time teaching jobs was at a university an hour's drive away. Because I had to leave for class early the next morning, my husband Dan made our family's call to the prosecutor's office. For an hour, he got busy signals, but was finally able to leave a message with White's secretary. White called him right back. The prosecutor was polite, but when Dan said, "A lot of people know and respect this family," White responded, "Yes, that was true of Al Capone, too. Character witnesses are not very relevant."

The mother of Nora's Scottish dance teacher also called White that morning. She told him that her daughter had been nervous about seeing the pictures but afterward had said, "Mom, you've got worse pictures of me from when I was a kid." The mother described those pictures to White, pictures she had taken years before of her infant son naked in the light from their fireplace. Her seven-year-old daughter had climbed out of the bathtub and come into the room wanting to be in the picture, too. "What you see through the lens is not always what comes out," she told the prosecutor. "I am from Lorain. This is not just an Oberlin problem."

When Marc Blecher called White that morning, he introduced himself as an Oberlin College politics professor. Marc told White a lot of people were angry and "if this comes out badly for Cynthia, it's going to get ugly fast." Marc found White surprisingly civil and willing to talk. White asked Marc what he meant by "badly for Cynthia."

"If Nora is taken away or Cynthia goes to jail," Marc said.

White brushed off those scenarios. He said it had never been their plan to take custody of Nora. The newspapers had misunderstood, he insisted. And as for Cynthia, there was no mandatory jail time attached to the statute. She would probably get probation.

Marc did not point out that a ruling of abuse or a criminal conviction could have other devastating consequences for Cynthia's livelihood and life. He just said, "Look, this is going to be a big problem for you, and I think it would be better for you and certainly better for Cynthia if we all could figure out a way to make this go away."

Marc asked if White would consider meeting with a small group of concerned Oberlin citizens. "Just to be clear," he added, "I'm not doing backdoor bargaining here. I haven't talked with Cynthia's attorneys." White offered to come to Oberlin on Monday morning. Marc thanked him and said he'd be back in touch.

Although Stan had sent out Cynthia and David's request to hold off on protests late on Wednesday night, e-mails had continued to be exchanged on the topic through the wee hours of Thursday morning. Around 3:00 A.M., the neighbor who had brought to Campeloupe the e-mail from "Deep Throat" was sending messages of his own, complaining, "It seems to me that waiting on a demonstration until a decision is handed down is a lot like closing the barn door after the horses are out, but that's the decision." Later, though, he was ready to take unilateral action, and he corresponded with several friends who wanted to bring their children and picket to show the prosecutor and the media "a spontaneous swell of support" from Cynthia's community.

The phone rang at Campeloupe before breakfast on Thursday morning. The call was from Deep Throat. She introduced herself to Cynthia and David and asked, "Did you really decide not to have a demonstration today? If you don't picket, it's a done deal. The prosecutor and court do what they want in this county. The only thing they're afraid of is picketing." She knew both Rosenbaum and White personally. "Rosenbaum doesn't care who he destroys," she said. "Greg, on the other hand, is very loyal to his people. Once he makes up his mind his people are right, he's adamant." She got along with White because "he likes *mean* people, like me. But he hates publicity." If Cynthia and David didn't call for an immediate protest, she warned, they would be making a catastrophic mistake.

When the phone rang again, Cynthia and David learned that some people were planning to picket "spontaneously" that evening, with or without their blessing. They knew these people had good intentions, but they also realized how quickly community support could take on a life of its own—and who knew if it would help or hurt? For advice, David called Kreig Brusnahan, who said he didn't think a demonstration would do any harm since public opinion seemed to be running 98 percent in their favor. But, Kreig cautioned, the organizers needed to get the proper permits and obey every city ordinance, and Cynthia, David, and Nora had to stay home and keep their hands off all organizing efforts.

By 10:30 Thursday morning, Cynthia and David gave Stan Mathews the go-ahead to organize a rally. Stan sent out an e-mail:

```
URGENT!!! DEMONSTRATION TODAY: Due to drastic turn
of events,

Cynthia Stewart has called for public action NOW!
Thursday, February 3, 2000 5:00pm
Lorain County Administration Building . . .
Bring signs and bring as many people as possible. We
will call press and TV to be there.

Important: THESE PEOPLE LOATHE PUBLICITY IN A
CASE LIKE THIS, SO BY ALL MEANS USE THEIR NAMES
PROMINENTLY ON YOUR SIGNS.
```

When I got home that afternoon, Stan's e-mail was printed out and waiting for me on the kitchen counter. My husband had scribbled on the bottom: "I'll be home from work in time for us to drive up together."

"Damn!" I muttered, tossing the e-mail into the trash. I was frustrated that a public event had been thrown together so quickly, without consensus on a message or a plan for what would happen once we got there. There was a high likelihood, I thought, that the whole thing would misfire—too few people would show up and those who did would not be coordinated enough to be effective. I put my daughter in charge of heating up leftovers for her and her brother's supper. I certainly was not going to drag my children to some disorganized rally and have their first taste of political action be a *fiasco*.

The demonstration was planned for the county administration building, where the prosecutor's office was located. When my husband and

I arrived in the lobby, I was surprised by the diverse crowd that had gathered, including a handful of elderly people and a good number of parents with their children in tow. Some people were holding homemade poster board signs ("Don't Take This Child!" "Protect Loving Families, Don't Bust Them!" "Girl + bathtub ≠ pornography") and others held pieces of paper with large letters printed on someone's computer ("Judge Boros: _Leave the kid alone!_" "Greg White: Call off Rosenbaum," "_Stop_ Ohio v. Stewart!!"). About a hundred people had gathered. I felt sheepish and sorry I hadn't brought my own kids.

At five o'clock, Stan announced that we would be marching across the street to the old county courthouse. As we headed out into the late light, walking in a thick line, I felt as if we were walking onto the stage of an empty auditorium. The town was almost deserted: there were no courthouse workers peering out their windows, no passersby to stop and gawk, no drivers to honk their horns in irritation or support.

But as we approached the courthouse, I saw three television cameras trained on us and several reporters with notepads and pens. Stan had assembled the crucial audience, after all. And with his architect's eye, he had realized that our rallying spot—a modern office building on a street corner—had no cinematic meaning. An iconic American courthouse on a town green did.

Someone in our crowd started chanting, "Stop this case! Stop this case!" Even those of us made squeamish by group chanting joined in. When we reached the courthouse steps, a few of us instinctively climbed up the steps and turned toward the cameras. Everyone else turned toward the cameras, too, and we all flourished our signs. Someone started chanting, "Listen to the truth! Listen to the truth!" and we all joined in. When silence fell, Stan leapt onto the steps and gave an impromptu speech about civil liberties. Then a dozen people took turns making spontaneous remarks. Some people spoke about First Amendment rights and censorship. Some parents, with their children beside them, made pleas on behalf of a good parent whose photographs had been taken out of context and misconstrued. Two of Nora's teachers praised Cynthia's family and urged Children Services to redirect their energies toward children who _did_ need intervention and help. Ann Cooper Albright took the courthouse steps to praise the feminist goal of raising girls who were unashamed of their bodies. Then, to prove her point, she added, "Anyone can take nude pictures of me anytime!" My born-and-bred-Baptist heart sank.

After forty-five minutes, the cameramen packed up, while reporters lingered to interview people in the slowly dispersing crowd. Many people were in high spirits, excited that we had taken a stand with TV cameras as witnesses. But as we drifted toward our cars in the chilly twilight, I wondered what all that ardor would look like on the eleven o'clock news.

Channel 8 Fox News ran the most extensive coverage of the rally that night. Over the title "Kiddie Porn Controversy," the segment opened with Stan in his stylish overcoat asking the crowd around him: "How many people in this crowd have photographs that would have gotten them obscenity charges?" Stan shot his hand up, and so did many of us around him. The camera cut to close-ups of a boy waving an American flag and of an elderly man holding a large sign: "In 1950 I took photos of my daughter bathing. Arrest me?"

Ann Cooper Albright, who was tall and regal with a mane of long, graying hair, looked striking on the courthouse steps in her black coat, purple scarf, and Russian black wool hat. She said forcefully, "These are not obscene images, but they are images of a naked girl who should be proud of her body, be proud that her mother took those pictures."

Nora's third grade teacher insisted, "I saw photocopies of these photographs. I saw *nothing* wrong with them. The only person I think who *could* would be someone who needs serious counseling." She was holding an orange poster mounted on a yardstick that read, "I wish every child had a wonderful, loving parent like Cynthia Stewart!"

As "Save this child! Save this child!" swelled in the background, Cynthia's sneering mug shot appeared on the screen, followed by a shot of her school bus and then a shot of Greg White, surrounded by law books. The reporter had gotten an advance reaction from White: "We all have photographs of our children when they're young, taking a bath or changing diapers. The question is—what's the context of those photographs and is there a sexual orientation to them?"

The report ended with the camera following Stan onto Campeloupe's front porch after the rally. When Cynthia came to the door, Stan told her there had been an incredible turnout. She hugged and thanked him: "It's wonderful for you to do this."

"It could be me, it could be any of us," Stan assured her. "It scares us all."

The next morning, Cleveland's *Plain Dealer* ran a small, front-page article with a black-and-white photograph on an inside page. The article included supporters' comments and noted that defense fund donations had come in from thirty-eight states, plus Greece, Germany, and England. It also included a provocative exchange, facilitated through a reporter who had interviewed both Stan and, later, Greg White:

> Mathews said White, a Republican prosecutor, is out of touch with the liberal community of Oberlin.
>
> White rolled his eyes at the comment.
>
> "This is not an issue of politics," said White, who has relatives living in Oberlin. "It is an issue of children."

In the county newspapers, the rally garnered big headlines and large color photographs. In the *Morning Journal*, Stan threw down a gauntlet for White:

> Stan Mathews . . . said nothing but a complete exoneration for Stewart is acceptable.
>
> "We will accept nothing but full exoneration and ideally an apology from Greg White," he said.

The *Chronicle-Telegram* highlighted inflammatory remarks made by both sides. The rally was described as a group of angry residents who "took turns on the county courthouse steps Thursday afternoon, decrying what they called a fledging 'police state' led by a prosecutor's

office in its moral crusade against a mother and her right to privacy."
Executive director of Children Services, Gary Crow, protested that
his agency had asked for protective supervision of Nora "only after
Stewart refused to cooperate or to allow investigators to speak with
her daughter." And Greg White reacted, "I'm not going to discuss
the merits of this case while it's still pending. For 20 years, I've said
it—'We'll do our talking in the courtroom.'"

The day after the rally, my son Jesse told Nora at school: "I wish I
could have stood on the courthouse steps for you yesterday." Ann
Cooper Albright's daughter Isabel chimed in, "Me, too!" It made
Nora feel proud to know that her friends wanted to stand up for her,
and it made her feel safe to know that her teachers and her friends'
parents had. Cynthia and David noticed an immediate difference
in Nora after the rally. She grew more cheerful and energetic. Her
nightmares vanished.

But as a lawyer in Lorain County, Tom Theado felt that somebody had to deliver the bad news. And the bad news from Tom's point
of view was that the rally at the courthouse had looked like a mob,
and Greg White hated mobs. Tom urged Cynthia and David to tell
their supporters to stay away from "cosmic" issues and stick with the
personal: "You can't convince Greg White it's a First Amendment
issue. And you can't get the county to care about a feminist issue.
The message has to be: this could be *your* family." Tom also urged the
supporters to rethink their tactics: "I don't care how many people sign
petitions in Oberlin—unless you get people signing petitions at the
Elyria mall, it doesn't mean a thing. And you could put a thousand
pickets in front of Greg White's house, day after day, and the rod in
his back would just get stronger. Greg's not going to say, 'Oh, my God,
I must be wrong!' He's going to say, 'Those people down in Oberlin
have to live under the same rules as the rest of the world.'"

The day after the rally, I received a call from another prominent
Lorain County attorney, a man I had never met. He had seen my
name in the newspaper and wanted to give me some off-the-record
advice. The legal community, he said, was abuzz with conversations

about Cynthia's case. He didn't know Cynthia, and he hadn't seen the photographs, but the prosecution made his blood boil. "What's the point of a prosecution like this?" he asked. "To teach her a lesson? If White wanted to teach Cynthia Stewart a lesson, he could have called her and her lawyer into his office, described the world of child porn, explained how her pictures could have been stolen from the photo lab and put online, frightened her with prosecution if this ever happened again, then stressed, 'We're not just whistlin' Dixie here, honey. This is the *real* world.' That would have cured Cynthia of her naïveté *fast*."

Despite his critique of White, the lawyer's message to me was much like Tom Theado's message to Cynthia: don't become militant against the court system, and especially don't alienate Judge Zaleski, "the only one in the courthouse not intimidated by the prosecutors"; don't back Greg White into a corner; do give White a face-saving way out of the case; don't emphasize Oberlin's differences, but do point out that none of us need police coming into our bedrooms or looking in our photo albums when no harm has been done. He gave me his office and home phone numbers and encouraged me to pass along his advice to the family's supporters. But he pointedly and re-peatedly asked me not to mention his name.

On Friday afternoon, Cynthia and David had a conference call with their attorneys. Even though the magistrate had told Amy that her Children Services ruling would be handed down by that day, Feb-ruary 4, no decision had been announced—which Amy found very, very interesting. "Everyone at juvenile court looked like they were feeling the heat today," Amy told Cynthia and David with delight.

Later, Cynthia consolidated the feedback they had gotten from Amy, Kreig, and Tom into a list of instructions for supporters. At the top of the list, Cynthia wrote "Nix on Planet O," which was short-hand for telling people to stop focusing on the ways Oberlin was dif-ferent from other places and start emphasizing the ways we were just like everybody else.

But Cynthia balked at giving White a way to "save face" after her own face had been smeared all over the media and her life turned upside down. Nevertheless, Tom Theado was adamant. He reiterated:

"You can't demonize your opponent, because the devil always wins. If he's a true demon, then you lose because there's no ground on which you can communicate, no incentive that will be enticing, no reason that will be understood, no rationale that can be explored. It's fun and cathartic to hate your opponent, but it's not productive."

At Cynthia and David's request, I sent out an e-mail late Saturday night asking everyone to stop calling White's office. Letters to White and to Children Services and to the newspapers were still encouraged, but calls were to stop immediately. And there were to be no more personal attacks on Greg White: "We need to keep sharing our views in a measured way," I wrote.

Virginia Behner's instinct, however, was the opposite of Amy's, Kreig's, and Tom's: she had been *thrilled* to read about the rally, and she wanted us to keep the pressure on, loud and strong. She left a message on Campeloupe's answering machine: "Hello, is this Politics Central? Well, I have a new thing that all your people can do to torment Children Services. Their meeting is the third week of the month on a Wednesday, at 4:00 P.M. If you could get a thousand people to crowd upstairs there to make their lives a living hell! In a nice way, of course."

Marc Blecher, Stan Mathews, Connie Grube, Rebecca Cross, and I were quickly emerging as the ad hoc leadership of the large but loosely organized group of supporters that had grown out of the meeting at my house only the week before. Marc, the China scholar, had started calling us "The Politburo."

That Sunday, the county newspapers ran sprawling lead stories recapping Cynthia's case and our protest, with more color photographs, lead editorials, and even a political cartoon. We combed through the articles for new information and insights into the police and prosecutors.

In the *Chronicle-Telegram*, the acting Oberlin police chief seemed to acknowledge the subjectivity of the case. He said the police found no evidence Cynthia planned to sell or distribute the photographs, but that "it's offensive to have them to begin with. My personal opinion [is] if a child's old enough to understand they should be clothed and not showing their body, then it's probably inappropriate to be photographing them and putting them in an awkward situation."

Greg White refused to make comments to the *Chronicle-Telegram*. "The jury will decide," he said. "I'm not trying it in the newspapers."

The *Chronicle-Telegram's* editorial, "When 'Protection' Goes Too Far," was pointed and acerbic, suggesting that the Children Services case existed merely to benefit the prosecutor's office since Cynthia "must now devote financial and emotional resources to two legal battles." The editorial cartoon showed a naked smiling baby, bottom-up on a living room rug, and a mother with a camera looking worriedly at the father who was peering out the window and saying, "Quick! Hide the camera and the baby! It's the prosecutor, a children's services worker and the sheriff's SWAT team pulling into our drive!"

White *had* spoken with the *Morning Journal*. He insisted that Children Services did not want custody of Cynthia's child, and he blamed the media for whipping the public into an overreaction. "This case has a lot of issues that have been aggravated by inaccurate news media accounts," he claimed. And Jonathan Rosenbaum gave a harsh rebuttal to Cynthia's supporters: "Children are not objects owned by their parents. I don't think the law permits parents to take pictures of their daughters with a shower sprayer pointed at their genitalia."

Those of us who expected the *Morning Journal* to be more supportive of the prosecutor than its rival, the *Chronicle-Telegram*, were surprised by the *Journal's* own Sunday editorial:

> There's a lot of "on the one hand, but on the other . . ." in this case. That's what makes it so interesting. There are a lot of well-meaning people on all sides. That's what makes it so public.
>
> There's a frightened, confused little 8-year-old girl in the middle. That's what makes it so sad.
>
> That's who we need to keep our eye on. Don't be distracted. If we keep our eye on her, I think justice will be served. If we don't, I think we're all in trouble.

~~~

On principle, Virginia had not made contact with any of Cynthia's supporters, but she was eager to keep abreast of our plans. On Sunday, she left several messages on Campeloupe's answering machine: "Hello, is this the home of the famous radicals? Yes, I've read about you in both papers today! I wonder what Greg White's thinking?" And later: "Famous political radicals home? I didn't know if you came up with a spokesman yet. We got to get this thing moving fast, as you know."

Over the weekend, Marc Blecher and Connie Grube *had* been moving fast. They had consulted with Amy and Kreig, who had given permission for a delegation to meet with White on Cynthia's behalf as long as they did not try to speak for the family or their lawyers. Marc and Connie had handpicked several people to join them, and they had scheduled the meeting for Monday morning, February 7, at 9:30 in the parish hall of Christ Episcopal Church.

Marc called White at home on Sunday to finalize details. He assured White that he would not be walking into a lion's den and predicted that dropping the charges against Cynthia would make White "a hero." White listened but told Marc he was angry about the rally. "People have misunderstood," White insisted. He wanted to know who had organized the protest and the phone calls. Marc told him it was a loosely knit group of people who were quickly becoming more organized.

The Politburo met that night to take stock and plan ahead. Stan would continue working with the regional media, while Connie would network behind the scenes. Marc was pleased with how different people in the group were carving out complementary roles. "Stan can be on the barricades," Marc told the group, "while I can work the back channels. We can play good cop/bad cop—give White a hard time and then give him a way out."

17

Improvisations

Marc and Connie had recruited three people for the meeting with the prosecutor. Marc had invited the Reverend Nancy Roth when she had shown up at the rally wearing her priest's collar. Connie had enlisted Gina McKay Lodge because she was a home-schooling mother whom White could in no way dismiss as a "liberal type." And Connie had hit upon her friend Alan Campbell when she had gone to the public library to browse through old Oberlin High School yearbooks, looking for someone who had grown up with the prosecutor.

In her flowing skirt and with her gray hair swept up into a wide bun, Nancy Roth looked and moved like a dancer. Now an associate priest at the Episcopal church, she had been trained in ballet, and all through her varied career she had sought "to join the body and spirit in prayer." Nancy could intuit people's personalities from the ways they moved their bodies. Even before they met, she had thought that Cynthia Stewart moved with a sense of pleasure and freedom, as if the earth beneath her were her friend.

Gina McKay Lodge lived on a farm, where she and her husband homeschooled their four children and ran a nationally respected art conservation business. Gina, like Cynthia, had been raised in West Virginia, but she had come from a family of conservative doctors and stockbrokers. Many years after moving to a liberal town in northern Ohio, she maintained her Southern identity and still considered her-self "a moderate Republican with conservative moral values." Gina's oldest children, like Nora, sang with Choristers and took violin les-sons from Molly.

As a teenager, Alan Campbell had been in a rock 'n' roll band
with Greg White's younger brother. Greg had been serving in Vietnam at the time, and the younger boys had nervously followed the
reports of his experiences there. Later, when Greg was working as a
carpenter and Alan as a house painter, they'd see each other on jobs
around town. Greg went on to law school, while Alan expanded his
house painting business into a family enterprise that included an-
tiques, estate sales, lawn care, stone casting, and rental properties.
When Greg was first elected county prosecutor, Alan's crew painted
and wallpapered the prosecutor's offices.

Alan believed there were two kinds of people in the world: those
who studied to get credentials and those who just *are*. Alan thought
of himself as "an *are* guy." During the years he had volunteered as a
wrestling coach, Cynthia had driven his high school team to tourna-
ments and taken an interest in their accomplishments. Ever since,
Alan had always waved to her around town. Alan considered Cynthia an "are person," too.

Registered as a Republican ever since he could vote, Alan had a
disdain for protests and chanting. But he did believe he was the kind
of guy Greg White would listen to.

On Monday morning, February 7, the delegation gathered in the
parish hall of Nancy's church. Nancy was wearing her priest's collar, Connie had put on makeup and ironed her slacks, and Gina
had donned her Southern heritage: her mother's pearls, a cashmere
sweater, a linen shirt, and a wool A-line skirt. Marc looked professori-
al in his tweed jacket, and Alan wore a flannel shirt and jeans because
he wasn't "a suit guy." The lounge had big, comfortable chairs and
windows overlooking a new prayer garden. When White arrived—a
taut, clean-shaven man in a starched white shirt and tie—they all
introduced themselves. Then they politely got down to business.

Everyone began by agreeing that child pornography was horrific, and they commended White on his desire to combat it. Nancy
assured him that her church took seriously every form of child abuse.
In her preparations to be a priest, she had been trained in the warn-

ing signs of abuse and in ways to intervene and get help for an abused child. But this group wanted to give White a different context for looking at Cynthia's photographs, she said. They wanted him to see Cynthia through their eyes—as a mother, a community member, and a photographer.

Listening as the women took turns speaking, Marc was pleased that White was hearing from people who clearly shared values with him. Connie mentioned that she was a registered Republican and taught natural fertility for the Catholic church. She spoke of Cynthia's generosity as a photographer and showed White a framed picture Cynthia had shot of her youngest daughter Mia leaping in midair during a soccer game. Mia kept the photo displayed on her dresser; it made her feel empowered and proud.

Gina mentioned she was a Republican, also. She explained to White that everybody in the community knew Cynthia, and if he just knew Cynthia the way everybody in town knew Cynthia, then he would know immediately that there couldn't possibly be anything going on. Cynthia put her heart into everything she did. She took school bus driving to a level most people would never dream of—she was a psychologist, friend, and second mother to the kids on her bus.

Alan had come to the meeting feeling like Cynthia's fate rested on their shoulders. He was proud they weren't a bunch of people waving signs. They were people who *knew* something, who wanted to share information with the man who controlled Cynthia's fate. The polite tone of the meeting encouraged Alan. Here they were, trying to help a person who had been wrongly accused, a mother who was helpless in the face of charges that could ruin her family's life. They had the accuser there, and nobody was mad. There had been no ugliness, no shouting, no crazy stuff. The system was working—they had asked for this to happen, and it was happening. And then the spotlight swung to him. It was Alan's turn to speak. And the prosecutor was listening.

Instead of speaking, Alan began to cry.

Marc was astonished. Here was Alan, the sturdy businessman with his down-to-earth gruffness, going to pieces, sobbing! Marc might have expected one of the women to get weepy, but not this tough guy.

Nancy was delighted and touched to see a man cry. Gina thought it was picture-perfect: Alan's tears were saying in a tangible human way what all of them had been trying to say in words. Unable to speak, Alan got up and left the room. He had no interest in sitting there and letting everybody watch him weep.

Like a good Marine, White kept his face impassive. He didn't move to pat Alan's shoulder or offer him tissues. Still, Marc was certain Alan's tears had made a big impression on White. Even a screenwriter couldn't have scripted a more surprising or effective scene, he thought.

Gina broke the awkward silence and began to tell a personal story she had planned to share, a painful story about Cynthia and David's intervention in a situation involving her daughter's safety and well-being. Gina would be forever grateful to them for perceiving harm in a situation she had misjudged as benign and for taking the initiative to protect her child. White listened but said little. Gina thought he harbored an impression of Cynthia as a radical who could not be reasoned with. She made a point of saying, "Cynthia's not your average suburbanite, and it's easy to judge someone like Cynthia because she can come across as this on-the-wild-side, hippie type. But you should not project onto her something she is not."

Alan eventually slipped back into the room. Composed now, he talked about his own experiences with Cynthia and shared his conviction that she would never do anything to hurt her child. Everyone watched White listen to Alan. Nancy thought White's stiff body revealed inflexibility and defensiveness—he was not the sort of person she would want making decisions about *her* life! Gina thought White was listening with an intent, puzzled interest and behaving like a consummate gentleman. Marc feared that White was unfazed by their testimonials because he had the mindset of Sergeant Friday in *Dragnet*: "Just the facts, ma'am."

Yet when someone mentioned Cynthia's "thousands and thousands of photographs," White complained that no one had ever shown *him* all those photographs. Then he made an offer: if Cynthia submitted more of her pictures as evidence, he would consider them as context for the ones she had been indicted for. Perhaps, then, he might see her bathroom pictures differently. Marc volunteered to pass along White's offer to Cynthia's attorneys.

"But what if there are other nude photographs of Nora in Cynthia's collection? Would that put her in even more trouble?" Connie asked.

"I don't see how she could be in *more* trouble," White said pointedly.

The meeting had lasted almost two hours. It ended as politely as it had begun, with White and Alan catching up for a few minutes before they all went their separate ways.

Later that day, White phoned Alan. He wondered if Alan had felt free to speak frankly at the meeting and if there was anything he'd like to say privately about Cynthia Stewart. Alan stood by his earlier remarks. "I haven't been in her house, I never dated her, but I've seen her a lot, I've seen her from different angles, and this accusation doesn't match," Alan told Greg. "Some people are kind of secretive, but she is so open about everything. She's not the kind of person who's doing sneaky, sordid stuff."

The next day, White requested a meeting with Kreig Brusnahan to discuss the Stewart case. He asked to see one hundred more of Cynthia's photographs as context for her bathtub shots. The men agreed to meet on February 18. Kreig would give White the one hundred pictures then.

Pleased with this new development, Kreig called Amy, who surprised him by fervently opposing the plan: she didn't trust White, and she feared he only wanted those pictures to fish for fresh evidence against Cynthia. Only if White would send written assurances that additional nude photographs would not put Cynthia in more legal jeopardy would Amy relent. Kreig contacted White, who sent the assurances.

Kreig then sent word via Cynthia and David that their supporters should cool it for a while and give him space to work things out
with the prosecutor.

The next afternoon, Tuesday, February 8, Amy called Cynthia and
David with news: Arredondo had just ruled Nora a dependent but
not an abused child. Over the phone, she read Arredondo's succinct
ruling and terse conclusion. The dispensational hearing was scheduled for February 17. That hearing, however, might never take place
since Amy planned to file a motion to stay the magistrate's ruling of
dependency.

Cynthia and David were relieved Nora had not been ruled
abused but angered she had been ruled dependent. In their opinion,
the ruling boiled down to: "Your child is dependent because of what
we're doing to you to make your child dependent."

But Amy pointed out that by *not* ruling Nora abused, the magistrate had potentially dealt a severe blow to the criminal case. List had
argued, "If this photograph is obscene, then Nora is abused." Logi-
cally, then, that meant that if Nora were *not* abused, then the pictures
were not obscene.

My phone was ringing as I walked in the door that afternoon from
my teaching commute. It was Cindy Leise, the reporter from the
Chronicle-Telegram whom I had spoken with several times now. She
wanted to know how Cynthia's supporters were responding to the
ruling. I hadn't heard about the ruling yet. Leise filled me in. I tried
to respond honestly to her questions, but I also felt uncertain about
which of my opinions were appropriate to share. I wanted to send a
message to the prosecutors that Cynthia had fierce support, but I also
didn't want to jeopardize Kreig's upcoming talk with Greg White.
Suddenly, I was in a role I had hoped from the beginning to avoid:
impromptu spokesperson for an ad-hoc group taking improvisational
political action.

The Politburo conferred by e-mail and phone that evening. We
felt we needed to have some kind of public response to the depen-

dency ruling, and we needed to keep some kind of steady presence in the press. But we also recognized that we needed to strike a different tone from the rally. We agreed that on Thursday, February 16, the eve of the dispensational hearing, we would hold a candlelight vigil in Tappan Square, the heart of Oberlin, to show that Cynthia's community was staying vigilant—that our eyes were open even if our mouths were, for the moment, cautiously shut.

I sent an e-mail to supporters about the upcoming vigil, using an excess of capital letters to make my point: "THIS EVENT WILL BE VERY DIFFERENT IN CHARACTER AND TONE FROM THE EVENT AT THE COURTHOUSE LAST WEEK. We request no signs or posters, no chanting of slogans, and no extemporaneous speeches." Only Nancy Roth and I would be making short prepared remarks, I added.

That evening, Virginia left a message on Campeloupe's answering machine in a sad voice: "Well, I'm sorry about the ruling. I wanted it to be dismissed. But I know for the greater good of other people, it might be better that this happened. Maybe God's going to use this to incite people to action, where if it had gone your way, maybe not. Anyhow, I'm sorry about this. But I think *they're* going to be sorrier! Bye!"

The next morning, the *Chronicle-Telegram*'s headline blared: "Agency Gets Role in Girl's Life." In Leise's article, Kreig claimed that Children Services and the county prosecutors "would disapprove of anyone but Ozzie and Harriet." Kreig also reacted to Children Services's assessment that Cynthia and David needed counseling in order to "understand how others with differing beliefs may view their actions":

> Brusnahan said the mention of "differing beliefs" in a court order "scares the hell out of me."
>
> "I thought that was what this country is about—differing beliefs," Brusnahan said.

Greg White blamed the media and Cynthia's supporters for traumatizing Nora:

White said the case would not be damaging to the 8-year-old girl if it wasn't handled in such a public way.

"I think it's time for everybody involved here to step back and end the media frenzy in this case," said White, who declined to answer other questions about the case. "The people involved in this process need to reflect on what has happened here without any more external forces being involved.

"No one is being harmed here more than this child because of the media attention that this case is receiving."

Marc and I both insisted in the article that it was the *prosecution* that had traumatized Nora, not her mother's pictures or the public support.

Cynthia phoned me right after she read the newspaper. She was furious at White's comments and frustrated she couldn't say so to the press. For the first time, she offered me some talking points. "Tell them the publicity has *not* had a negative effect on Nora or any of us," she insisted as I scribbled down notes. "Since the rally, Nora hasn't had a single nightmare, and we all have felt so much more energetic. There's a big difference between fighting a battle by yourself and fighting it with lots of people beside you. And tell them," she added hotly, "it's *wonderful* Greg White is now so concerned about Nora. I just wish he had been concerned about her feelings when Rosenbaum wanted to wipe her pictures off the face of the planet!"

White himself was chafed by the "Ozzie and Harriet" jibe. He called Kreig and threatened to call off their February 18 meeting. White also called Marc and wanted to know how to square Marc's and my comments with the group's diplomatic outreach to him earlier in the week. Marc tried to soothe White, telling him we had just been speaking out of our concern for the family. "If you've got concerns, call me, not the media," White instructed Marc. Marc encouraged White to keep doing the same.

White, in turn, had raised the hackles of the *Chronicle-Telegram* editor, who wrote in an editorial that White "apparently isn't enjoying all the attention this case is generating, so he decided to shoot the messenger." Many of Cynthia's supporters were angry about White's comments, too. Stan wrote a scathing letter to the editor, submitted it to the Oberlin newspaper, and e-mailed a copy to Marc. The letter began:

> *It's more than a bit self-serving for Prosecutor Greg White*
> *to claim that emotional damage to Cynthia Stewart's child is*
> *being caused by media attention to this case. I think he and his*
> *henchmen, along with the nincompoops at Children's Services*
> *have already done an admirable job of terrorizing this little girl,*
> *long before the media got involved. . . .*

When Marc read Stan's letter, he panicked, phoned Stan, and persuaded him to retract the letter. He also convinced Stan to cool the rhetoric generally. But Stan was reluctant to cancel any of the upcoming media interviews he had lined up. In particular, he had arranged an interview with a reporter for WKSU, the National Public Radio station in Kent, Ohio. The report would air on the Kent station, though it could possibly get picked up for larger distribution. I was supposed to participate in the interview, too. Stan promised we wouldn't say anything inflammatory.

Late that evening, Marc sent an e-mail around encouraging supporters to lay low for now in order to increase our credibility and foster an atmosphere in which an agreement could be worked out. "Further attacks," Marc warned, "will probably just make Greg dig in his heels further."

The next morning, Marc e-mailed me a copy of the fax he had just sent to his "new pal Greg":

Dear Greg,

Thanks for the call yesterday. I'm sorry if it
seemed like we did anything to stoke up yesterday's
Chronicle story. Lynn and I were honestly trying to

```
balance some wish to be responsive to reporters'
inquiries--they called us, we certainly didn't call
them--with our desire to cool things down at this
point.
      . . . I want you to know that I managed to get
one citizen to retract from one of the local papers
a letter to the editor that had already been sent
and that would have made your hair curl. In short,
there are some pretty angry people out here, but we
are trying, with reasonable hopes of success, to
persuade them to hold off. . . .
```

When Amy went to the courthouse that day, she heard another reaction to the *Chronicle-Telegram* article. A bailiff pulled her aside and whispered, "The headline shouldn't have read, 'Agency Gets Role in Girl's Life.' It should have read, 'Pictures Found Not Obscene!' That was the *real* news! You didn't lose. You won!"

18

Watching Out and Watching Over

B efore he had even read the newspapers the next morning, Marc received a call from Greg White. It was a preemptive call: an inexperienced member of the court staff had "misspoken" in the *Morning Journal* and suggested that the court might still opt to remove Nora from her home. White wanted to assure Cynthia's supporters that taking custody of Nora was not an option they were pursuing. After the call, Marc sent around a reassuring e-mail, concluding: "Greg's call is another indication that we have a good channel open to him. He urges calm on this latest media blip, and so do I."

When I read the *Morning Journal* later, I noticed that the "inexperienced member of the court staff" was actually the Lorain County Juvenile Court administrator—someone whose word I, and others, would certainly have taken as authoritative. I also noticed that White had not mentioned to Marc his own statements in the article, in which he criticized the "tremendous media attention" the two cases against Cynthia had generated and the ramifications for the child. "I think we really need to take a look at where we're at," White said. "I have never seen a case in which the child victim was so exposed and I'm very, very concerned about that."

On Friday morning, February 11, Vincent Duffy, the WKSU reporter, interviewed Stan and me at Stan's house, in a room filled with paintings, plants, and windows full of snowlight. Despite my promise to Marc to be judicious, as soon as the microphones were turned on, I realized how hard it would be for me to speak both honestly *and* diplomatically. When Duffy asked what my reaction to seeing the photographs had been, I blurted out: "I was *shocked* by how *un*-shocking they were." And when he asked, at the end of our interview, how I expected the case to end, I boasted, "We will win because we are right!" Then I paused, embarrassed, imagining Jonathan Rosenbaum saying the same sentence with that same degree of certainty and self-righteousness.

Amy was now receiving a steady stream of inquiries from the regional press; she was also receiving new offers of help and support. The most significant offer came from the Lorain County lawyer who had phoned me after the rally. He invited Amy to come to a working dinner at his home with several attorneys who wanted to share their expertise *pro bono* and talk strategy with her. Amy found the overture a bit condescending since the attorneys were clearly worried that she was in over her head. On the other hand, she believed their intentions were good, and she knew she could use all the help she could get. She accepted the invitation.

Tom Theado had suggested early on to Cynthia and David, to Amy, and to anyone else who would listen that a diversion program was the best hope for resolving Cynthia's situation. In diversion programs, low-risk, nonviolent, first-time offenders were offered probation in lieu of trials and the threat of incarceration. Tom knew a diversion program would be a hard sell to Cynthia since diversion agreements usually required some admission of guilt from defendants. It would be an even harder sell for Greg White, who had always refused to institute a diversion program in Lorain County and who never dropped indictments without a defendant pleading guilty to *something*.

When Amy or others would point out that Lorain County didn't have a diversion program, Tom would say, "Who cares? If you have the acquiescence of both parties and the permission of the court, you can structure any agreement you want." Tom believed both sides in this case would eventually want a resolution, and the most probable outcome then would be a deal in which no one was the winner.

Over Sunday night pasta and wine, Amy heard similar advice

from her new advisors. The attorneys discussed the criminal statutes, the politics of the county, and the players in the prosecutor's office. They also discussed White's and Rosenbaum's political aspirations. It was an election year, and that meant White would change course in this prosecution only if it made him look like a *protector*—not a protector of an odd woman's right to take naked pictures of her daughter, but the protector of a child who was being buffeted by the media and the justice system. "If you want to prevail in negotiations with Greg White, you're going to have to make him look like a hero," the lawyers counseled her.

White, they said, had political ambitions beyond the county. If the Republicans won the White House in 2000, White hoped to be appointed U.S. attorney for northern Ohio by the new president. He was already quietly lobbying the leaders of the local Republican Party to appoint Rosenbaum as county prosecutor in his place if he rose to the federal position. The Stewart prosecution ultimately had to reflect well on both Rosenbaum and White. "If you don't make White and Rosenbaum the victors, you will never get what you need for your client," they warned.

The Politburo met on Sunday night, too—at my house, over cups of tea, with about a dozen volunteers and two agenda items: the upcoming vigil and the opportunity to address the Children Services board, whose meeting was scheduled in Elyria an hour before the vigil. We had no interest in trying to pack the board meeting with a thousand supporters, as Virginia had suggested, but we did think it wise to send a small delegation. Marc offered to be part of that delegation, along with three people who had been subpoenaed but not allowed to testify at the Children Services hearing. Since Virginia was still actively serving as Nora's guardian ad litem, she could not speak publicly about the case. But she had registered an official complaint, so the agency's ombudsman would apprise the board of her concerns. Marc would draft a letter to be read at the meeting, expressing the community's concerns, too.

The rest of us volunteered for vigil-planning jobs. Everyone would post the fliers I had made around town. Nancy Roth would ask her church to donate candles, and she and I would write prepared remarks to be vetted by Connie and Marc. Stan had already sent out press releases and would follow up with phone calls to reporters. He would bring matches, lighters, and Dixie cups to use as candleholders and set up a table at the event with petitions and information sheets. A member of the Unitarian Fellowship would record and make CDs of the event.

Connie would advertise the vigil by painting Tappan Square's two large boulders—"erratics" left by the ice age glacier, which now functioned as billboards for community announcements, birthday greetings, and declarations of love. If you painted one of The Rocks, you could depend upon your message staying up only a day or two before someone else painted over it with their own urgent news. So Connie said she would wait until late Tuesday to take over her buckets of house paint and her spray cans.

Snow started falling again Sunday evening, and by morning the schools had been canceled for the day. That afternoon, Cindy Leise called from the *Chronicle-Telegram*. She told me that the dispensational hearing scheduled for Thursday had been postponed. Because of Amy's motion to stay the magistrate's ruling, Judge Boros was suspending further action on the case and would consider whether or not to uphold the magistrate's ruling in a hearing on April 7. Would we still go forward with the vigil? I assured Leise that, yes, we would, since a show of support for the family was certainly relevant on the eve of a meeting between Cynthia's lawyer and the prosecutor. I tried to choose my words carefully, tiptoeing through her questions, but when Leise asked if Cynthia would plead guilty in order to cut a deal, I didn't mince words.

It was late in the evening before I could e-mail my vigil remarks to Cynthia and David and follow up with a call to get their response. David gave me a thumbs-up on the speech, then told me about a poignant call he'd gotten from his friend Kevin, the father of Nora's friend Hannah. Kevin had helped Hannah make "snowpersons" in their yard that day, including one snowwoman with breasts. Afterward, while admiring their handiwork, Kevin had asked Hannah to run inside and get the camera so they could take pictures of their snowpeople. But Hannah had refused, declaring, "No way! They'll come and take me away just like they did Cynthia!"

"And that," David observed dryly, "is what we call 'The Chilling Effect.'"

The next morning, the *Chronicle-Telegram* reported that Kreig Brusnahan was hopeful that criminal charges against Cynthia would be dropped. White maintained that nobody was talking about dropping charges. My afternoon phone chat with Leise had made it into the article, too. I had said, diplomatically enough, that Cynthia's supporters are "guardedly hopeful that talks between Cynthia's lawyers and the prosecutor's office will be fruitful" and that we were encouraging people to remain vigilant "but to quiet their voices for a while." But my last no-minced-words comment now gave me a twinge of concern:

> Powell said she does not think Stewart will admit to any wrongdoing in a plea bargain with prosecutors.
>
> "I cannot in my wildest imagination see Cynthia pleading guilty to any charge, because she's absolutely innocent and it would be a disservice to families everywhere," Powell said.

On the other side of town, Marc read my words and felt more than a twinge of concern. He fired off a reprimand to me and the Politburo:

> The story in this morning's *Chronicle* is NOT helpful at all. We should NOT be talking about legal strategy in public. The upshot of Kreig Brusnahan's ill-considered statement that he hopes charges will

be dropped, and of Lynn's statement to that effect,
is to back Greg into a corner--making it harder for
him to drop the charges by forcing him to discuss it
in public. His reply comes very close to saying he
will not drop the charges; if he says that, Cynthia
is in deep shit. Luckily, he does not go all the
way. But let's lay off this sort of thing, please.
   Sorry to sound critical, but we are playing with
fire here, and I know you will understand where I am
coming from. . . .
   I am going to call Greg and try to do some damage
control on this one.

Marc couldn't get through to White on the phone right away,
so he faxed him:

Dear Greg,

Apropos of today's Chronicle story, I wanted you to know two
things:
   1) I was pretty unhappy with several of the statements made
on Cynthia's behalf, because I fear they might have put you
in a difficult position on the case. I have said as much to the
maker of the statements, and to other members of our support
group.
   2) I noticed and very much appreciated the careful way you
responded. Thanks, Greg. And I hope that the Friday meeting
[with Kreig] goes well.

Cheers,
Marc Blecher

After reading Marc's e-mail, I agonized about my remark. I apologized to Marc and worried out loud to my husband and to several
friends about jeopardizing Cynthia's chances of a resolution. But the

more I worried, the more I wondered if I was right to worry. Maybe
Marc was getting a bit too protective of—and chummy with—Greg
White? I remembered Deep Throat's warnings to Cynthia and David
about White and Rosenbaum; she knew them up close, and she counseled confrontation. White and Rosenbaum had certainly used their
own dismissive and critical statements in the newspapers to send
strong signals to us. Why couldn't we do the same? The strong signal
I wanted to send was that Cynthia's supporters could be tenacious,
even if we looked like what we were—a group of small-town folks
unpracticed in the gamesmanship of politics and litigation. Marc was
uneasy about provoking White too much, but I had become uneasy
about reassuring him too much. Somehow Marc and I had switched
roles since that first meeting at my house a few weeks back.

But there was larger criticism circulating in Oberlin toward *all*
of Cynthia's supporters. One of my husband's colleagues pulled Dan
aside at work and said sternly, "Lynn should stop interfering with the
legal system." A carpenter stopped me on the street and said he liked
Cynthia but didn't think a good parent would take photographs of
her naked daughter. I asked him if he let his children watch television whenever they liked. When he said yes, I responded sharply:
"Well, some people think a good parent wouldn't do *that*." An English professor flagged me down in a parking lot and said that he heard
that "the rally was a *total* disaster." His assessment was based on one
thirdhand negative report. But as I tried to fill him in, I realized how
hard it had become to give the whole story succinctly and how futile
it felt to try.

The comments of my husband's colleague, however, bothered
me. I wondered if we were indeed "interfering" in the legal system.
And, if so, was this interference corrosive—or necessary—to justice?
Yes, it would be chaotic if every action by the police and prosecutors
were met with protests. But wouldn't it be dangerous if the police and
prosecutors were *never* questioned?

The next morning, I e-mailed Marc my vigil remarks, and he
e-mailed me the letter he was preparing to present to the Children
Services board. We were quick to praise and encourage each other's

work. Marc thought my remarks were "beautiful," and he gently rec-ommended that I tone down only one sentence, which I did. And I had only tiny suggestions for his letter, which effectively urged the board to review how the Children Services case against Cynthia had been conducted. His three-page letter ended: "An innocent woman and a healthy child who is not in any danger whatsoever (except from the effects of the case that LCCS and the Prosecutor have brought) are being tormented daily by these proceedings. Swift action is need-ed to return them to the peaceful lives they need and richly deserve." I was pleased that Marc was not mincing words, either.

Wednesday, February 16, dawned dry and mild. A good omen, I thought, as I drove Jesse, who still refused to ride a school bus unless Cynthia was driving, to school that morning. As we passed Tappan Square, I saw that Connie had painted The Rocks. Both boulders were white and proclaimed in big, black letters: "Candlelight Vigil in support of Cynthia Stewart, Wed 2/16, 5:30 P.M., Bandstand."

In warm weather, the bandstand in Tappan Square was the focal point for outdoor concerts and community celebrations. It was de-signed to resemble a giant Chinese rickshaw with a two-tiered pagoda roof. In April, it was surrounded by blooming daffodils and magno-lias. In June, it was visited by wedding parties, with photographers in tow. In February, it looked like a whimsical, oversize prop of summer, abandoned among the snow and barren trees.

When I arrived at the bandstand late that afternoon, the P.A. system had been set up and tested, recording equipment was ready to go, a banner was waiting to be unfurled, Stan had tables set up where people could sign petitions or donate money, and Connie had brought two buckets of large permanent markers for people to add messages of support for Cynthia's family on The Rocks. Candles had been stuck through Dixie cup holders, and lighters distributed to the pockets of several volunteers. Stan was speaking quietly with several strangers, who, I realized, were reporters. I slipped Stan photocopies of my vigil remarks to give to them. I wanted to be quoted exactly.

We had remained lucky with the weather. The snow from earlier in the week had mostly melted. The sidewalks were dry, and the air still. It was chilly but not uncomfortably cold.

By 5:30, the sun had sunk low in the sky, spreading the square with a last, thick rosy gold. About three hundred people had gathered, including senior citizens from the nearby retirement community, a few college students, and all sorts of families with all ages of children, from teenagers to babies in Snuglis. As I looked out at the crowd, I was surprised to see faces of people I hadn't known were supportive of Cynthia, plus a few of Oberlin's "luminaries" (as a newspaper would call them the next day): the chair and the vice-chair of the city council, and the college's dean of students. This time my children were present, too; they had walked to Tappan Square with my husband and were each holding candles in Dixie cups, standing with small groups of their own friends.

Someone started the lighting of the candles, and soon the crowd was hushed and solemn, passing the fire, wick to wick. I stepped to the microphone and read a poem Nora had written at school the previous April, a poem which I now offered back as a kind of prayer for her:

Magnolia Bud

Soft little buds
on the magnolia,

the wind gently
sways them but

they are unharmed,
soon to become beautiful
flowers.

I talked about the poem's delicacy, optimism, and attentiveness to beauty. I talked about Cynthia and David as parents and as citizens and how it was an honor to stand in solidarity with them. I spoke of Cynthia's passion for photography and the chronicle she had kept of her family's everyday life. And then I spoke to the skeptics I had been arguing with in my mind all day:

> Every family is different. Every parent makes countless judgment calls in raising a child which the neighbors next door might question. There are good parents who would not take photographs of their child in the bathtub and there are good parents who would. There are good parents who forbid television because of violent and sexual content, and there are good parents who freely allow television so their children can be "in touch with the world." And certainly good and loving parents disagree vehemently about education, discipline, and religious training.
>
> We are all grateful for laws that protect our children from exploitation. And we appreciate the efforts of police and prosecutors and social workers as they work to keep our communities free from child pornography. But we do not believe the laws they seek to enforce are meant to criminalize mothers taking innocent pictures of the children they love. Surely this is not what we as citizens want from our government.

Nancy Roth spoke next, noting that the word "vigil" came from a Latin word that could be translated as "watching" or "being awake." Nancy explained we were watching in two ways: "We are watching that justice may be done," and "we are trying to watch over Cynthia and her family, to assure them that this community cares about them." She spoke, too, about the spiritual dimensions of a wakeful silence:

> Silence helps us to move *inward*, to the center of our being where we can be awakened to the truth of our own and others' existence. But silence also helps us gather our interior thoughts and send them *outwards* in what some

call "being a witness" and others might call "sending good
energy" and others would label "prayer."

As Nancy finished, the sun was almost down, and the candles
seemed to burn more brightly. We all stood for a few moments of
silence, then two middle school boys unfurled the banner—"In Support of Cynthia Stewart & Family"—and led the candlelit procession
down through the square to The Rocks. As we watched the crowd
walk somberly away from us, Nancy was thinking how proud she was
of Oberlin and how moved she was by our community's solidarity. I
was having more selfish thoughts: "If the police ever come after *me*,
these are the people who would stand by my family. I'm never leaving
this place!"

For half an hour, The Rocks were quietly swarmed with people
writing messages of support. Then as everyone drifted away in the
chilly dusk, Connie and Stan packed up the tables, markers, candles,
and Dixie cups. Stan handed me a donation jug with $100 or so in
small bills and change. Connie's older daughter took flash photographs of The Rocks. Since the boulders got repainted so frequently,
those messages for Cynthia's family might not even be there the next
morning.

Much to everyone's amazement, though, no one repainted The
Rocks for weeks. The messages stayed untouched day after day, ex-
tending the vigil and, as Nancy had hoped, both "keeping watch" and
"watching over" not only Cynthia's family, but, somehow, all of us.

The delegation to the Children Services board meeting had also
gone well. After Marc's letter was read, the president of the board
asked the executive director to respond. Gary Crow confirmed that
the agency had found a very nice family and a happy, well-adjusted
child and that they had no issues with the family except whether the
pictures were appropriate and whether or not nude pictures of the
child would continue to be taken. Addressing the delegation, Crow
said he "certainly understood" that Cynthia's supporters did not be-

lieve Children Services should be involved with the family, and that he had "talked with many people who agree with you." The board president said they would consider the delegation's letter later in a closed-door session.

That night Marc sent an ebullient e-mail to a friend, reporting on the success of both events. "We can strike on two fronts simultaneously!" Marc exulted. Then he sobered up: "But so could Hitler, and see where it got him."

The next morning, Stan received exciting news from Vincent Duffy: his radio news story about Cynthia's prosecution would be broadcast on NPR's *All Things Considered* that evening at 5:20. On the eve of Kreig's meeting with Greg White, we would be striking on a third front, too.

19

A Thousand Pictures' Worth

In the fall, when she had been working through her pictures to find every nude shot of Nora, Cynthia had been cheered by her visits to Amy's "all-girl office." She admired the camaraderie that Amy and her co-lawyer shared with their secretary and legal assistant. She had come and gone freely from Amy's basement, putting her lunch in the office refrigerator and optimistically bringing in healthy snacks, like hummus and pita or popcorn dusted with brewer's yeast, to share with a staff that actually preferred French fries and pizza. Cynthia had even brought in bottles of cod liver oil to make sure everyone in the office got the vitamins they needed as winter approached. Someone diplomatically filed the bottles in the refrigerator, and they were never touched again—except when Amy caught a cold and Cynthia coaxed her to gag down a smelly spoonful.

Now Cynthia was again spending every day in Amy's basement, combing through her pictures to choose the hundred she would give to Greg White. She was distressed about any of her prints leaving the protection of Amy's office and being delivered into the prosecutor's hands. Yet she also found herself wanting to give White *more* pictures than he had asked for. A mere hundred, she felt, could not convey her family's life, the constancy of her camera, or the mammoth size of her photographic project.

Cynthia wanted White to understand her family. And so she wanted to include *yearly* examples of each of her series of Nora: Nora on her birthday, Nora on the first day of school, Nora with gifts from the Easter Bunny. . . . And she wanted to include photographs of Nora with each of her relatives, family friends, teachers, playmates, and animals; photographs of the places they had traveled; photographs of Nora playing her violin, singing in Choristers, dancing Scottish dances; photographs of Nora in various bathtubs. Cynthia wanted White to know how her family was both *like* and *not like* his.

As she chose each picture, Cynthia placed it in a fresh white envelope on which she noted a description of the image and its negative, roll, and box number. Once all the pictures had been chosen, she planned to make an album for White, slipping the prints into archival plastic pages and affixing the envelopes with their crucial data onto those pages. Cynthia wanted to ensure that every picture would eventually be returned safely to its proper place in her archives.

On Wednesday morning, February 16, as her supporters had been preparing for the vigil, Cynthia had been entering a state of panic: she was supposed to have the photographs ready for Amy to look over by noon and for Kreig to pick up that afternoon. But she had only made her way through half of the boxes, and she had already identified five hundred pictures she felt were crucial to include.

Amy downplayed the importance of exactly which pictures Cynthia chose. "White just wants proof that you've been photographing Nora all along," Amy urged. "Proof that you didn't just pick up a camera one day and start shooting naked pictures of your daughter."

But Cynthia couldn't stop agonizing over her decisions. She missed Amy's noon deadline. Then she missed Kreig's afternoon deadline. At six o'clock, she still wasn't done. Amy called downstairs to tell Cynthia it was time to wrap up for the day—she would need to put the finishing touches on the next morning. But Cynthia came up from the basement to report that she wasn't anywhere near done and to ask if she could stay and work a few more hours.

Amy didn't believe Greg White cared one whit about the story of Nora's life. She believed he was looking for an excuse to drop charges, and any reasonable group of one hundred photographs from Cynthia would provide that. If it had been up to Amy to make a selection, she would have sat down for an hour, pulled out a hundred pictures, stuck them in an album, and sent them off to White, for whom, she believed, the whole exercise was a face-saving farce.

But Amy could see that the slow, exacting work of choosing those photographs was Cynthia's way of fighting for her family. She didn't understand Cynthia's passion for her pictures, but she understood Cynthia's passion for her daughter. Amy gave Cynthia the spare key to the outside door and showed her how to lock the deadbolts once she was done for the night.

Over supper that night, Amy mentioned offhandedly to her husband that Cynthia was still at the office sorting pictures. He was incredulous. There had been tension between Amy and her husband for some time about Cynthia. Amy had, understandably, not been home much during her mother's illness. It had been a hard time, and everything had been much harder because of this case. Her husband thought that Amy spent too much uncompensated time talking on the phone to Kreig or Cynthia or Tom Theado, and she had developed a new habit of slipping into her office on weekends to work. Most seriously, she had let essential attorney-client barriers come down. As a physician, he had strict rules about "work being at work and home being at home."

This time, he and Amy got into a fight. He argued, "You have confidential files in there! You have to remember that she is a *client*. You can't let her have free access to your office. You can't let her have free access to *you!*" Amy argued back, but she knew deep down that her husband was right: she was no longer making professional decisions as Cynthia's attorney; she was making decisions as a grieving daughter and as a mother who could not bear to think of losing her own child.

Amy arrived at her office early the next morning and was astonished when Cynthia climbed up from the basement to say hello. Cynthia had never gone home. She had slept a little while on the waiting room couch, but mostly she had worked through the night, sustained by Earl Grey tea and hummus and calls home to Nora and David before they had gone to sleep.

Cynthia told Amy that she would not have the photographs ready by noon to deliver to Kreig. Amy was alarmed at how tired and stressed Cynthia looked, so she soothed her with an offer to drive the pictures over to Kreig's office anytime that afternoon. Cynthia disappeared again into the basement.

At noon, David arrived with lunch for Cynthia and helped her for a couple of hours. At four o'clock, Amy herself began to panic. Not only was Kreig still waiting for the pictures he needed to give to White the next morning, but she needed to be home by five o'clock to take care of her son. It was her husband's bowling night—a nonnegotiable outing in their household.

When Amy went down to check on Cynthia, she could see that it would be disastrous to leave her alone again. Cynthia had almost finished making her choices, but she had chosen a *thousand*, not a hundred, pictures. Now she needed to slip each photo into a plastic sleeve and staple on its envelope of identifying data. Amy didn't think Cynthia was calm or rested enough to finish the job alone.

Amy called her mother-in-law and asked her to babysit. Then she called her husband to inform him of the arrangements. She explained, "I don't want to leave Cynthia alone because, my God, she would stay up another twenty-four hours." Her husband was not pleased: "If she wants to be that ridiculous, that's her problem, not yours. You need to come home." But Amy had made up her mind— she was staying until Cynthia handed over those pictures and went home herself.

Amy's secretary and assistant, Chris and Charlene, volunteered to stay and help. So while they went out to buy snacks, Cynthia lugged her photographs, plastic pages, and envelopes up the basement steps and piled them on Amy's dining room table. Everyone would gather there to keep Cynthia company and see her through.

At five o'clock on weekday evenings, the radio at our house was often tuned to NPR because I half-listened to the news in the kitchen while I cooked supper. But that Thursday evening, my family and

I nervously gathered around the big stereo speakers in our living room. Although we were expecting Cynthia's story at 5:20, I was still startled to hear Linda Wertheimer's familiar voice, at that exact moment, begin to talk about our small town. After her introduction, Vincent Duffy's voice took over. He described the circumstances of Cynthia's prosecution, then turned to sound clips from White, Kreig, Amy, and me.

Everyone reprised the positions they had staked out in the local newspapers. White said there was a line where naked pictures of children became "inappropriate and unlawful." Kreig said that White was looking for something in Cynthia's photographs that wasn't there. Describing the shower sprayer photographs, Kreig argued: "Some people have said, Isn't that somehow wrong or doesn't that simulate masturbation? My answer to that is, no, what that simulates, and what that actually depicts, is someone *washing* themselves. And because it's captured on film that makes it somehow sinister? I don't buy that."

Duffy described the community support Cynthia had been receiving and introduced me as someone who had started a defense fund and who had seen the pictures. "I was shocked by how *un*-shocking they were," I heard myself say.

Kreig explained how the vague and overbroad Ohio law allowed prosecutors to place their own interpretations on photographs, and Duffy finished up the four-and-a-half-minute report with a dramatic flourish: "Brusnahan says that unless the law is changed, parents in Ohio and states with similar laws will be at risk when they take any naked photographs of their children. For Cynthia Stewart that risk has become a nightmare. She remains free on $10,000 bond, but is on unpaid leave from her job, could lose her child to foster care, and is likely to face a criminal trial in May. For NPR news, I'm Vincent Duffy in Oberlin, Ohio."

At those words, my family burst into applause, cheers, and yelps. My daughter Anna-Claire, who had recently been going through her early adolescent my-mother-is-a-dork phase, gave me a huge hug and said, "That was *awesome*, Mom!"

All over town, in fact, Cynthia's supporters were ecstatic. Marc called Stan to congratulate him on arranging the interview and then e-mailed me:

> Very nice work on the NPR interview! That was a
> beautiful story--Greg stated his case, and the
> rest of the story rebutted it. I am very proud of
> everything we have done so far. We could not have
> set the table better for tomorrow's meeting.

Fueled by potato chips, onion dip, and beer, Amy, Chris, and Charlene were trying, as the evening wore on, to be helpful to Cynthia and to keep her spirits up. As they worked, Cynthia told funny and touching stories about the photographs—stories that, Amy could see, were all part of the larger story Cynthia was trying to tell Greg White.

Along with the laughter, though, there was a good bit of tension in the room. It was hard for Cynthia to accept the other women's help because she had such a particular method for slipping, in strict chronological order, the pictures into their plastic pages and attaching the notated envelopes. With four people working, the job went more quickly, but with more opportunities for error and confusion. Frequently, Amy felt like shouting: "Goddamn it, Cynthia, if you tell us one more time not to mess up these pictures I'm going to throw you out of my office!" But she also understood how vulnerable Cynthia felt preparing her pictures for an antagonist.

Late in the evening, someone made a mistake, and a picture got misplaced. Cynthia wanted to backtrack through all the work they had done to see if they could find the missing picture. When Amy chided, "Oh, come on. We'll figure it out when we get them all back," Cynthia burst into tears. Amy hastily apologized, and they all worked backward until they found and fixed the mistake.

Through the evening, Amy stayed in touch with Kreig, who was waiting for the photographs with increasing irritation. And then Amy's husband returned home from his bowling night and called her.

"What the *hell* are you doing? You left home at 7:30 this morning!" he shouted. "Where are your priorities?"

Close to midnight, the four women finally finished putting the pictures into the albums. Chris and Charlene left for home, and Cynthia and Amy carried six huge binders out to the parking lot to Amy's car. In the process, the new locking system on the building malfunctioned, and they got locked out of Amy's office.

Now it was Amy's turn to burst into tears. Cynthia tried to soothe her, "Oh, Amy, this isn't your fault!" But all Amy could think was: it's really late, Kreig's pissed off, my husband won't speak to me for two days, and Greg White will hardly even look at these damn pictures anyway. To Amy, the night seemed emblematic of the whole case: part heroic, part *Three Stooges*; part beautiful and moving, part neurotic as hell.

20

One-on-One

The next morning, Friday, February 18, a producer for ABC News called me. He wanted to know if Cynthia and her supporters would be willing to appear on *20/20*. If so, they could begin shooting right away.

I had anticipated the NPR story generating calls to Cynthia's lawyers; I had not imagined getting calls from TV producers myself. Our small, twenty-year-old television was hooked up to a VHS player, but we had neither cable nor antenna to connect our set to the outside world. I finessed my TV ignorance, trying to sound pleasantly interested but not overly eager. "Please remember," the producer told me as we were hanging up, "I was the first to call you."

He was not, however, the first to reach Amy. A producer from NBC's *Dateline* had already called. And by the time Kreig left his office that morning with six bulging binders to give to Greg White, CBS's *60 Minutes* had called him.

Kreig had promised Cynthia and David that he would not explore any plea deals with White. His bottom line was going to be: "There *has* to be a dismissal of this case and let me tell you why—it's in the best interest of the child."

When Kreig presented White with the six albums, he tried to convey just how much care Cynthia had put into compiling the context White had asked for. The two men did not look through the albums together, but Kreig asked White to notice that Nora often had the same expression fully clothed as she had in the nude photographs—obviously, that expression was not intended to incite lust. As White began to disagree, Kreig said, "Don't tell me what you think now. Look at these first. You've said you want context. Here it is."

White acknowledged it was not a crime to take a nude photograph of a child. But he insisted that sexually suggestive photographs were not okay. Kreig said, "My client would not want to disagree with you." He tried to impress upon White that Cynthia's family was different from the mainstream. "She's an old hippie," Kreig explained. "These people go down to their farm in West Virginia, and they swim around with no clothes on, but they're not hurting anybody."

Neither man spoke about what conditions they would require for a resolution to the case, but they agreed Nora's welfare was the central concern. Kreig said that the best interests of this child were not being served by the prosecution of her mother; White said he might want to meet Nora in order to judge that for himself.

The two men agreed to meet again the following Wednesday, after White had had a chance to look at the pictures. Kreig stressed that the national media was "turning up the heat." White complained about Cynthia's supporters and told Kreig to "get those people under control." Kreig replied that Cynthia's supporters had agreed, at his and Amy's request, to stay quiet for a while. "But," he emphasized to White, "we don't *control* those people."

After the meeting, Kreig gave an optimistic report to Cynthia and David. The prosecutor had not foreclosed any possibilities. Kreig did wonder, though, how White's tone might change if Rosenbaum balked at the idea of a resolution. "Greg White is a completely different person with Jonathan Rosenbaum in the room," Kreig warned.

The weekend brought a welcome lull for the Politburo. For the first time in three weeks, there was nothing to plan or hash out. Everywhere I went that weekend, though, people were pulling me aside with advice, brainstorms, news scoops, and secrets. One prominent supporter wanted to try out "a crazy idea" on me: since only a few people had seen Cynthia's pictures, I should re-create the pictures with my own daughter, show the shots to ABC News, and "thereby take a lot of steam out of White's statements." I agreed the idea was crazy.

When I went to get my hair cut, my hairdresser confided that she knew from two *very* reliable sources that a certain woman in the county government—a woman who just happened to have a role in Cynthia's case—had put herself through school as a topless dancer. "I hope that information will be useful to you," she said with a knowing look. I relished the gossip but had no idea how it might be useful.

Back home, the phone rang frequently. One call came from a man who worked as a guardian ad litem. He gave me his savage assessment of Lorain County Children Services: "If there's a fire, you call the fire station, but if you want to protect children, the last place you should call is Children Services. The joke about 'protective supervision' is that it's not." He told me about Ryan Scott, a two-year-old who had died in a foster home while under the protective supervision of Children Services. The coroner had ruled the child's death a homicide, but in the two years since the death, White's office had not made an arrest. "Children Services needs a watchdog," my caller insisted. "They're not used to having to be accountable." He ended by giving me a little pep talk: "The prosecutor has met his match in you folks. If it wasn't for you guys, Cynthia Stewart would be gobbled up."

The phone was busy at Campeloupe all weekend, too. Virginia called, critical of the vigil, which she had read about in the newspapers. "Nobody in the rest of the county pays any attention when a bunch of Oberlin people march around Tappan Square!" she complained. "Your people need to come back and keep picketing at the courthouse. That's what puts Greg White on the spot." When Cynthia explained that her supporters didn't want to alienate the prosecutor as long as he was meeting with her lawyers, Virginia was disgusted. "Oh, they don't want to upset Greg White!" she whined, her voice dripping with sarcasm. Then she growled, "Well, *upsettin'* him was what was *doin'* it for ya!"

Virginia kept worrying that Cynthia could end up in jail like

Nancy Smith, the Head Start bus driver. "You've got to put up your fight *before* you're convicted," Virginia declared. "You may think justice will prevail. Well, I've got news for you: justice doesn't prevail. You gotta get up and *fight* for justice!"

The woman who had met furtively with Rebecca Cross and me in late January had kept in private touch with both Cynthia and me since the rally. Cynthia and I had begun calling her the "Guardian Angel" to keep ourselves from slipping and referring to her by name in front of anyone else. Now the Guardian Angel sat on Campeloupe's couch with a worried look. "Avoid mudslinging," she advised Cynthia and David. "Mudslinging causes a reaction, not a response." She thought the vigil had been poignant and timely and any other public actions should be in the same tone. And she urged them to avoid the national media as long as they could. "It's your trump card," she cautioned. "Once you play it, it's gone."

Deep Throat, the Republican activist who had e-mailed dire warnings before the rally, phoned Campeloupe with different advice: "Play the press for all it's worth! Unless there is constant coverage of this case, you won't win." She harbored a jaded view of any behind-the-scenes diplomacy. "The prosecutors are playing games," she warned. "Greg White can build Marc Blecher's ego all he wants—that's all he's doing. White will just keep your supporters off his back till you're in jail!" She suggested that Cynthia's supporters picket outside the prosecutor's office with signs that read "*Persecutor* Rosenbaum."

When David checked his e-mail late Sunday night, he found a message from Sally Mann, whom Cynthia had not spoken to or written since November. Sally was writing from her new house on a large, secluded farm in the Shenandoah Valley: "A friend, from England for Chrissake, sent me an NPR piece on you—I assumed the charges had been dropped. Guess not. Nothing like those terrier prosecutors."

No one knew how quickly things might move once White had looked at Cynthia's pictures, but by Monday morning, reporters were calling anyone who might have a scrap of information. Cynthia's supporters didn't have much to report, but an expectation was circulating among us that as soon as White looked at the albums he would have the excuse he needed to drop charges.

The Politburo's understanding was that we could speak judiciously to local newspaper reporters, but should not agree to any interviews with national TV without Kreig and Amy's approval. When a very polite reporter from *USA Today* called, we felt we were walking a fine line—by talking with a national newspaper, were we staying within the bounds or not? We decided we were. Marc, Stan, Rebecca, and I were all interviewed. The reporter didn't want to reprint Cynthia's mug shot, so Cynthia scissored a smiling portrait of herself from a family photo, and I sent it by Fed Ex.

Kreig felt emboldened as he walked into the county administration building on Wednesday, February 23, in the late afternoon. He was coming over from the courthouse, where he had been delighted to find that Cynthia's case was *the* topic of conversation.

As they sat down in White's office, White told Kreig that, in looking through her photographs, he could see that Cynthia was an artist. Still, he was uncomfortable with some of her pictures.

Kreig pointed out that just because they made White uncomfortable didn't mean that Cynthia's pictures were illegal or harmful to Nora. "Greg, you know that famous photograph of the girl sticking the daisy in the barrel of the gun of the National Guardsman?" Kreig asked. "That's you and Cynthia. That's how different you two are. She has a right to stick that flower in the gun, and you have a right to stand there and glare at her. That's okay. But it doesn't mean either one of you is wrong."

Like Tom Theado, Kreig had come to believe that a diversion program was the most promising way out of this prosecution for both the defendant and the prosecutor. But when White suggested that Cynthia might be a good candidate for a diversion program, Kreig said dryly, "Greg, we don't have a diversion program in Lorain County." White said perhaps he could create one.

When Kreig asked what kind of diversion program he imagined, White said his diversion program would work the same way most diversion programs do—a guilty plea, probation, then dismissal—though his program would also be tailored to address the needs of individual cases. In this case, White would require psychological counseling for Cynthia and Nora, a period of monitoring by Children Services, and the destruction of the two shower sprayer photographs.

Kreig tried to impress upon White that Cynthia would not plead guilty to anything. And he did not know if she would agree to the destruction of any of her pictures.

White wanted to meet Nora to assess her well-being for himself. Kreig didn't know if Cynthia and David would allow Nora to meet alone with White, but he said he would consult them. Then Kreig had a more radical idea: "Greg, why don't you come over to Amy's office, just down the street, and meet Cynthia? I'll let the two of you go into a room alone together. This won't be a lawyer talk. I won't be in there, and Amy won't be in there. And if you can come out of that room after an hour alone with Cynthia Stewart and honestly tell me that she is a child pornographer, then we'll go to trial. We'll try the case, and I won't bother you again."

White listened, but only said that he would talk with Kreig again on Monday. Kreig promised that he and Amy would hold the media off until then.

When Kreig told Amy that White had uttered the words "diversion program," she was ecstatic. But when Kreig told her that he had proposed a private meeting between Cynthia and the county prosecutor, with no legal counsel present, Amy thought Kreig had gone stark raving mad. "That could be malpractice!" she cried.

Kreig assured Amy that Cynthia would need to sign a release absolving her lawyers of liability and that White would need to sign a statement ensuring that nothing said in the meeting could be used against Cynthia in court. Amy cringed at the thought of Cynthia, uncensored, alone in a room with the county prosecutor. But she knew defendants often felt frustrated when out-of-court settlements denied them the chance to tell their stories and make their case. Amy sensed that speaking face-to-face with White would make Cynthia feel more in control of her fate and give her the satisfaction of having her story heard by the man sitting in judgment of her parenting and her pictures.

As Amy anticipated, Cynthia and David recoiled at the idea of sending Nora alone into Greg White's office. However, they *were* willing to let White meet with Nora if other adults she trusted could accompany her. They suggested several names to Amy, including mine.

Over the weekend, Cynthia brooded on the possibility of meeting with White herself. She did feel eager to explain her pictures. And she wanted to suggest a way out of the prosecution for both of them: she and White could become allies in changing a bad law. Cynthia imagined a joint press conference in which she and the prosecutor called on the state legislature to change a vague and overbroad law that had caused them both so much unnecessary trouble.

Everything that weekend seemed charged with meaning to Cynthia, from the dead mouse one of the cats brought in, to the movie *The Hurricane* she saw at the town's vintage Apollo Theater. As she left the theater, an older African American woman she knew slightly was also coming out. The woman stopped Cynthia in the middle of the street, grabbed her hand, and, with tears suddenly streaming down her face, said, "I've seen you with your daughter, and I'm praying for you and hoping that people who know nothing of you won't do you in." But "it happens," she kept saying, clasping Cynthia's hand, "it happens." As the two women were holding on to one another, a police cruiser drove slowly past, with Detective Anadiotis at the wheel.

Back home, Cynthia called her friend Ruthie, who lived in New Haven, and asked her to throw the I Ching. Cynthia turned Ruthie's reading over and over in her mind. Sunday night, she meditated in her notes:

> *hexagram thunder over water*
> *I read it every 2 or 3 hours and its meaning deepens each*
> *time . . .*

> hexagram—there was a single bolt of lightning and clap of
> thunder tonight at supper—thunder over water—a rainstorm
> washes everything clean—

David was soliciting a different kind of advice from friends and lawyers, including Tom Theado, who stopped by Campeloupe to talk to both of them. Tom couldn't imagine a worse idea than Cynthia going into a room alone with Greg White. If she did decide to go, Tom counseled her to control her temper: "Don't go in and dress White down for fucking up. Remember, White *has* to be decisive and strong. That's his shtick. And it makes sense because you don't want a weak prosecutor."

Tom also warned Cynthia that inviting White to work with her on changing the law was hopelessly naive. "A prosecutor isn't going to say, 'What we've got is a problem with the law.' Greg White can't speak out against a Republican legislature! And if Greg White says no, *then* what?"

But Tom was thrilled that White was floating specifics of a diversion agreement. "Remember," Tom encouraged Cynthia, "sometimes compromise is not an admission of anything. It's just a recognition of the realities of going to trial."

On Monday morning, February 28, Cynthia picked up a copy of *USA Today* at Drug Mart. On page five, under the headline "Pictures of Daughter in Bath Submerge Mom in Hot Water," she saw herself smiling. Cynthia was irritated to read that she dressed in "quilted skirts and Birkenstocks." She had never worn a quilted skirt in her life. But otherwise, she was grateful for the article, which gave more column inches to the words of her supporters than to the words of the prosecutors. She was sorry to learn, though, that there was another woman in the same legal boat in New Jersey:

> Stewart and a New Jersey grandmother are the latest
> photo-taking defendants to face charges in today's sensi-
> tized society. The lines have blurred between family pho-

tography and potential pornography. . . .

Marian Rubin, 65, of Montclair, N.J., is on paid suspension from her job as a school social worker. Described by her lawyer as a serious portrait photographer, Rubin's charged with endangering the welfare of a child because of revealing photos of two granddaughters, ages 4 and 6. Her lawyer calls the charges "absurd."

The article noted that "sensitive negotiations" were underway between Cynthia's lawyers and White's office and that "those close to the case say a settlement might be announced as early as today."

At 10:03 that morning, a reporter from a talk radio station left a message on Campeloupe's answering machine. By 10:47, there were messages from KTSA in San Antonio, KTRS in St. Louis, ABC in Los Angeles, and CNN in Atlanta.

Calls continued to come in every twenty to thirty minutes. Sarah from *The Early Show with Bryant Gumbel* laughed off David's request for callers to sing their messages, then continued, "I'm sure you've been inundated with calls this morning. I'd really love to talk and see if we could get you on our program."

Connie from KFYI in Phoenix assured Cynthia that "we're very supportive of your position. We want you on this afternoon."

Josie from *Good Morning America* wanted Cynthia to know that ABC had a "great interest in having you on air to talk with Diane Sawyer."

A producer from WKRK in Detroit exclaimed, "Okay, you don't need to hear me sing! I'm looking for the Cynthia Stewart that is involved with a rather silly case. Sorry if this is an intrusion."

Sabine from German television said in a strong accent, "We think that that is really unbelievable. Maybe you are free to talk to the press?"

Even more calls were pouring into Amy's and Kreig's offices. By afternoon, Amy had collected a thick stack of pink phone slips, with messages from CNN, the Associated Press, *Dateline*, *The Today Show*, *Good Morning America*, *The Chicago Tribune*, *Fox News* in Chicago,

Court TV, *The Early Show with Bryant Gumbel*, German television, KFYI Phoenix talk radio, and a half-dozen other talk radio stations from Tennessee to Las Vegas. Local and regional reporters who had been covering the case for months were also calling for updates. Some of these people were also calling Marc, Stan, Rebecca, and me.

White had agreed at their previous meeting to be in touch again on Monday, and Kreig had agreed not to speak with TV reporters until they had talked. But now it was Monday, and, with impeccable timing, the *USA Today* article had brought the media banging on his door. Since White did not contact him that morning, Kreig began to call White's office. Amy called White's office, too. By mid-afternoon, White had not returned the call from Amy or the two calls from Kreig. Kreig told White's secretary that he needed to speak with White urgently, but she didn't know if the prosecutor would even be available the *next* day, much less today.

Irritated, Kreig took a call from *Good Morning America*. Diane Sawyer wanted to interview Amy and Kreig the next morning, in the show's first hour. They could go to ABC's Cleveland affiliate for a live feed. Kreig told the producer he would get back to her later in the day. Then he left messages on White's pager and home phone.

Kreig believed White was stalling, and he wondered if White was getting resistance from Rosenbaum. Amy feared White was just stringing them along until the media interest died down, at which point he would return to his old position of "We'll do our talking in the courtroom."

By the end of the workday, White had not returned Kreig's or Amy's calls. After consulting David and Cynthia, Kreig called *Good Morning America* and scheduled an interview with Diane Sawyer. Kreig and Amy would need to report to the Cleveland studio by 6:30 the next morning. The GMA producer would contact Greg White, who, he hoped, would also agree to be interviewed.

At 7:30 that evening, Kreig's home phone rang. It was an angry Greg White. He thought the two of them had made an agreement not to discuss Cynthia's case with the media.

"And I thought we had an agreement to talk *today*," Kreig pointed out. "I was under the impression that we were in serious negotiations, but you haven't been returning my calls."

White said he didn't want Amy and Kreig to be interviewed on *Good Morning America*. Hold off on the media for another week, he told Kreig, or we're going to trial.

Kreig pushed back, "We need a resolution in this case, Greg. We haven't even received an update from you."

White again brought up the idea of a diversion program. Kreig said Cynthia would not plead guilty to anything.

But every time they seemed to reach an impasse, the two men kept talking, leaving the door ajar to some kind of compromise. By the end of the conversation, Kreig agreed to cancel the *Good Morning America* interview and White promised to be in touch with Kreig and Amy the next day.

At noon the next day, Tuesday, February 29, Marc Blecher was scheduled to give a talk at a Lorain County Rotary Club luncheon. Months before, the Rotarians had scheduled him to speak that day about political developments in China. Marc had published a recent book on the subject, and he was pleased at the local interest. He was also pleased to learn through the grapevine that Greg White usually attended those Rotary lunches.

As Marc was chatting with people after his presentation, he noticed that White was hanging around chatting with people, too. Marc and White slowly began to work their way toward each other. When they met, White told Marc that he was thinking of having a one-on-one meeting with Cynthia. Marc discouraged him. Marc thought a meeting between White and Cynthia might be catastrophic, with tempers flaring on both sides, though he tried to express that concern diplomatically to White.

Then the two men began to disagree about the merits of Cynthia's case. White kept insisting that if Marc had seen the pictures, then he would know they had gone over the line. Marc argued that people he knew and trusted had been subpoenaed and had seen the pictures as completely innocent.

Marc said he was getting regular calls from the national and international media. Pretty soon, he warned, this case was going to blow wide open. It needed to get settled *now*. Once this case became a national media circus, it wasn't going to be much fun for anybody.

White bristled. He told Marc that Cynthia's supporters could call in the TV cameras anytime. *He* had seen the photographs, *he* had the law on his side, *he* was going to do what he thought best. And he was *not* going to be intimidated by the threat of national TV.

White called Amy that afternoon. He had decided to accept Kreig's offer to meet with Cynthia. He suggested the following morning at eleven o'clock at her office.

White also asked about meeting with Nora. Amy explained that Cynthia and David were willing for him to meet her in the company of several adults she trusted. She mentioned my name as one of those adults, and White snapped, "I won't be in the same room as that woman." Amy said she would consult with her clients about a substitute.

When Amy told Cynthia and David that "Greg White won't be in the same room as Lynn Powell," they instantly agreed that if White couldn't put Nora's interests above his own in so small a matter, then Nora would not be meeting with him. Period.

Cynthia, though, was ready to meet with White herself. She would come to Amy's office early the next morning with the list of questions she had been drawing up. Among the many questions she had written in black ink was one written in red: "How and in what context did White say he wanted my pictures destroyed?"

Cynthia called that evening to tell me I had earned the opprobrium of the county prosecutor. A few months earlier, I would have been frightened to hear that Greg White knew my name and harbored ill will toward me. Now I was more than a little pleased with myself. "Greg White should see me now," I laughed, standing at the stove in my khaki apron, holding the phone with my shoulder and brandishing a wooden spoon.

But Cynthia was not as pleased or amused as I was. She wrote in her notes that night: "Lynn—poet/mother too threatening. We have to make the most powerful man in Lorain County feel safe, and to hell with the 8-year-old kid."

The next morning at her office, Amy had an answer for Cynthia's red-ink question. White's absolute bottom line for proceeding with negotiations was the destruction of the two shower sprayer shots. Every copy and photocopy of those two photographs, along with their negatives, had to be destroyed—"removed from the face of the planet," as Rosenbaum had threatened earlier—or Cynthia was going to trial.

Cynthia was horrified. To rub out two moments of Nora's life was more than an act of censorship; it was a personal violation.

And it made Cynthia heartsick to think of the message that destroying those two pictures would send to Nora: the message that her nakedness was shameful. To agree to the destruction of those images would be to agree to a pervert's view of her daughter's body. Cynthia did not see how she could possibly agree to White's bottom line.

So she began tearfully offering ideas for compromise: the photographs could be locked up for ten years in the prosecutors' files, for twenty years, for fifty years. No, Amy said, White was *adamant* about the photographs' destruction. On this point, Amy saw no room for compromise.

Cynthia saw no room for compromise, either. And as they talked, Amy grew exasperated. "It's just two pictures!" Amy finally burst out. "You have a half-million other pictures of Nora!"

"It doesn't matter how many others I have," Cynthia protested. "Those two are just as important as all the others. I'm *not* going to agree to their destruction."

"Then I don't understand you," Amy shouted, tears flaring in her eyes. "If you choose those goddamn photos over your daughter, then everything I thought I knew about you has been a lie. You are not the mother I thought you were." Amy swept up her stack of papers and walked out of the room, leaving Cynthia sobbing at the table.

Greg White had just arrived, and Kreig had met him in the office waiting area. Amy calmed herself for a moment. She thought she had been inexcusably harsh to Cynthia. As she showed White into her conference room, she felt as if she were ushering a lion into a den where she had abandoned a helpless client. Agreeing to this meeting ran counter to everything in Amy's education as a lawyer and to all her professional principles. Every second White spent with Cynthia behind that closed door was going to be agony for her.

Kreig, on the other hand, was pleased as he watched White stride into the conference room. Kreig was excited that this was a "first"—the Lorain County prosecutor meeting with a criminal defendant one-on-one! And there could be other firsts in this case, too, if White created a diversion program for Lorain County.

Kreig believed there were no two people in the world more opposite than Greg White and Cynthia Stewart. But he also believed, at least at this moment, that they were the two best-suited people in the world to change each other's minds.

Cynthia was quiet, with her head in her arms on the table, when the prosecutor walked into the conference room and shut the door. When she lifted up her tear-streaked face, there was no exchange of pleasantries.

"I've taught my daughter that her body is healthy and pure. How do I explain to her that an image of her body must be destroyed?" Cynthia asked.

White told Cynthia he was sure she could find a way to explain the situation.

"But what does it *teach* my daughter for you to destroy those pictures?" she persisted. "And what does it teach my daughter for me, her mother, to consent to their destruction?"

White told Cynthia he was not trying to teach her or Nora a lesson.

Cynthia begged White to lock up the photographs in his files for twenty years, for fifty years, but every suggestion she made was met with a firm no.

Cynthia told White of the bathing ritual Nora had had since she was small, and of the context of the "yoni/rosebud" shots. "That's all they are," Cynthia explained.

White said that he would never have taken those pictures.

"We're very different," Cynthia pointed out. "We've lived opposite lives."

Over and over Cynthia insisted that by asking her to consent to the destruction of her photographs, White was asking her to do wrong, asking her to hurt Nora, asking her to destroy something innocent. But over and over, as Amy had warned, White was clear that the photographs had to be destroyed.

Cynthia told White that she was not capable of seeing the pictures of her daughter as lewd. Cynthia acknowledged that sometimes she was surprised by how differently a photograph turned out from what she had expected. Sometimes a photograph disappointed her at first, but the more she looked at it, the more subtleties and beauty she noticed. Other times she was immediately swept away by a photograph so beautiful that she just couldn't stop looking at it. "That's the magic of photography," she told him. "That's what keeps drawing me back. You never know in advance what you're going to capture in the frame."

Cynthia explained that she wanted to change the law so that other children and families would not suffer as her child and family had. She invited White to join with her in that cause.

White declined but said he didn't begrudge anyone else their causes. Cynthia was aware that White was treating her gingerly, as if she might start screaming or as if, at any moment, she might explode.

Cynthia kept coming back to her plea that White should not ask her to do something that she could not, in good conscience, do.

"You're asking me to do wrong," she kept repeating. "I can't do that. I just can't do that."

White pointed out that he had always said he would only do his talking in court. And yet he was willing to act differently this time, for Nora's sake.

Cynthia insisted that it was for Nora's sake that she did not want the photographs destroyed.

As they talked, Cynthia noticed that White sat ramrod straight. She also noticed that he never mentioned Jonathan Rosenbaum. He seemed to be taking all the responsibility for the prosecution—and all the responsibility for what happened next.

Finally, exhausted and convinced that he was unmovable, Cynthia told White that, although it was absolutely against her sense of what was right, she would allow the destruction of the two photographs, for Nora's sake and Nora's sake only. She did not want Nora in a courtroom. Nora had had enough.

Cynthia repeated, however, that she would never admit to any guilt or wrongdoing. That was *her* bottom line.

White listened, but did not respond. And when it was clear that there was nothing else for either of them to say, White shook Cynthia's hand and left.

Kreig and Amy had been watching the closed door of Amy's conference room for an hour. Amy had spent that hour pacing up and down the hallway's blue carpet. When White finally emerged, he said to Amy and Kreig, "We need to talk." He asked them to fax over a proposal for a diversion agreement, based on their previous discussions.

Kreig was elated; he was confident their gamble had paid off. Amy was too exhausted, physically and emotionally, for elation. But she did go into the conference room and tell Cynthia that she had a good feeling about the case for the first time. "I no longer think we're being screwed," she said, in the biggest surge of optimism she could muster.

Amy apologized to Cynthia for being harsh before the meeting. She said she would keep giving the most honest advice she could.

"But," she acknowledged, "I understand you have to do what you have to do. And whatever you do, I will back you up."

Amy had never seen Cynthia look so shaken and depleted. She said they could debrief later, and she watched as Cynthia silently gathered her things and headed home.

21

"I Expect You to Be Honorable"

Faxes and phone calls kept the lines busy between Amy's office, Kreig's office, and Campeloupe the next morning, Thursday, March 2. Amy and Kreig needed to craft an agreement that they could approve legally, Cynthia and David could live with personally, and Greg White would accept. It became immediately clear that satisfying all three of those conditions would not be easy.

Cynthia had promised White that she would allow two of her photographs to be destroyed. But she balked at any wording that made it seem as if she *approved* of the destruction. Kreig warned Cynthia not to push White too far. Remember, he told her, White not only had to save face, but he also had to support the police and the grand jury, both of whom had found the photographs lewd.

Cynthia fumed to David that the "suave bulldog" she had once been so impressed with was now too eager to placate the prosecutor. Being the first lawyer to wrest a diversion agreement from Greg White, she feared, was becoming more important to Kreig than defending her innocence. David understood that Kreig had plenty to gain by landing a diversion agreement, but he thought Cynthia was being too hard on him. David still believed both of their lawyers had the best interests of their family at heart.

Despite—or because of—tense exchanges throughout the day, Amy, Kreig, Cynthia, and David eventually reached consensus on the document's language. The agreement began with an assertion that "there would be no admission of any wrongdoing or illegal activity by Ms. Stewart." That assertion was followed by an acknowledgment that "although it was not Ms. Stewart's intention to take photographs of her minor child that were sexually oriented, the photographs in question could be interpreted in that manner."

The diversion program would last six months and require Nora and Cynthia to attend counseling sessions, Children Services to monitor the family with monthly home visits, and Cynthia to refrain from taking "photographs of her minor child that Ohio law would deem to be sexually oriented." Cynthia would be allowed to return immediately to her job with the Oberlin Schools. At the end of September, if Cynthia had not violated the terms of the agreement, all criminal and Children Services charges against her would be dismissed. All of Cynthia's photographs—except the two controversial ones—would be returned to her. The proposal concluded: "Our client understands . . . that the two photographs in question and all copies and negatives will be destroyed at the end of the diversion program. . . . The destruction of these photographs will be without Ms. Stewart's consent or approval."

Late that afternoon, the diversion agreement was faxed to White's office. Cynthia assumed she would be signing the official document within a few days. She wasn't happy with the agreement, but she was resigned to signing it.

Cynthia and David had been ignoring the messages collecting on Campeloupe's answering machine for several days, but over the weekend Cynthia played them all back. Virginia had called twice. She had heard about Cynthia's meeting with White and was wondering "if anything got signed, sealed, and delivered."

There were more "you-don't-want-to-hear-me-sing" jokes left by radio talk show hosts and more reporters singing soprano and tenor requests for interviews. German television was proving especially persistent. The most recent call was from Hans who said his network was willing to pay for the story: "Maybe *that* is incentive to talk to us?"

Two calls particularly interested Cynthia. "Not sure if I'm calling the right number," the first caller ventured. "My name is Leslie, and I'm in a very similar situation in New York." The second caller had a bolder voice: "Well, it's very creative, but I can't sing worth a *damn*. However, this is Marian Rubin. I don't know if you may have read about me, but I would like to talk with Cynthia Stewart if I may. Obviously, if I have the right number, she'll know what it is about."

Cynthia called both women back. Leslie had taken some snapshots of her daughter playing dress up. She had been arrested in early December, not long after she had taken her photographs to be developed. Now she was allowed to visit her own home only when her children were at school, and she was allowed to see her children only if she was accompanied by "a bodyguard."

Marian in Upper Montclair, New Jersey, was an avid photographer who had taken nude photographs of her two granddaughters as they played around after their nighttime bath. A New Jersey law required photo developing lab workers to report child pornography to the police; a worker at a local lab had been bothered by her pictures and reported her. When she went to pick up her prints, police were staked out to arrest her on seven counts of child endangerment. Of the photographs the police found offensive, one was a photograph of her older granddaughter mooning her, and another was of her younger granddaughter lying naked on the bed with her grandmother's glasses on. To make the picture funnier, Marian had put a book in her granddaughter's hands so that she could pretend to be reading. Because the book was titled *How to Make Money in Stocks*, the police thought Marian was advertising her granddaughter's body.

Marian had been immediately suspended from her decades-long position as a public school social worker. She had already paid $25,000 in legal fees and $4,000 in nonrefundable bail. Most distressing to her, however, was the loss of her own innocence. She told Cynthia, "These two little girls are the light of my life. What I do out of love has been turned into something twisted and disgusting and dirty. I resent that."

Marian's attorney didn't want to involve the ACLU, and he didn't want any more publicity for her case. It probably didn't help that the front page of a New Jersey tabloid had recently featured the gigantic headline: "Granny Busted for Nude Pics. Cops Think She's a Perv!" Cynthia advised Marian to switch lawyers and to keep her case in the public eye. Public pressure, aided by media attention, had certainly been helping *her* family, she said.

After they had faxed White the diversion agreement, Kreig had left for a week of vacation, so Amy had been the one to follow up with White the next day. The only point of contention seemed to be who would formulate the goals for Cynthia's counseling. White wanted Children Services to formulate those goals, and he wanted those goals to include a review of materials on adolescent sexuality, a review of materials on child pornography, and an evaluation of how well Cynthia understood those materials. Amy thought it was inappropriate for the prosecutor to tell professional therapists how to conduct their psychological work. White relented a bit and agreed to let Cynthia's therapist formulate goals in consultation with Children Services.

By Wednesday of the following week, March 8, Amy had heard nothing more from White, so she faxed him a letter requesting a counterproposal by the next day. "In addition," Amy concluded, "I am still receiving five to ten daily phone calls from national media who are becoming impatient with my staff. I do not know how much longer the media will refrain from doing stories based on our request."

White fired off a testy fax to Amy the next morning, chafing at her comments about the national media, warning that pressures from the outside could give him second thoughts about the merits of resolving this case, and scolding, "Perhaps you do not intend the result, Amy, however, sometimes what you write appears to be less than cordial."

As it turned out, White had "less than cordial" interactions with at least one other person on Thursday, March 9—and rumors traveled quickly about that fractious exchange. Stan left a message at Campeloupe: "Just got a call from Cindy Leise at the *Chronicle-Telegram*. She was asking me all kinds of questions that I couldn't answer. But she *did* tell me that she got a call from several lawyers who said that White and Rosenbaum got into a huge shouting match at the courthouse today. Apparently a big blowup and reports of a potential shakeup in the prosecutor's office!"

The next morning at the courthouse, Amy heard that White and Rosenbaum had been arguing—loudly and publicly—about the Cynthia Stewart case.

Two days later, on Saturday, March 11, the *Morning Journal* published a startling piece of news: Rosenbaum had resigned as the chief assistant criminal prosecutor for Lorain County. Rosenbaum had given the juicy scoop to the *Morning Journal*. On Sunday morning, the *Chronicle-Telegram* followed up with their own long feature article and a headline blaring: "Rosenbaum Quits."

According to the papers, Rosenbaum's resignation had been turned in on February 14 and would become effective in early April. A quick look at the calendar showed that Rosenbaum had resigned one week after White had met with the delegation at the church, and four days before White accepted Cynthia's one thousand pictures from Kreig. The connection between White's actions and Rosenbaum's resignation was obvious to Cynthia's supporters. The *Chronicle-Telegram* made the connection, too. But White insisted that Rosenbaum was resigning to pursue a career in civil law, and he declined to say whether he and Rosenbaum were having a disagreement. "Jonathan has decided that he wants to move on and do other things," White told a reporter. "Obviously, that's a decision that we respect. We'll do whatever we can to help in that effort."

Among the Politburo, Rosenbaum's resignation caused glee and more than a little gloating. "*Happy days are here again!*" sang Stan into Campeloupe's machine. "Looks like we've had a big effect!"

Virginia was ecstatic, too. She read the *Chronicle-Telegram* out loud on Campeloupe's answering machine and then, in a voice of fake sympathy, said, "It's *your* fault the poor man had to quit! What a *shame*, right?"

The editorial page of the *Chronicle-Telegram* assessed Rosenbaum's nineteen-year tenure with quotes from his admirers ("One of the best prosecutors in the state") and his critics ("An insolent, renegade prosecutor who believed himself above the law"). The editorial closed with a hope that "the Stewart case might be resolved out of court once Rosenbaum steps aside. . . . We think a resolution of the case without going to trial would benefit everyone involved, particularly the innocent little girl who unwittingly is in the center of a storm."

The following Tuesday, March 14, Amy gave White a call to check on the status of the diversion agreement. White told her frankly that things were kind of a mess around his office since Rosenbaum had quit, but he hoped to have the paperwork done by the end of the week.

Rosenbaum's resignation fueled more phone ringing from the press at Campeloupe. And another mother in trouble called, this time from Pennsylvania: "Hi, I wanted to offer my sympathies and also to tell you that I'm in the exact same situation myself. I'm headed to court on Monday. So I wanted to talk to you to see if you could give me any advice and to let me know what happened with the American Civil Liberties Union. Maybe if we could console each other? Or do you have any words of wisdom for me? I could sure use it."

Cynthia called Lisa, the young mother, back. Lisa had shot a roll of film quickly to test out a new camera. Her three-year-old daughter had been playing around half-naked in their home, and she had taken some pictures of her on the couch, on the floor, and on the potty chair. A seventeen-year-old clerk at Kmart had turned the pictures over to the police. Now, as Lisa and her husband struggled to pay their mounting legal fees, they were in danger of going bankrupt and losing their home. They couldn't afford to pay both their attorney and their mortgage.

On Friday afternoon, March 17, two weeks and a day after Amy and Kreig had sent over their proposed agreement, White faxed them back the official version, with lines for everyone's signatures. When Cynthia stopped by Amy's office to pick up copies, Amy told her that Kreig was convinced she would need to sign the document *as is*. Kreig had spoken with White, and White seemed to have no interest in

u are *not* the only client I have," he had said in a tone that she
condescending.

ynthia kept talking to David about getting rid of Kreig and
ng him with another lawyer. But David continued to appreci-
eig's pragmatism and experience with Lorain County realities.
or no Kreig, Cynthia did understand that to ask White for any
ges was to risk going to trial. "After all, Kreig *could* be right," she
tted to me. "White might be all too happy to tell the world: 'We
to negotiate with that woman, but she was intransigent.'"

That afternoon, David, Cynthia, Amy, and Kreig gathered in
y's conference room. Cynthia announced right away that she
ld need changes before she could even consider signing this
ument.

"It's taken a lot of people a long time to get to this stage," Kreig
tested. "You really need to sign this agreement, or I don't feel like
an continue working for you."

"Well, I *can't* sign it," Cynthia insisted. "And I'm still smarting,
reig, from the phone conversation we had the other day."

"That's it. I'm out of here," Kreig burst out, slamming his fist
own on the table.

Cynthia's throat tightened. She felt like she could only force a
few words out over her strong impulse to cry, but the words she did
get out were: "Okay. Fine. *Go.*"

Kreig began to write vigorously on a notepad. Otherwise, no one
moved or spoke for several long minutes.

Finally, Kreig stopped and asked, "Well, what are we going to
do here?"

"I think I've made my wishes clear," Cynthia said as evenly as
she could in her raw voice.

"Yes," Amy said quickly, ignoring Cynthia's obvious meaning.
"She's made her wishes perfectly clear: she can't abide by this provision, so we'll need to make some changes."

Kreig was exasperated: "You're expecting those people to be sane
and rational!"

"No, I'm expecting Greg White to be a man of his word," Cyn-

further compromise. Amy, Kreig, Cynthia, and David would meet on
Monday to go through the document together and perhaps Cynthia
could sign it then.

Amy was keenly aware that she could never have gotten this far
by herself. Not only did she lack the experience and the good ol' boy
connections, but the case made her too emotional and the prosecutors made her too angry. As they had worked together the past few
months, Kreig had coached Amy, "You've got to check your temper
at the door. Whether you like it or not, you've got to do these things
to let the prosecutor save face. You've got to go through these hoops
in order to get what your client needs." As she read White's version
of the agreement that afternoon, Amy guessed she would soon be
coaching Cynthia the same way Kreig had been coaching her.

Late Saturday morning, Cynthia called me. She said the document
from the prosecutor's office was terrible. "I can't agree to this," she
moaned. "White took out everything favorable to us and put in all
sorts of language I could never accept. Either it's going to take a *lot*
more negotiations, or it's over." She said she had had nightmares all
night, including one in which a cloaked and hooded "Mr. Graves"
had broken into her house, knocked her to the floor, and threatened
her with a bludgeon. All morning she had been crying and occasionally yelling and was generally so upset that Nora had even come to
her and said, "Mom, if you can't sign it, you can't sign it. It's okay.
I understand." Cynthia recognized the courage it took Nora to say
those words since Nora's logic so far had been: Continuing with the
case equals Mom going to jail. Mom must not go to jail. Therefore,
Mom has to sign the agreement.

As Cynthia calmed down on Saturday afternoon, she and David
began marking up their copies of the document (David using pencil, Cynthia using red pen) and calling more friends and family for
advice. Cynthia particularly wanted to speak with Sally Mann, and
she left urgent messages on Sally's voice mail. Finally, on Sunday,
while the family was away from the house, a Southern voice appeared
on Campeloupe's answering machine: "Well, I can't sing because I

lost my voice when I got the flu. Otherwise, I do a perfect rendition of Emmylou Harris. This is Sally Mann. I'm returning your several calls."

On Monday morning, March 20, as soon as Nora and Jesse were off to school, Cynthia dropped by my house. I handed her a cup of tea, and she handed me the two marked-up copies of White's document.

Glancing through the pages, I could see that White's version was twice the length of Amy and Kreig's original, with many more conditions that Cynthia was now supposed to agree to. Still, I was surprised at Cynthia's despair and her looming sense of crisis. Yes, this document was written in cold legalese and, yes, White's wording had slid into punitive language from the original proposal's more neutral tone. But from the point of view of a writer who had gone through countless drafts on numerous collaborative writing projects, I saw these pages simply as the next draft of a piece of writing that everyone was, presumably in good faith, working on together. Looking at the lines scratched out in red ink and the neatly penciled inquiries and objections, I didn't think consensus looked all *that* far away.

I asked Cynthia which changes made by White most upset her. Some were changes in language that implied guilt or caving in. Amy and Kreig's proposal, for example, had stated, "Ms. Stewart will attend counseling sessions." White's version read, "the Defendant shall . . . submit to counseling." In another section, White had added a clause that indicated Cynthia had committed an "offense."

White had also added a provision that the Defendant must pay all court costs. David and Cynthia did not want to pay court costs; paying court costs, they felt, implied guilt. And they strongly objected to the limitless power White seemed to give to Children Services. The section of his document detailing the role of Children Services began: "In addition to any terms and provisions imposed by the Monitoring Agency, the Defendant shall do or comply with all of the following." David had marked through the opening clause and written in large letters beside it: "TOO BROAD. Any additional

terms & provisions would have to be giv
Most upsetting to Cynthia, though, was th
sentence most crucial to her: "There would
wrongdoing or illegal activity by Ms. Stewar

I asked Cynthia why she thought Greg W
to destroy those two pictures. Since she posse
tographs the police had never looked at, includ
naked, going to all this trouble to rid the world
derstood snapshots seemed rather absurd, not to
resources and an exercise in futility if the Interne
in horrific child porn.

"It's all about appearances—that's what my
thia said. "White gets to say to the voters of Lorai
has eliminated porn, but preserved a family."

"But it also solves a problem for White, doesn't
"If those two photographs vanish, then no one else w
to decide for themselves whether or not they were lew

I encouraged Cynthia to use White's eagerness to
pictures as leverage to get what *she* wanted in the diversi
"Just keep politely sending back the document with th
doing' sentence written back in until he incorporates it,"
"Treat his version as a good draft that needs a few small
was hard for me to believe that White would scrap the agre
because he couldn't tolerate one sentence stating the obv
Cynthia Stewart did not believe she had done anything wro

Cynthia, though, was convinced that Kreig was unwillin
proach White for even small changes because he feared White
perceive any request as a throwing down of the gauntlet. I was
fied by that attitude. "But isn't that what negotiations *are?*" I
"A back and forth and back and forth?"

"Yes, but Kreig's staked his lawyerhood on getting this diver
agreement signed, and that's made him timid," Cynthia complai
Her exchanges with Kreig had grown sharp lately. He had barked
her on the phone when she had called him during a busy time. "Cy

thia declared, finding her voice again. "The man who sat across from me at this table was an honorable man. The man I shook hands with was an honorable man."

"Okay," Kreig relented, "then that's how we'll play it."

Early the next morning, Virginia called Campeloupe. "Look at today's newspaper," she said glumly. "I think this news is timed to put pressure on you to *sign*."

David fetched the *Chronicle-Telegram* from the mailbox and read the headline to Cynthia: "Rosenbaum to Keep County Job Part Time." Rosenbaum would not be leaving the prosecutor's office completely, after all. He would be continuing "as a prosecutor at half salary" when he began practicing civil law. Greg White called the new arrangement "the best of both worlds for the county." When the reporter had asked White if Rosenbaum "would continue to prosecute the case against Cynthia Stewart," White had responded, "Nothing has changed in the Stewart case."

When Cynthia and David arrived at Amy's office that morning, Kreig and Amy handed them a memorandum marked "Confidential." The memorandum laid out the positives and negatives of the two choices before them—accepting White's diversion agreement or risking a trial by asking for changes. The "Benefits of the Offered Settlement" and the "Negatives of a Trial" were long, detailed lists. The "Negatives of the Settlement" and the "Positives of a Trial" were tiny lists, each with three single-line items. The document concluded with Amy and Kreig's advice to their clients "to accept the settlement proposal from the State of Ohio"—although they also affirmed Cynthia's "absolute right to have a trial."

Studying the lists, David asked how likely it was that Cynthia would be sentenced to jail time if a jury convicted her. Amy said that it was very rare for someone convicted of a felony *not* to go to jail. Kreig emphasized that everyone in their family would be subjected in a trial to tough questioning, presumably by Jonathan Rosenbaum, about their intimate family life, and that Nora was first on the list of witnesses Rosenbaum would call.

But Cynthia and David had already decided to ask for changes that would bring the agreement back in line with what Cynthia had committed to in her meeting with White. They signed the memorandum and spent the rest of the day hammering out revisions with Amy and Kreig.

By late afternoon a number of changes had been made. Cynthia's claim of no wrongdoing had been added back. White's requirement that Cynthia pay court costs had been dropped. "Submit to counseling" had been changed to "continue counseling." The word "offense" had been deleted. Language that gave Children Services unspecified power over the family had been narrowed. The passage about Cynthia's employment had been clarified by adding one sentence.

The thorniest problem had been Cynthia's continuing agony over the destruction of her two pictures and her refusal to indicate approval of the destruction. Finally Kreig had suggested that the order to destroy the photographs should be given not by the prosecutor but by the court—a destruction Cynthia could acknowledge without giving assent to. The judge would order the destruction "over the objections of the Defendant."

Before she left her office that evening, Amy faxed the revised agreement to White with a brief cover letter, noting: "It is our belief that this document more fully sets forth the terms and conditions contained in our March 2, 2000 correspondence."

Cynthia had arranged for Nora to come home from school that afternoon with Jesse. As Nora and Jesse spilled out of my car and into our yard, I was struck by how much happier and more secure Nora seemed than the last time she had visited us, on the final day of the Children Services hearing. In the car, she and Jesse had decided to switch shoes, so Nora was now wearing Jesse's scruffy tennis shoes and Jesse was wearing Nora's silver, fur-lined boots. They instructed me to call them by each other's name—Nora was now the boy, and Jesse was now the girl. I tried to split the difference by calling them "Norbert" and "Jessica," but that was not acceptable to either of them.

By the time Cynthia had finished with the lawyers and arrived at our house, Nora and Jesse had abandoned their shoes and pseudonyms and were in our family room flying the helium-filled, remote-controlled blimp Jesse had gotten for Christmas. Nora announced to her mother that she was not ready to go home. So Cynthia sat down in the kitchen and told me of the past two days' meetings with Amy and Kreig while I chopped vegetables for the roasting pan.

Cynthia said things had gotten heated between Kreig and herself the day before, culminating in an exchange during which, at least in her mind, she had fired him. Kreig had rehired himself a few minutes later, and they had all moved forward. But her differences with Kreig still rankled Cynthia. When she had said that she expected White to be "an honorable man," Kreig had thought that would be a good angle to try. Expecting someone to be honorable should not be an *angle*, Cynthia complained.

But Cynthia did worry about how White, honorable or not, would respond to the new document they had just faxed him.

"Maybe he will take out everything you changed," I suggested. "But you should keep putting those things back in with the attitude, 'I expect you to be honorable.' You might have to do that several times. Just keep looking at the process the way an anthropologist would."

Cynthia jumped to her feet. Crouching gorilla-like, she began to swing her long arms, grunt, and pound her chest with her fists.

"Yes," I grinned, "and when White says *that*, your response will be: 'I know, but I expect you to be honorable.'"

"And then *he'll* say—," Cynthia growled, beating her chest and grunting.

I affected a dignified pose and with exaggerated gravity replied, "And then *you* must say, 'Sir, I *do* understand. But I still expect you to be honorable!'"

That evening Cynthia finally spoke with Sally Mann. Cynthia was interested in hearing Sally's reaction to White's plan to destroy her two photographs. As Cynthia had expressed anguish about the destruction to friends and family, everyone had been sympathetic with her principles. But almost everyone had also been convinced that sacrificing two pictures was a small price to pay for freeing her family from this ordeal. Only one friend had advocated going to trial.

"What do *you* think?" Cynthia asked Sally.

"Terrible, horrible," Sally gasped. "That takes my breath away. That's too much of a concession. Untenable, unthinkable!"

Sally's response was just what Cynthia had been longing for. As an artist, Sally understood the horror of being told by the state what she could and could not take a picture of. And as a mother, Sally understood the horror of having an image of her child's body perceived as obscene. "Your reaction makes me feel sane," Cynthia said, gratefully. Hoping she had found the ally who would tell her to ditch the diversion agreement and vindicate herself in the courtroom, Cynthia implored Sally, "Stiffen my resolve!"

But Sally said, "I can't get up on my high horse and tell you what to do. You need to bounce this stuff off someone other than a knee-jerk radical like me. I'm a pugnacious person, but I still took some pictures off the wall of an exhibit because I didn't want to be a sacrificial lamb."

Cynthia told Sally that she worried about the effects of a trial on Nora. But she also worried about the effects on Nora of watching her mother capitulate and agree to something she knew was wrong.

"Kids can be stronger than we think," Sally pointed out. "The times I've stood my ground, my kids have been proud." Sally said she would talk to her husband when he got home from a city council meeting, and she would call a couple of lawyers she knew for advice.

Later that night, Sally sent an e-mail letting Cynthia know that she had left a message for "the noble soul who volunteered to be on tap for me if there were ever any First Amendment rumbles." Then she reiterated: "I feel quite strongly that you should not destroy the images, or the negatives. That is a completely knee-jerk, unlegal opinion, which may be revised after I have the bigger picture drawn out for me."

David wrote Sally right back:

Thanks for your interest and support--it has meant a great deal to us to know that we're surrounded by so many people who are so concerned about our situation. I became all the more aware of this today after speaking with a woman in Pennsylvania who is being prosecuted for taking what sound like perfectly innocent naked photos of her 3-YEAR-OLD. She's just an ordinary person, doesn't even take that many pictures, has no real community and no contacts, and--if it's possible--the misapplication of the law appears to be even greater in her case than in our own.

I wish I knew the answer to the bigger problem of how to keep this from happening to others, but the first order of business is to resolve our own sticky situation. For the moment, the ball is in the prosecutor's court.

22

Bottom Lines

On Wednesday, March 22, White called Kreig and threatened to call off the negotiations. He said he had not sent the diversion agreement to Kreig and Amy for changes; he had sent it to be *signed*.

Kreig reminded White that Nora's well-being was the goal of this process. He also enumerated the political consequences for White if negotiations failed. Eventually, as they talked through the document point by point, White accepted some changes, but he refused others. On one point in particular he would not budge: he would not allow Cynthia under any circumstance to claim in the agreement that she had done nothing wrong.

Early the next morning, March 23, Amy faxed Cynthia and David a rough draft of the agreement Kreig and White had worked out. Some of the changes rankled them, but David had also penciled "OK" and "Good" in a number of places. The biggest problems for Cynthia were the excisions of her no-wrongdoing clause and of her objection to the destruction of her photographs.

Cynthia pored over the document all morning, then called and asked if I would take a look at it. I told her to give me a few minutes and I would bicycle over.

It was a late March day, with a big blue sky, a warm wind, and forsythia and daffodils blooming from my house to hers—the sort of weather that made you wonder why people ever disagreed about anything.

Inside her house, Cynthia pushed newspapers and a pizza box to one end of the dining room table and tossed the current diversion further compromise. Amy, Kreig, Cynthia, and David would meet on Monday to go through the document together and perhaps Cynthia could sign it then.

Amy was keenly aware that she could never have gotten this far by herself. Not only did she lack the experience and the good ol' boy connections, but the case made her too emotional and the prosecutors made her too angry. As they had worked together the past few months, Kreig had coached Amy, "You've got to check your temper at the door. Whether you like it or not, you've got to do these things to let the prosecutor save face. You've got to go through these hoops in order to get what your client needs." As she read White's version of the agreement that afternoon, Amy guessed she would soon be coaching Cynthia the same way Kreig had been coaching her.

Late Saturday morning, Cynthia called me. She said the document from the prosecutor's office was terrible. "I can't agree to this," she moaned. "White took out everything favorable to us and put in all sorts of language I could never accept. Either it's going to take a *lot* more negotiations, or it's over." She said she had had nightmares all night, including one in which a cloaked and hooded "Mr. Graves" had broken into her house, knocked her to the floor, and threatened her with a bludgeon. All morning she had been crying and occasionally yelling and was generally so upset that Nora had even come to her and said, "Mom, if you can't sign it, you can't sign it. It's okay. I understand." Cynthia recognized the courage it took Nora to say those words since Nora's logic so far had been: Continuing with the case equals Mom going to jail. Mom must not go to jail. Therefore, Mom has to sign the agreement.

As Cynthia calmed down on Saturday afternoon, she and David began marking up their copies of the document (David using pencil, Cynthia using red pen) and calling more friends and family for advice. Cynthia particularly wanted to speak with Sally Mann, and she left urgent messages on Sally's voice mail. Finally, on Sunday, while the family was away from the house, a Southern voice appeared on Campeloupe's answering machine: "Well, I can't sing because I lost my voice when I got the flu. Otherwise, I do a perfect rendition of Emmylou Harris. This is Sally Mann. I'm returning your several calls."

On Monday morning, March 20, as soon as Nora and Jesse were off to school, Cynthia dropped by my house. I handed her a cup of tea, and she handed me the two marked-up copies of White's document.

Glancing through the pages, I could see that White's version was twice the length of Amy and Kreig's original, with many more conditions that Cynthia was now supposed to agree to. Still, I was surprised at Cynthia's despair and her looming sense of crisis. Yes, this document was written in cold legalese and, yes, White's wording had slid into punitive language from the original proposal's more neutral tone. But from the point of view of a writer who had gone through countless drafts on numerous collaborative writing projects, I saw these pages simply as the next draft of a piece of writing that everyone was, presumably in good faith, working on together. Looking at the lines scratched out in red ink and the neatly penciled inquiries and objections, I didn't think consensus looked all *that* far away.

I asked Cynthia which changes made by White most upset her. Some were changes in language that implied guilt or caving in. Amy and Kreig's proposal, for example, had stated, "Ms. Stewart will attend counseling sessions." White's version read, "the Defendant shall . . . submit to counseling." In another section, White had added a clause that indicated Cynthia had committed an "offense."

White had also added a provision that the Defendant must pay all court costs. David and Cynthia did not want to pay court costs; paying court costs, they felt, implied guilt. And they strongly objected to the limitless power White seemed to give to Children Services. The section of his document detailing the role of Children Services began: "In addition to any terms and provisions imposed by the Monitoring Agency, the Defendant shall do or comply with all of the following." David had marked through the opening clause and written in large letters beside it: "TOO BROAD. Any additional

terms & provisions would have to be given to us now, in writing."
Most upsetting to Cynthia, though, was that White had excised the
sentence most crucial to her: "There would be no admission of any
wrongdoing or illegal activity by Ms. Stewart."

I asked Cynthia why she thought Greg White was so determined
to destroy those two pictures. Since she possessed thousands of photographs the police had never looked at, including hundreds of Nora
naked, going to all this trouble to rid the world of a couple of misunderstood snapshots seemed rather absurd, not to mention a waste of
resources and an exercise in futility if the Internet was already awash
in horrific child porn.

"It's all about appearances—that's what my lawyers say," Cynthia said. "White gets to say to the voters of Lorain County that he
has eliminated porn, but preserved a family."

"But it also solves a problem for White, doesn't it?" I observed.
"If those two photographs vanish, then no one else will ever be able
to decide for themselves whether or not they were lewd."

I encouraged Cynthia to use White's eagerness to get rid of the
pictures as leverage to get what *she* wanted in the diversion agreement.
"Just keep politely sending back the document with the 'no wrongdoing' sentence written back in until he incorporates it," I suggested.
"Treat his version as a good draft that needs a few small changes." It
was hard for me to believe that White would scrap the agreement just
because he couldn't tolerate one sentence stating the obvious: that
Cynthia Stewart did not believe she had done anything wrong.

Cynthia, though, was convinced that Kreig was unwilling to approach White for even small changes because he feared White would
perceive any request as a throwing down of the gauntlet. I was mystified by that attitude. "But isn't that what negotiations *are*?" I asked.
"A back and forth and back and forth?"

"Yes, but Kreig's staked his lawyerhood on getting this diversion
agreement signed, and that's made him timid," Cynthia complained.
Her exchanges with Kreig had grown sharp lately. He had barked at
her on the phone when she had called him during a busy time. "Cyn-

thia, you are *not* the only client I have," he had said in a tone that she found condescending.

Cynthia kept talking to David about getting rid of Kreig and replacing him with another lawyer. But David continued to appreciate Kreig's pragmatism and experience with Lorain County realities. Kreig or no Kreig, Cynthia did understand that to ask White for any changes was to risk going to trial. "After all, Kreig *could* be right," she admitted to me. "White might be all too happy to tell the world: 'We tried to negotiate with that woman, but she was intransigent.'"

That afternoon, David, Cynthia, Amy, and Kreig gathered in Amy's conference room. Cynthia announced right away that she would need changes before she could even consider signing this document.

"It's taken a lot of people a long time to get to this stage," Kreig protested. "You really need to sign this agreement, or I don't feel like I can continue working for you."

"Well, I *can't* sign it," Cynthia insisted. "And I'm still smarting, Kreig, from the phone conversation we had the other day."

"That's it. I'm out of here," Kreig burst out, slamming his fist down on the table.

Cynthia's throat tightened. She felt like she could only force a few words out over her strong impulse to cry, but the words she did get out were: "Okay. Fine. Go."

Kreig began to write vigorously on a notepad. Otherwise, no one moved or spoke for several long minutes.

Finally, Kreig stopped and asked, "Well, what are we going to do here?"

"I think I've made my wishes clear," Cynthia said as evenly as she could in her raw voice.

"Yes," Amy said quickly, ignoring Cynthia's obvious meaning. "She's made her wishes perfectly clear: she can't abide by this provision, so we'll need to make some changes."

Kreig was exasperated: "You're expecting those people to be sane and rational!"

"No, I'm expecting Greg White to be a man of his word," Cynthia declared, finding her voice again. "The man who sat across from me at this table was an honorable man. The man I shook hands with was an honorable man."

"Okay," Kreig relented, "then that's how we'll play it."

Early the next morning, Virginia called Campeloupe. "Look at today's newspaper," she said glumly. "I think this news is timed to put pressure on you to *sign*."

David fetched the *Chronicle-Telegram* from the mailbox and read the headline to Cynthia: "Rosenbaum to Keep County Job Part Time." Rosenbaum would not be leaving the prosecutor's office completely, after all. He would be continuing "as a prosecutor at half salary" when he began practicing civil law. Greg White called the new arrangement "the best of both worlds for the county." When the reporter had asked White if Rosenbaum "would continue to prosecute the case against Cynthia Stewart," White had responded, "Nothing has changed in the Stewart case."

When Cynthia and David arrived at Amy's office that morning, Kreig and Amy handed them a memorandum marked "Confidential." The memorandum laid out the positives and negatives of the two choices before them—accepting White's diversion agreement or risking a trial by asking for changes. The "Benefits of the Offered Settlement" and the "Negatives of a Trial" were long, detailed lists. The "Negatives of the Settlement" and the "Positives of a Trial" were tiny lists, each with three single-line items. The document concluded with Amy and Kreig's advice to their clients "to accept the settlement proposal from the State of Ohio"—although they also affirmed Cynthia's "absolute right to have a trial."

Studying the lists, David asked how likely it was that Cynthia would be sentenced to jail time if a jury convicted her. Amy said that it was very rare for someone convicted of a felony *not* to go to jail. Kreig emphasized that everyone in their family would be subjected in a trial to tough questioning, presumably by Jonathan Rosenbaum, about their intimate family life, and that Nora was first on the list of witnesses Rosenbaum would call.

But Cynthia and David had already decided to ask for changes that would bring the agreement back in line with what Cynthia had committed to in her meeting with White. They signed the memorandum and spent the rest of the day hammering out revisions with Amy and Kreig.

By late afternoon a number of changes had been made. Cynthia's claim of no wrongdoing had been added back. White's requirement that Cynthia pay court costs had been dropped. "Submit to counseling" had been changed to "continue counseling." The word "offense" had been deleted. Language that gave Children Services unspecified power over the family had been narrowed. The passage about Cynthia's employment had been clarified by adding one sentence.

The thorniest problem had been Cynthia's continuing agony over the destruction of her two pictures and her refusal to indicate approval of the destruction. Finally Kreig had suggested that the order to destroy the photographs should be given not by the prosecutor but by the court—a destruction Cynthia could acknowledge without giving assent to. The judge would order the destruction "over the objections of the Defendant."

Before she left her office that evening, Amy faxed the revised agreement to White with a brief cover letter, noting: "It is our belief that this document more fully sets forth the terms and conditions contained in our March 2, 2000 correspondence."

Cynthia had arranged for Nora to come home from school that afternoon with Jesse. As Nora and Jesse spilled out of my car and into our yard, I was struck by how much happier and more secure Nora seemed than the last time she had visited us, on the final day of the Children Services hearing. In the car, she and Jesse had decided to switch shoes, so Nora was now wearing Jesse's scruffy tennis shoes and Jesse was wearing Nora's silver, fur-lined boots. They instructed me to call them by each other's name—Nora was now the boy, and Jesse was now the girl. I tried to split the difference by calling them "Norbert" and "Jessica," but that was not acceptable to either of them.

By the time Cynthia had finished with the lawyers and arrived at our house, Nora and Jesse had abandoned their shoes and pseudonyms and were in our family room flying the helium-filled, remote-controlled blimp Jesse had gotten for Christmas. Nora announced to her mother that she was not ready to go home. So Cynthia sat down in the kitchen and told me of the past two days' meetings with Amy and Kreig while I chopped vegetables for the roasting pan.

Cynthia said things had gotten heated between Kreig and herself the day before, culminating in an exchange during which, at least in her mind, she had fired him. Kreig had rehired himself a few minutes later, and they had all moved forward. But her differences with Kreig still rankled Cynthia. When she had said that she expected White to be "an honorable man," Kreig had thought that would be a good angle to try. Expecting someone to be honorable should not be an *angle*, Cynthia complained.

But Cynthia did worry about how White, honorable or not, would respond to the new document they had just faxed him.

"Maybe he will take out everything you changed," I suggested. "But you should keep putting those things back in with the attitude, 'I expect you to be honorable.' You might have to do that several times. Just keep looking at the process the way an anthropologist would."

Cynthia jumped to her feet. Crouching gorilla-like, she began to swing her long arms, grunt, and pound her chest with her fists.

"Yes," I grinned, "and when White says *that*, your response will be: 'I know, but I expect you to be honorable.'"

"And then *he'll* say—," Cynthia growled, beating her chest and grunting.

I affected a dignified pose and with exaggerated gravity replied, "And then *you* must say, 'Sir, I *do* understand. But I still expect you to be honorable!'"

That evening Cynthia finally spoke with Sally Mann. Cynthia was interested in hearing Sally's reaction to White's plan to destroy her two photographs. As Cynthia had expressed anguish about the destruction to friends and family, everyone had been sympathetic with her principles. But almost everyone had also been convinced that sacrificing two pictures was a small price to pay for freeing her family from this ordeal. Only one friend had advocated going to trial.

"What do *you* think?" Cynthia asked Sally.

"Terrible, horrible," Sally gasped. "That takes my breath away. That's too much of a concession. Untenable, unthinkable!"

Sally's response was just what Cynthia had been longing for. As an artist, Sally understood the horror of being told by the state what she could and could not take a picture of. And as a mother, Sally understood the horror of having an image of her child's body perceived as obscene. "Your reaction makes me feel sane," Cynthia said, gratefully. Hoping she had found the ally who would tell her to ditch the diversion agreement and vindicate herself in the courtroom, Cynthia implored Sally, "Stiffen my resolve!"

But Sally said, "I can't get up on my high horse and tell you what to do. You need to bounce this stuff off someone other than a knee-jerk radical like me. I'm a pugnacious person, but I still took some pictures off the wall of an exhibit because I didn't want to be a sacrificial lamb."

Cynthia told Sally that she worried about the effects of a trial on Nora. But she also worried about the effects on Nora of watching her mother capitulate and agree to something she knew was wrong.

"Kids can be stronger than we think," Sally pointed out. "The times I've stood my ground, my kids have been proud." Sally said she would talk to her husband when he got home from a city council meeting, and she would call a couple of lawyers she knew for advice.

Later that night, Sally sent an e-mail letting Cynthia know that she had left a message for "the noble soul who volunteered to be on tap for me if there were ever any First Amendment rumbles." Then she reiterated: "I feel quite strongly that you should not destroy the images, or the negatives. That is a completely knee-jerk, unlegal opinion, which may be revised after I have the bigger picture drawn out for me."

David wrote Sally right back:

Thanks for your interest and support--it has meant a great deal to us to know that we're surrounded by so many people who are so concerned about our situation. I became all the more aware of this today after speaking with a woman in Pennsylvania who is being prosecuted for taking what sound like perfectly innocent naked photos of her 3-YEAR-OLD. She's just an ordinary person, doesn't even take that many pictures, has no real community and no contacts, and--if it's possible--the misapplication of the law appears to be even greater in her case than in our own.

I wish I knew the answer to the bigger problem of how to keep this from happening to others, but the first order of business is to resolve our own sticky situation. For the moment, the ball is in the prosecutor's court.

22

Bottom Lines

On Wednesday, March 22, White called Kreig and threatened to call off the negotiations. He said he had not sent the diversion agreement to Kreig and Amy for changes; he had sent it to be *signed*.

Kreig reminded White that Nora's well-being was the goal of this process. He also enumerated the political consequences for White if negotiations failed. Eventually, as they talked through the document point by point, White accepted some changes, but he refused others. On one point in particular he would not budge: he would not allow Cynthia under any circumstance to claim in the agreement that she had done nothing wrong.

Early the next morning, March 23, Amy faxed Cynthia and David a rough draft of the agreement Kreig and White had worked out. Some of the changes rankled them, but David had also penciled "OK" and "Good" in a number of places. The biggest problems for Cynthia were the excisions of her no-wrongdoing clause and of her objection to the destruction of her photographs.

Cynthia pored over the document all morning, then called and asked if I would take a look at it. I told her to give me a few minutes and I would bicycle over.

It was a late March day, with a big blue sky, a warm wind, and forsythia and daffodils blooming from my house to hers—the sort of weather that made you wonder why people ever disagreed about anything.

Inside her house, Cynthia pushed newspapers and a pizza box to one end of the dining room table and tossed the current diversion agreement down between us. She asked if White's language made her sound guilty.

"It sounds to me," I said, after studying the various *whereas*'s, "like you accidentally did something wrong, and that you're promising you'll never do it again."

"As opposed to," Cynthia suggested, "I did a reasonable thing, and they misconstrued it?"

"Right."

"Which is why I can't sign this," she sighed.

I looked at the small number of marks in pencil and in red ink. "Can't your lawyers just go back to White and say, 'Thank you for this document. It looks like we're getting very close. There are just two or three small points that need refinement?'"

"No! They won't go back to White."

"Why not?" I asked.

"Because he's the silverback! He's the king!" Cynthia said, with disgust. "They're afraid they'll get their heads chopped off."

Yet Cynthia was certain she could not sign her name to the agreement as it now stood. And that made her despair. "I'm beginning to remind myself of my father," she said quietly.

I asked Cynthia whether having a strong Stewart will was a gift or a burden right now. She said she honestly didn't know.

Later that afternoon, Amy received a courier-delivered letter from Greg White, which she faxed on to Campeloupe. The letter deepened Cynthia's despair. White was "extremely distressed" about the suggested changes to the agreement's language. He questioned Cynthia's sincerity and expressed pessimism about whether therapy would do her any good. He justified his own efforts to resolve the case but reiterated his view that a conviction would have been attainable. He also asserted that he was behaving in Nora's best interests. Now, though, he was reconsidering his position. He was enclosing a "final draft" of the diversion agreement and warned that if Cynthia did not sign it as is, the prosecution would proceed. "We have made a proposal that is more than fair," he concluded. "I have gone as far as I will go."

Kreig and Amy conferred that afternoon. Kreig wanted to know if Cynthia was now willing to sign. Amy told Kreig that if they pressured her to sign today, Cynthia would probably say, "Fuck off."

"Well, what does she want me to do? I've used up all my cards!" Kreig protested. He told Amy that White would not include a no-wrongdoing clause because he didn't want "to get into a pissing match in the media with Cynthia Stewart." White didn't want Cynthia to be able to point to the document and tell reporters: "See, this proves I never did anything wrong. I was *forced* to sign this agreement."

Amy called Cynthia and assured her that Kreig had gotten more out of White than she had ever dreamed possible. Cynthia was skeptical and distraught and argued that perhaps it would be best for Nora if her mother stood up and fought and won exoneration in the courtroom.

"Look," Amy begged Cynthia, "this agreement guarantees *it will all go away*. Sure, the lawyer in me would love to try this case. This case is a lawyer's dream, a once-in-a-lifetime chance to take on a big constitutional issue and make a splash! But the mother in me—going to trial scares the *shit* out of me."

That evening Cynthia and David went round and round about how to proceed. Cynthia didn't see how she could sign her name to a lie. The thought of taking up a pen and writing "Cynthia Stewart" at the bottom of statements she found reprehensible and untrue—she didn't see how she could even physically do it.

"It doesn't matter whether or not they're absolutely true," David argued. "There's been nothing honorable about this whole prosecution—why should you insist on honor?" He was terrified of their family being worn down by months more of prosecution or, worse, being broken apart by Cynthia going to jail. He had strong principles, too, but he didn't think they were more important than protecting his family. "Sign your name, and get us out of this nightmare," he pressed her.

The phone rang, interrupting their argument. It was Cynthia's brother Patrick, the wild-man owner of Gonzo's Garage and the sibling, she thought, who was most like her. She asked his advice, and Patrick didn't hesitate: "Choose survival over heroism."

Long after David had gone to sleep, Cynthia was still awake, her mind churning. At 1:30, she began writing a letter to Greg White. She began the letter, which eventually sprawled over eleven hand-written pages, by calling White "an honorable man" who had shown "great sensitivity" to her family by attempting to reach a settlement. She appealed to him as someone like herself, "a person who means what he says and who would stand by what he believed even at great personal cost. It is because I see this in you that I hope you will understand why I cannot sign this agreement as it now stands."

Cynthia acknowledged some responsibility for what had happened: "I am tremendously sorry that I did not realize the possible implications of sending this picture to a public processing plant (nothing in my previous experience led me to think of getting my film developed as a public act)." But about taking the pictures and about the pictures themselves, she was unapologetic: "Even now with you and two police departments and two grand juries telling me the pictures are over the line, all I see is my daughter goofing in the bathtub."

Cynthia referred to her private meeting with White repeatedly, trying to refresh his memory about what they had discussed and what they had agreed to. "One possible misunderstanding in our conversation," she wrote, "involves the destruction of my pictures. I think you know what it cost me to agree to it. I thought we had an understanding that when the destruction of the pictures is publicly mentioned, it would also be noted that I object to it." And she appealed to White's own principles: "Remember when I asked you how could I explain to my daughter that the pictures of her playing a game in the bathtub had to be destroyed? You told me surely I could find a way to explain it to her. How do I explain to her that I lied, that I signed my name to something that I did not believe to be true?"

Cynthia concluded the letter with an appeal to the "spirit of seriousness about these negotiations that I believe we have both shown throughout" and with her own final offer: "If the agreement we got today additionally somehow said that I do not believe my pictures are a mistake and that I object to their destruction, I will sign it."

At 3:00 A.M., with her letter written, Cynthia finally felt calm enough to sleep.

She awoke at 7:00 and called her friend Ruthie in New Haven to read the letter. Ruthie felt the letter was too long and too complicated, she didn't like the word "goofing," and she thought the prosecutor might not want to be complimented on his sensitivity. "I've got a strong gut feeling," she observed, "that Greg White is into being tough."

David had a negative reaction to the letter, but he didn't want to get into an argument with Cynthia about it. He faxed the letter to Amy.

Amy called Campeloupe right away. "You'd have to *fire* me to send that letter," Amy told Cynthia bluntly. "You'd be giving Greg White your head on a platter!"

Cynthia asked if, instead of sending the letter, she could meet alone again with White. "I have a really strong feeling I should talk to him," she told Amy.

"And I feel just as strongly that that would be a huge mistake," Amy said. "I have stretched those boundaries as far as I possibly can. Realistically, this is the fairest agreement you're ever going to get out of Greg White. If he let you claim no wrongdoing in this agreement, he would look like an asshole for prosecuting you."

David suggested drafting a new introductory *whereas* with neutral language both Cynthia and White might be able to live with: "*Whereas* the office of the prosecutor and the defendant disagree as to the nature of the pictures. . . . "

Amy said she would check with Kreig, and Cynthia finally relented, "I will bow to your greater knowledge and experience, Amy."

"Okay," Amy replied, "then let me give you some advice: never pursue *principles* through a court of law."

Cynthia and David had been trying to shield Nora from the stress and uncertainties of the negotiations, but with the days increasingly consumed with poring over documents and hashing out possibilities,

Cynthia had sat Nora down and explained to her why they still might be headed to trial, why she objected to the destruction of the pictures, and why she could not sign the agreement unless it made clear she believed she had done nothing wrong in photographing the daughter she loved. Nora had told her mother that she understood.

But on Friday night, Nora had the first nightmare she had had in a couple of months. In the long, complicated dream, her mother was taking photographs of a mummy in a museum. Those pictures had caused a commotion and a crisis, and Cynthia had gone back into the museum to negotiate alone with the mummy. Nora and her dad were waiting and worrying outside. Her dad was trying to comfort her, but they were both terribly afraid.

As days had passed with no news about a resolution, Cynthia's friends and supporters had grown anxious. Though the Politburo's official line was that serious negotiations were ongoing, those of us close to the deliberations worried out loud to each other, and we let supporters know what the sticking points were.

Connie Grube decided to focus her energy on spiritual needs. She lay in bed at night praying for Cynthia, David, and Nora. And, like Ruthie, she spent several days throwing the I Ching. Connie was hoping Cynthia would "rip up the two pictures and move on!" But with both her Catholic prayers and her Chinese hexagrams, Connie tried not to ask that her own will be done.

Connie's prayers weren't only for Cynthia's family. When she mentioned to me that she was praying for Jonathan Rosenbaum, I asked if she were praying for Rosenbaum to *change*. "No," Connie said. "I would never pray for anyone to change. I'm praying for his mind and his spirit. I figure his job is probably the hardest one and that he needs spiritual support. It's as difficult to carry through with a prosecution as it is to back down."

As word spread that negotiations were stalled over Cynthia's reluctance to let two of her pictures be destroyed, some supporters expressed impatience. Gina McKay Lodge, who had spoken so passionately in Cynthia's defense at the church meeting with White, now vented privately at our children's violin recital, "How can Cynthia be so naive and out-there liberal? Can't she just get off her platforms a while and see that this is *real life?*" Gina felt terrible criticizing a woman she empathized with and supported. "But," she pointed out, "I'm a different person. I would be very pragmatic in a situation like this."

Tom Theado was unapologetic about his similar point of view. Although he kept his words measured when talking to Cynthia, to others he said more candidly, "I understand we don't kowtow to censorship, but two fewer photos in Cynthia's oeuvre seems like a small price to pay for a Get Out of Jail Free card!"

Virginia, too, thought it was high time for Cynthia to sign. She didn't trust Greg White and was afraid he'd use any excuse to back out of instituting a diversion program in Lorain County. She called Campeloupe regularly to see if Cynthia had put her name on the dotted line.

The Guardian Angel phoned Campeloupe on Saturday morning, March 25. Cynthia read her the current version of the agreement. "Considering who it's coming from, it's an extremely generous offer!" she exclaimed. "White is really bending over backward." She cautioned Cynthia not to count on supporters sticking by her through a drawn-out trial and appeal process. Expecting people to give this much time and energy over the long haul was unrealistic and untenable. "Even people with the best intentions get tired. The momentum is *now*," she urged Cynthia. "I may sound like the voice of doom, but the reality is, without public support, you *are* doomed."

Moments after they hung up, the phone rang again. "I'm calling to double check," the Guardian Angel said, "that I impressed upon you that going to trial would be a *tragedy*."

That evening, Cynthia called Ruthie and asked her to throw the I Ching once more. Ruthie called back Sunday afternoon with the reading: "The 'heads of two warring villages' must come together for union, unity, further consultation."

On Monday morning, March 27, the front page of the *Chronicle-Telegram* featured two adjacent stories involving Children Services.

One article reported on a candlelight vigil held on the second an-
niversary of the death of Ryan Scott, the two-year-old who had died
in foster care.

The adjacent article contained grim news about two young
brothers found living in an Elyria house "filled with garbage, un-
washed clothes, fecal matter, no food and no running water," and
with "blood, ants and flies all over the floors and furnishings." The
boys ate their meals and used the bathroom at a nearby pizzeria. The
police placed the boys in the care of their elderly grandmother until
Children Services could be notified on Monday morning.

Cynthia handed the newspaper to David over breakfast and
asked, "Why the hell are the prosecutors wasting their time on us?"

In Amy's conference room that morning, Kreig had a suggestion:
if a couple of crucial changes would enable Cynthia to sign the document right now, right here at Amy's table, then Kreig and Amy could
take the signed document to White that afternoon. An agreement
with Cynthia's signature and today's date might tempt the prosecutor
to accept changes he might otherwise resist.

With David's and Amy's encouragement, Cynthia accepted
Kreig's idea. So they made the two changes most important to
her: they inserted David's neutral language at the beginning of the
whereas, and they noted that Cynthia would file an official objection when the prosecutor sought a court order for her photographs'
destruction.

Amy printed out a clean copy of the agreement with those
changes and dated it March 27, 2000. Cynthia signed her name with
a tight flourish over the word "Defendant."

When Amy and Kreig met with White in his office that afternoon,
he immediately scotched their new whereas. And he was indignant
about the formal objection Cynthia wanted to file concerning the
destruction of her pictures. He found it illogical that she wanted to
simultaneously consent to and object to the destruction.

Amy assured White that Cynthia appreciated the lengths he
had gone to to find a resolution, but that she did not believe it would

be truthful for her to sign an agreement which did not make her own views clear.

White rolled his eyes and complained that *he'd* tried to protect Nora, *he'd* tried hard to put the child first, why couldn't *she* put her child first now and just sign the agreement he had offered her?

"It's because she loves her daughter that she needs to be able to sign truthfully," Amy insisted. "And it's because of Nora that I'm here, too—on bended knee."

White was unmoved. He said it was fine to discuss their disagreements in public later, but he could not and would not have any disagreement evident in the diversion agreement.

Amy tried again: "Cynthia's a mother, and she can't see her child, or her photographs of her child, through any other eyes."

White said he didn't believe the pictures were good for Nora and that he hoped after six months of counseling Cynthia would agree.

"What if counseling *doesn't* change her mind?" Amy asked.

White hoped it would.

"But what if it *doesn't?*" Amy persisted.

Then there was nothing he could do about it, White conceded.

Eventually, late in the afternoon, it was White who formulated a new *whereas*, utilizing a phrase Amy had used earlier in their conversation:

WHEREAS, the Defendant acknowledges that the two photographs at issue can be interpreted as sexually oriented in nature, although it was not the Defendant's intention to take photographs of her minor that were sexually oriented in nature, *and as a mother, she cannot see them that way;*

White also acknowledged verbally to Amy and Kreig that Cynthia was free to file an objection with the judge when he sought a court order for the photographs' destruction, though he would not put that acknowledgment into the document.

As the meeting ended, everyone understood that negotiations had come to an end. Amy and Kreig would see if Cynthia would sign the agreement as it now stood. It was quite clear they had wrung the last concession out of Greg White.

That night Cynthia phoned me with the afternoon's news. She wasn't sure whether or not she was going to sign. She and David had had very little time to talk, right now they had a houseguest, they hadn't had supper, and they were exhausted. But even in that brief exchange, I heard something new in Cynthia's voice—a kind of restless resignation, an irritable resolve, a need to get off the phone and get on with her life.

The next morning, Nora wanted to go with her parents to Amy's office. Cynthia and David said no, there wouldn't be much to see, just a bunch of paper shuffling and crossing of t's and dotting of i's with the lawyers. Nora would have a better day at school than schlepping up to Elyria to the law office.

But Nora wondered what would happen if Greg White had put something new in the agreement that her mother couldn't accept. If something went wrong, Nora wanted to know what was going on as it was happening. She wanted to be there for the figuring out of what to do next.

Cynthia gave Nora a large hug and assured her that she really and truly was going to sign that morning. "I know you don't want to sign, Mom," Nora told Cynthia, hugging her back hard. "And I know you're signing it for me."

Kreig was waiting at Amy's office when Cynthia and David arrived. He had prepared the diversion agreement and the necessary motions to stay the proceedings in both the criminal and Children Services cases. Charges in both cases would be dismissed on October 2, pending Cynthia's successful completion of the diversion program.

Cynthia asked if White could revoke the agreement and consider her participation "unsuccessful" if she spoke her mind to the media. Kreig said she would need to measure her words until the diversion program ended in October. Once the charges were dismissed, she could say anything she wanted.

As Cynthia signed her name to the documents, the moment felt hollow. Signing felt like the least acceptable thing she could do and still live with herself. She moved through the morning as if it were happening to somebody else.

Back in January, Virginia had asked a woman at a church prayer session to prophesize about Cynthia's case. Virginia hadn't told the woman any details, only that she was the guardian ad litem of a child whose mother was being prosecuted and that she was concerned about the family's well-being. "I'm about to go to court," Virginia had told her, "and I want God's will to be done."

After they had prayed, the woman had shared with Virginia her prophecy: "It won't come out like you want at first. But then God will make a way. God will use a man to save the mother from prosecution."

Virginia had been certain that Judge Zaleski would be the man God would use to save Cynthia. Now, euphoric, Virginia marveled at God's mysterious ways—the man God had actually used was Greg White himself!

"Well, God runs everything," Virginia observed to Lillian the next morning. "Greg White may think he owns this county. But he *doesn't*."

23

Almost Normal

Nora was turning nine years old that Friday, March 31. Usually Cynthia and David organized a big party for Nora with the coolest party favors in town. But Cynthia and David weren't up for partying anytime soon, even for Nora's sake. As it turned out, David needed to fly that weekend to Charlotte, where he would be hawking the digital archives of *The Nation* at the American Library Association's convention. As an alternative to a party, he suggested that Cynthia and Nora come along for a getaway weekend and birthday adventure. Nobody needed convincing, especially Nora, who would get to miss school on her birthday.

Everything about that weekend seemed carefree and exciting to Nora: making garlands for her hair from dandelions; picking droopy bouquets of wisteria; eating dinner at a fancy Japanese restaurant; making funny faces with her dad in the hotel room's mirrors; posing in front of sculptures and fountains for her mom's camera; and pretending at her dad's convention that she, too, was there on business. David had given Nora a set of convention ID tags to wear around her neck, and Nora liked wearing those tags with her black suit coat and the pants and pretty rose petal shirt her Gramma Freda, David's mother, had just made for her. Nora felt so grown-up in her outfit and ID tags that, as she explored the booths in the exhibition hall, she was convinced people there would not even know she was a child. She was pretty sure they would mistake her for a petite librarian.

On the way home, Nora told her parents how much she had loved her birthday trip with the two of them. "It's been really nice to be who we were before the case happened," she told them. "Really nice to be normal again."

The reprieve for the family was welcome, but short. Back home, on Monday, they awoke to good news and bad news. The good news was that Amy had gotten word that Judge Zaleski was about to officially approve the diversion agreement. The bad news was that the press would soon be breathing down their necks. Cynthia was eager to break her silence. But she and David worried about the effects on Nora and their family of a media blitz.

David called Victor Navasky, the editor of *The Nation*, for advice. Victor shared David's worry that the press—particularly national TV—would commercialize their family's trauma. He offered to contact a high-powered New York agent whom he trusted.

The agent didn't mince words. "I live, eat, breathe New York media," she told them, "and knowing what I know, if I were you, I would walk away. Everyone *regrets* the circus." David, taking notes, underlined the word "regrets" three times. "No matter how sympathetic a reporter might seem, the media always serves its own purposes. They eat people up. They're vultures. And I'm saying that even though they're my friends."

On Tuesday morning, April 4, Judge Zaleski stayed the criminal case pending Cynthia's successful completion of the diversion program. A hearing would be held on October 2 to evaluate her adherence to the agreement.

On Wednesday morning, the resolution was big news in area newspapers. The story had gone out over the AP wire, too. My parents clipped a story from the *Knoxville News-Sentinel* with the headline: "Mom Accused of Taking Lewd Photos Accepts Deal." The words "plea deal" appeared in the headlines of other newspapers, including Cleveland's *Plain Dealer*. Kreig was so indignant about the use of that phrase—a phrase that implied his client had pleaded guilty to some reduced charge—that he served notice to the *Plain Dealer* that they had published false statements. He demanded a correction.

The *Plain Dealer* issued no correction. Instead, it ran a follow-up feature about Cynthia the next day which began: "In a town where different is normal, Cynthia Stewart is a model citizen." The article cataloged only the eccentricities of "free-spirited" Cynthia and the Stewart family, and it exaggerated, to the point of offending Oberlin readers, the "quirkiness" of our small town. Cynthia's brother Eric, who taught yoga in Oberlin, joked that the newspaper made the Stewarts look like Noble Savages.

The day after the AP story went out, Cynthia and David received sixty-seven phone calls. Some of those were from well-wishers, but most were from the media. The major television news shows and stations—60 Minutes, Dateline, 20/20, Good Morning America, The Today Show, ABC News, Fox News, The Early Show, Inside Edition, German television—were all calling, along with countless radio talk show hosts and newspaper reporters. Cynthia and David gave them all a uniform, "No, thank you."

They did decide, though, to accept an offer from the Politburo to organize a public event at which Cynthia would thank her supporters. Reporters could come if they liked, but she would not answer any questions.

Deciding to forgo the pressures and repercussions of being in the national spotlight brightened the mood at Campeloupe considerably. When Amy called with the news that Glamour magazine was preparing a story on her anyway, Cynthia laughed, "Tell Glamour I'm willing to make an exception. They can interview me if they promise to use a photograph that includes my hairy legs!"

Cynthia did grant interviews to the two county newspapers that had covered her case so consistently and fairly. In the Morning Journal article that followed, Cynthia spoke of the prosecution as "surreal," and she questioned "what kind of logic one would have to use to reach the conclusion that the pictures . . . are sexual." She wondered why, if there had been real concern about her daughter's safety, there had never been a full investigation. She insisted—and the article highlighted these words in quotes above the headline—"Those pictures should not be destroyed."

The Chronicle-Telegram's article was illustrated with a photograph Cynthia had taken of Nora as a five-year-old whirling in leaves on a windy autumn day, wearing a long swirly dress, with her head bowed and her loose hair streaming in the sun. Cynthia poignantly recalled the birth of her daughter and the beginning of her passion for photography. But when discussing the diversion agreement, Cynthia sounded defiant: "If it weren't for my daughter, I'd have gone to trial in a heartbeat. . . . What does it teach my daughter about standing up for what you believe in? She knows that I believe destroying those pictures is wrong." Cynthia equated the destruction of her pictures with book burning, and she praised her new therapist, who, she said, had affirmed the way she and David were raising their daughter.

The editorial pages of both Lorain County papers praised the diversion agreement for putting the interests of the child first. Only the *Plain Dealer*'s editors, in an editorial titled "Much Left to the Imagination," regretted the resolution because, they punned, "the case has been airbrushed away by a plea bargain. It might have been better if some of the questions it raised could have been settled in a court of law."

On April 13, the 257th birthday of Thomas Jefferson, the Thomas Jefferson Center for the Protection of Free Expression, in Charlottesville, Virginia, announced that Greg White had been selected to receive one of its annual "Muzzle" awards. An AP wire story announced the tongue-in-cheek honor. Each honoree would receive a portrait of Thomas Jefferson with thick black tape over his mouth.

Besides White, the dozen honorees for 2000 included: the Clinton administration for its continuing "don't ask, don't tell" policy toward gays in the military, a school superintendent in Georgia for ordering the alteration of 2,300 textbooks because he feared George Washington's watch fob could be mistaken for his genitals, and the George W. Bush Presidential Campaign for seeking to have the Federal Election Commission regulate a parody of the Bush campaign's official Web site.

The Lorain County and Cleveland newspapers ran stories with headlines such as "Group Razzes Greg White." In those articles, White claimed to view the award as "a badge of honor," and he thanked the Thomas Jefferson Center for letting him join "some very distinct company." He noted, "It's definitely a bipartisan effort here."

But Amy wondered if the award had actually rankled White since he had called Kreig that week and thrown a tantrum. White had asked Kreig if Cynthia was really committed to the diversion program. If so, then she needed to stop saying things to the press like "the counselor agrees with me" and "I didn't do anything wrong."

Cynthia asked Amy if White were threatening to cancel the diversion program. Amy guessed he was just blustering. "If he were making a serious threat, he would have called *me*," Amy said. "I think he just called Kreig to piss and moan."

In mid-April, a succinct e-mail from Sally Mann popped up in David's inbox: "I guess you never needed any extra help?"

Cynthia called Sally, and they had a long talk. Sally had heard about the resolution of the case on NPR. Cynthia told Sally how terrible she felt about the loss of her pictures and how she carried around Sally's horror about their destruction like a talisman. She explained that the prosecutor had insisted those pictures were dangerous because they could have fallen into the hands of a pedophile and ended up on the Internet. She wondered how Sally dealt with that possibility in her own work.

Sally said that in 1991, the year before she published *Immediate Family*, she met with the head of the FBI's behavioral sciences department, a man who was an authority on child pornography and who had spearheaded many child-porn investigations. Sally took her husband, her children, and all her pictures to the meeting and told the FBI expert that she needed to know two things from him before she published her work: "Are you going to arrest me?" and "How do you feel about these pictures?"

The man had been very kind to her. He dealt with pedophiles and pornographers all the time, and he knew Sally was neither. He assured her, "You can't limit yourself to pictures that a pedophile won't find arousing. A pedophile will masturbate to a Sears, Roebuck catalog. There's not a picture you can take of *anything* that won't arouse *somebody* out there. If you're going to make this kind of art with your children, you can't let that stop you."

Sally and the FBI man had been friends ever since, and he had stayed supportive of her through various controversies surrounding her work. "He hates cases like yours," Sally told Cynthia.

Cynthia promised to fax Sally the recent press coverage of her case. Sally offered to help Cynthia any way she could. "I'm not a religious person," she said, "but our callings come through strange adversity. What you've been through is biblical."

The next morning, Sally penciled a note to Cynthia on the back of one of her own original 8x10 photographs:

> *Dear Cynthia, Our talk yesterday had a profound impact*
> *on me, & my fax machine is spitting out pages of stuff that*
> *I know will make me crazy. Before I get all lathered up, I*
> *want to write to you of my unflagging admiration for all you*
> *have done, and stood for, and for all I am sure you will do.*
> *My husband glanced at the texts just now and remarked that*
> *you and I are so much alike—right down to the little sign you*
> *posted in the school bus.*

The photograph had been folded into thirds to fit into a business-sized envelope. It was a picture of Sally's husband, naked and rinsing off with a garden hose, its nozzle held high above his head with his right arm. He was facing forward, in front of a lush, blurred canopy of trees, with his eyes closed, his mouth slightly parted, and his face turned up into the soft mist fanning out from the nozzle. Scrawled in blue Magic Marker around her husband's body were these words: "I can't wait until my series of pictures of my husband comes out—(not until children are grown). . . ." Perhaps the photograph was a witty version of the Garden of Eden, with the serpent now domesticated as a garden hose. Perhaps it was a technical experiment: the body veiled in misty light against the voluptuous dark of the earth. Perhaps it was feminist mischief: the male nude lavished with the kind of airbrushed attention traditionally lavished on the female nude. Perhaps it was an allusion to a Rodin nude or to early Renaissance paintings in which a saint is baptized by light fanning out from a single point in heaven. Or perhaps it was an ordinary moment Sally had snatched away from death: her husband rinsing off the sweat of a summer's day.

Whatever Sally intended the picture to be, it did not satisfy her. She had written a postscript on the bottom of the twice-creased photograph: "This one is not very good, is it?"

24

Gratitude

A hundred and fifty people filled the folding metal chairs in the First Congregational Church Fellowship Hall late Monday afternoon, April 17. The Politburo had planned the Community Gathering for Cynthia Stewart & Family, divvying up the jobs of e-mailing supporters, posting fliers, painting the rocks, rounding up a PA system, setting up chairs, deciding on speakers, and preparing for the media.

There was a serious but excited mood in the crowd—a sense that we had accomplished something unusual and that people had noticed. Reporters from the region were scattered through the audience, and a group of Cleveland TV cameramen were lined up at the back of the standing-room-only hall.

Eight of Cynthia's supporters spoke. Marc Blecher recalled the Kafka-esque beginnings of Cynthia's prosecution; Rebecca Cross announced that the Cynthia Stewart Legal Defense Fund had raised $40,000; Stan Mathews described how more than a thousand people in Lorain County had signed the petition; Nancy Roth quoted St. Paul, comparing our community to a human body, with all the various parts contributing to the whole; Scott Bailey, a neighbor who had started a Web site for the defense fund and whose roses Cynthia loved to photograph, rejoiced that "a special family was emerging from the tunnel in time to see the roses bloom"; I spoke of the lessons we had learned from each other in countless phone calls, e-mails, late-night talks, and sidewalk conversations, and I expressed a hope that other communities would learn from our experience; Tom Phinney, a longtime friend, told a moving story of rescuing his own young daughter from a cold river, a memory that provided him with an apt image of Cynthia and Nora during the past few months; and Ann Cooper Albright told a feminist parable for "Cynthia's daughter, my daughter, and many of our daughters in this community," a parable whose moral was: "As a girl in this culture, your body is never simply your own. No, you have to claim and reclaim it again and again, every single day. Let that reclaiming be a joyous practice, an act of love that will confuse, irritate, and ultimately defeat the powers that be."

Amy and Kreig also spoke, touching on the legal and constitutional issues raised by the prosecution. Both lawyers gave Cynthia's community enormous credit for the historic diversion agreement. Kreig said: "Without the support of Cynthia's friends, neighbors, and family, we would not be standing here today. We would be preparing for a trial in which a little girl, who just turned nine, would have been forced to take the witness stand in a case brought by the State of Ohio against her mother. There could be no winner when a little girl is placed in the middle of a criminal case involving her mother. Only losers."

Everyone kept his or her remarks brief in order to give Cynthia ample time to speak. Wearing a long black wool skirt and matching jacket—hand-me-downs from Eileen Fisher—Cynthia was nervous and emotional when she stepped to the podium. But her voice steadied as she began to thank all those who had helped her family, in ways she knew and in ways she never would know.

The last person she thanked was the least expected: "I would also like to thank Greg White. I think Prosecutor White is an honorable man. And I suspect the diversion agreement was probably as hard for him as it was for me."

Cynthia spoke about the dilemma the diversion agreement had presented her and how her new therapist had observed that the two main roles of parenthood—to guard and to guide—had come into conflict for her. Instead of being able to perform both roles, Cynthia had had to choose between them.

Cynthia spoke of how her daughter was "navigating and making sense of the events that have swirled around us." And she spoke of the future. She hoped other cases like this in Lorain County would go straight to Children Services, where they would be given a thorough investigation before being passed along to criminal prosecutors. She hoped state legislators would change a vague and overbroad law. She hoped other parents in similar situations would receive the kind of support from their communities that she and her family had received.

Cynthia closed with personal words for her supporters: "I had no joy in the resolution of this case. It came at too great a cost. And, then, a funny thing happened. I received another gift from my community. Your joy and your relief have become mine." The crowd rose to its feet and gave Cynthia—and ourselves—a long, proud, emotional ovation.

The immediate press coverage of the community gathering was uniformly positive, although the AP wire story included a thinly veiled threat from the prosecutor:

> White said yesterday that he has been paying attention to what Stewart says about the case to make sure she doesn't violate the agreement.
>
> "We obviously are watching the situation. If she does something that repudiates the agreement, then we will deal with that," he said. "The case has not been dismissed. It will go forward if it has to."

The wire story continued:

> During her remarks at the church, Stewart also thanked White for his willingness to settle the matter.
>
> "I think that prosecutor White is an honorable man and I suspect that the diversion agreement was as hard for him as it was for me," she said.

This time, neither Amy nor Kreig received a phone call from Greg White to complain about Cynthia's words.

But a few of Cynthia's supporters raised their eyebrows at Cynthia's compliment to White. One man e-mailed me, wanting Cynthia not to "be misled by the people she is dealing with":

> Greg is anything but gracious. In fact, he is dangerous. And there is absolutely nothing good about his assistant, JR. There's an old Italian proverb, "Tell me with whom you go and I'll tell you who you are," or words to that effect. And if Greg White has kept Rosenbaum on all these years, that should tell you something about White.

Tom Theado disagreed with this skeptical view. He thought Cynthia had been right to praise White. "There's another way to look at Greg," Tom pointed out, "which is: having stayed too long in the fortress of righteousness, when you finally hear the voices of dissent, and they're not just the rabid rabble but thoughtful people who are willing to discuss with you, you think, 'Wait, I may be wrong. I've never been wrong before, but I may be wrong here.' It takes a tremendous amount of courage to rethink basic decisions, which would make Greg fairly heroic."

After reading of the resolution and the community gathering in the newspapers, the Guardian Angel phoned me and began to weep with joy and relief. I invited her over to my house for a celebratory beer.

After dark, when I answered the doorbell, I noticed that she had parked up the street so that no one would recognize her car in my driveway. We sat in my family room with the shades drawn. "There are big changes underway in Lorain County. This is a great victory!" she exulted, clinking our glasses. We both hoped Cynthia and David would soon feel like celebrating, too.

But exhaustion was the main physical and emotional reality at Campeloupe. Cynthia felt a fatigue and depression she had never felt before. After the agreement was signed, she resumed driving her school bus in the afternoons. She didn't have the energy yet to face those early-morning runs.

David had essentially been working a double shift since September: his real job at *The Nation*, plus his unreal job of doing everything he could to pull his family out of their legal nightmare. His relief at the outcome was mingled with bitterness. His friend's early warning that "the best you can hope for is to throw massive amounts of money at lawyers and hope they can make the prosecution go away" had proved prescient. The saving grace for their family had been the $40,000 raised by the legal defense fund, which had just barely covered their legal fees, therapy costs, and other assorted expenses. But no fund could restore the lost year of their family's life.

One person who was *not* feeling exhausted was Virginia Behner. Virginia felt energized and excited. She dropped by Campeloupe with a stack of applications: she wanted Cynthia's supporters to become guardians ad litem and to apply for positions on the Children Services board. She believed she had found in Oberlin a hotbed of moral guerrillas like herself, ready to fan out and right the wrongs of the world.

Virginia phoned and introduced herself to me. There was a training session for GALs coming up, and she hoped I would volunteer. She also encouraged me to investigate a day-care center she was suspicious of. And she hoped I would take up the cause of Nancy Smith, the incarcerated Head Start school bus driver.

I listened, but I was tired. I begged off of everything. Summer was coming, and I needed to recuperate and attend to my own family, my own home, my own work.

In late May, Virginia left a dejected message on Campeloupe's answering machine:

> *I called and called everybody that they go down to that daycare and just look at it. And I couldn't get one person to go! That's*

*why Lillian is probably going to quit the court by the end of
the year because we go through this, and nobody wants to
get involved, and nobody cares about injustice or evil. They
say they do, but they actually don't unless it directly involves
them. They really don't care. Or else they'd do somethin'. It's
that simple. Anyhow, that's all I was going to tell ya. I will
talk to you later. Bye-bye!*

Throughout the summer, reporters continued to call to see if Cynthia and David had changed their minds about giving interviews. *60 Minutes* called. So did *Court TV*, who promised to do a "tasteful job." Nancy from German television tried, "The Germans are often mystified by how puritanical the Americans can be. We'd love to come out and do an interview—and perhaps look at the pictures?" Two producers from a radio station in Birmingham, Alabama, sang their request to the tune of *The Beverly Hillbillies* theme song. They had read about Cynthia in *Glamour* and assured her, "We're really on your side!"

The one journalist Cynthia did choose to speak with was Richard Cohen, a columnist for the *Washington Post*. In a column in June titled "Reeducating Cynthia Stewart," Cohen pronounced the diversion agreement "repulsive." He was alarmed by White's demand that Cynthia go into counseling, as he saw that as an effort to control the thoughts of a citizen and to make her renounce her beliefs. Usually, Cohen pointed out, criminals know that they've committed crimes. From White's point of view, Cynthia persisted in the delusion that she had done nothing wrong. Thus, she needed "to undergo a little work on her sick mind." Cohen found this new penchant of prosecutors for sending defendants to counseling similar to the Soviet Union's efforts to reprogram the minds of dissidents. American prosecutors, of course, would be indignant at the comparison of their rehabilitation efforts to Soviet reeducation programs. But riffing off the language of the diversion agreement, Cohen suggested that White and the state legislators who had framed the Ohio law might need counseling themselves because, "while it was not their intention to impose thought control, they had managed to do it anyway."

Throughout the summer, Tracy from Children Services visited Campeloupe once a month. Those visits remained short and perfunctory, more an inconvenience to the family than a real intrusion. Tracy assured Nora that she could confide in her anytime and call on her as a friend. Nora believed those words were code for: "I know you can't talk right now about your horrible parents and how they are abusing you, but you can tell me later in some secret way." Nora thanked Tracy in words that were her own polite code for: "You drive me crazy, and I want you out of my life!"

Throughout the summer, Nora and Cynthia continued seeing their therapists, both of whom sent regular, glowing reports to the prosecutor's office.

When school started again in September, Cynthia returned to driving both her morning and afternoon runs, this time on a shiny new school bus—the newfangled kind with a snub nose. During the first week of September, a boy Nora didn't know teased her on the bus ride: "Your mom went to jail for taking pictures of you naked!"

"No, she didn't," said Nora, surprised.

"Yes, she did!" the boy mocked.

"No, she *didn't!*" Nora argued.

The boy persisted until Nora, exasperated, got the better of him: "If my mother is in jail, then how can she be driving this brand-new school bus!"

On the last working day of September, Rob Corts, the assistant prosecutor who had originally been put in charge of Cynthia's case, gave Amy a call. He needed Amy and Kreig to turn over their copies and photocopies of the two photographs destined for destruction. Corts encouraged Amy to come on over and bring the pictures so they could be done with the process.

Amy joked, "Are we going to wear trench coats and meet in the park and exchange briefcases?"

Because she was in the process of packing and moving to a new office, Amy actually headed over to the prosecutor's office in jeans and a sweatshirt. She met with both White and Corts and read the journal entry they had prepared to submit to Judge Zaleski. It requested the destruction of the two pictures and the dismissal of criminal charges, but it contained no mention of Cynthia's objection to the destruction.

Amy said, "That's fine as long as you understand that we're going to file a statement that Cynthia objects."

White reacted irritably. He was hoping counseling would have changed her mind about that. This made him question all those great reviews he'd been getting from her counselor. It made him think that Cynthia still didn't *get it.*

"Greg, you can't believe that!" Amy exclaimed. "Did you really think when she went to counseling that she was going to come out thinking that it was *okay* for you to destroy her pictures? That would be like me saying, 'Greg, go to counseling for six months and when you're done you are going to find these pictures completely fine.'"

White was not satisfied. He wasn't sure if the counseling had made any difference.

"That's not what the counseling was about!" Amy argued. "Cynthia really *did* do well in counseling. Counseling *did* help her in a lot of ways. And you can rest assured she is not going to take this kind of picture ever again in Lorain County!"

Corts asked why Cynthia needed to file an objection with the court since she had already made her point loudly and clearly in the press.

"Because it's important to her," said Amy. "I don't control Cynthia. Nobody controls Cynthia. Yes, the whole general public knows that she doesn't want these pictures destroyed, but she also wants it on the official record. I'm her lawyer. I'll do what she wants. That's how it works."

Corts and White didn't say much else. The two prosecutors and Amy scoured White's office for the one picture—a family Halloween shot—that Cynthia had noticed was missing from the six photo albums White had returned. They lifted up couch cushions and looked under desks but couldn't find the stray picture anywhere.

Finally, Amy handed White the prints and photocopies she had brought for him to destroy, and she left.

On Monday morning, October 2, Cynthia felt agitated and angry. She had been wondering at what moment and in what way her photographs would be "wiped off the face of the planet." Would the prosecutors burn those images of her daughter? Shred them? Pour acid over them? Flush them down the toilet?

Cynthia's only comfort was that Amy filed a journal entry in court that morning: "The defendant wishes to state that she finds the destruction of her pictures reprehensible and unnecessary."

Later that day, a photographer for the *Chronicle-Telegram* asked to meet with Cynthia. He shot a number of straight-on portraits of her with her yellow bus stretched across the background. Then, for his last shot, he asked Cynthia to flex her muscles. She was wearing a sleeveless black shirt. She propped one hand on her hip and flexed her other arm—he-man style.

The next morning, the muscle-flexing shot was in full-color on the front page of the *Chronicle-Telegram* over the headline: "Stewart Charges Dismissed." Cynthia looked cocky and defiant, and the picture's caption said that she "remains concerned about prosecutors' handling of the case."

Greg White claimed in the article that he had no regrets about the prosecution. "There's no need to do an autopsy on this case," he told the reporter.

Within a couple of days, a letter arrived at Campeloupe from Children Services. Tracy thanked the family for their cooperation "in completing the goals and objectives that we discussed during home visits." Because "obvious" progress had been made and the initial risk factors "reduced," the agency believed there was no longer a need for their involvement with the family. She wished the family "good luck in the future."

But Tracy's letter—the last official correspondence of the case—was almost overlooked by Cynthia and David in the flood of congratulations and good wishes pouring into their mailbox.

As soon as she got word that Judge Zaleski had dismissed the charges, Cynthia borrowed her brother Eric's truck, and the family drove to Elyria to haul her boxes of photographs back from Amy's office. It took a good bit of hefting and lugging to get all the boxes up the narrow basement steps and out to the truck. Nora felt proud and excited to be helping this time. As she shoved a large box down Amy's hallway, she admired her own nine-year-old strength. She told her mother and father that she felt "buff."

Once all the boxes were back in place, Cynthia stood in Campeloupe's dining room and gazed at them, satisfied. It was such a round, full, happy feeling, she thought, to have her pictures back home.

The Ohio ACLU named Cynthia one of their five honorees for 2000 for "taking on the system to defend the Bill of Rights." When executive director Christine Link invited Cynthia to speak at the awards banquet, under the program's theme "With the Courage of Their Convictions," Cynthia protested that she *hadn't* stood up for her convictions and that she had been cowardly, not courageous. But Link said the Ohio ACLU board saw things differently, and she persuaded Cynthia to accept the honor.

The awards dinner was held in late October in a Columbus high-rise hotel. After telling the story of her own prosecution, Cynthia described the worse ordeals of Marian in New Jersey, who still did not have her job back, and Lisa in Pennsylvania, who, with her husband, had just filed for bankruptcy and lost their home. Trying to find the silver lining, Lisa had told Cynthia recently, "I'm not that sad we have to move because the neighbors won't let their children play with our daughter anymore."

Cynthia estimated that "for the last year, two to three people every month have called us with their lives turned upside down, sometimes ruined, because of misguided, overzealous prosecutors who are so eager to protect us all from pornography that they do not bother to check their own facts. Ironically, some of the best parents seem to be at greatest risk because they care enough to want to document their children's lives and because they try to teach their children to be comfortable with their own bodies."

She closed by insisting, "I do not deserve this award. We made the decision we had to make, but it was not a decision that furthered civil liberties." Cynthia accepted the award on behalf of everyone who had helped her family.

A few days after the ACLU ceremony, a young mother called Cynthia from a nearby Ohio county. Married to a truck driver, Karen was a stay-at-home mom who loved taking pictures of her two children. One day in the summer, Karen and her six-year-old daughter had showered together. Afterward, as they were getting dressed, her daughter picked up their new digital camera and began snapping pictures, including a couple of Karen naked from the waist up. Karen took a few snapshots, too, including three of her daughter playfully mooning her.

When her estranged husband later found a computer disk containing images of their naked daughter, he took the disk to the police in a fit of suspicion and rage. He was convinced that Karen was sending the images to a man she had met on the Internet. The police raided their home, taking Karen's computer and cameras and charging her with five felonies—one felony for each after-shower shot. The county family services agency took custody of Karen's daughter and ten-year-old son in the middle of the night and put them in foster care. Two weeks later, they gave the children to Karen's husband and ordered Karen to move out of the house. Even though Karen had voluntarily turned herself in to the police, they had put her in shackles for her arraignment. Out on bond and awaiting trial, Karen was now living with her parents and could see her children only two hours per week, with a chaperone.

The irony was that Karen and her husband had since reconciled, and he had tried to undo the damage to their family by apologizing to the police and explaining that he had jumped to conclusions—those pictures truly were just his daughter playing around. But it was too late. The prosecutor was determined to prosecute his wife to the fullest extent of the law.

Karen had found, via the Internet, a young lawyer from Cleveland whom she liked and trusted, but she had no idea how they were going to pay his fees. She told Cynthia in her girlish but determined voice, "The prosecutor offered me a deal if I would plead guilty to some of the charges, but I am not going to agree to be guilty of something I know I'm not guilty of. We're going to have to go to trial."

Cynthia told Karen what she had been telling all the parents in similar situations that had been calling her: "Let people know what's happening to you so they can help you fight back!" Cynthia asked Karen to keep in touch, and, in the meantime, she encouraged her to look for a copy of Sally Mann's *Immediate Family*.

On a cold, snow-bright Saturday morning in early December, I threw a collating, envelope-stuffing, stamp-licking party at my house. Cynthia had written a thank-you letter to be sent to the more than six hundred people on the defense fund's mailing list. The letter updated far-flung supporters on the outcome of her case and described the ongoing ordeals of two other mothers who had been arrested for taking nude photographs of their young daughters, Lisa in Pennsylvania and Karen in Ohio, and one grandmother, Marian in New Jersey. Organizing the mass mailing was the last official task of the Politburo.

The hefty mailing included Cynthia's three-page letter, various news articles and editorials, a double-sided Action Page with the addresses of Lisa's, Marian's, and Karen's defense funds, and a black-and-white postcard Cynthia had had printed from one of her photographs. It was the picture of Nora whirling in the autumn leaves as a five-year-old. The caption on the back of the postcard read: "It takes a community of friends to right a wrong."

A dozen of us walked circles all morning around my dining room table, collating the photocopies, while a half-dozen kids, including Jesse and Nora, licked stamps and stuck them onto envelopes. When the kids complained of tired tongues, we put kitchen sponges in bowls of water to keep them going. The children were proud of how hard they were working. They finished the stamps and started in on the address labels.

Although all the envelopes—to thirty-eight states and three foreign countries—got stuffed, stamped, and addressed in a few high-spirited hours on that Saturday morning, Cynthia wanted to take dozens of letters back to Campeloupe so that she could add handwritten notes. It took a couple of weeks, drafting a few at a time on scratch paper, but she finally dropped the last batch in the mail on the winter solstice. That batch included notes to her Aunt Sue in West Virginia, Katha Pollitt at *The Nation*, Sally Mann, Virginia Behner, and her father.

~~~

Dear Old Sue,

I can't tell you how much it meant to me, you sending us money. You don't have that much money, and so your doing that made me feel like maybe things would come out all right after all. If my Old Aunt Sue believes in me, then, Prosecutor, Beware!

~~~

Dear Katha,

Out of the 672 people that we're thanking, we probably have you to thank the most.

It was a pretty awful thing to have happen, but it could have been oh, so much worse.

Without what you wrote, we could have been like Lisa and lost our house, or like Karen and lost our kid. (You <u>know</u> national attention made that prosecutor think twice about just what he was going to do.)

I don't even want to think about the worst that could have happened. Because of you, it didn't, and we are very grateful.

—

Dear Sally,

Karen, one of the women mentioned on the (enclosed) Action Page, went and got a copy of <u>Immediate Family</u>, and it blew her mind. Clearly, whole new vistas opened for her. It was a lovely thing to watch.

Thank you for your help.

—

To the Unsung Hero,

If not for you, our lives would have been very different and much harder.

I'm hoping you get the rightful recognition and credit for helping us as you did.

Well, we know, and God knows. Thank you, Virginia.

—

Grampa,

Thanks for the upbringing.
  Your wild child,

Cynthia

25

A Memory of Spring

A year after Cynthia signed the agreement, I visited Nora on an April Saturday to talk about her tough third-grade year. She had just turned ten years old and was almost finished with fourth grade. She began by giving me a tour of Campeloupe.

"We don't use gravestones, we use trees," she announced, as we walked in her big yard sprinkled with saplings. Lily, a plecostomus, a kind of catfish that lived in her aquarium, was buried under a Japanese maple. A purple smoke tree marked the grave of WaWa, the cat who had witnessed Nora's birth. "And this is the grave of Sammie, the little gray cat who wasn't a year old when she died in the street. Since she was fuzzy, we buried her under a cottonwood tree," Nora explained, touching the buds that would soon burst open and offer their wisps to the wind. "We're really looking forward to when this tree gets big, because these little branches will be *wonderful* to sit on!" I imagined Nora as a young woman climbing up and lounging in the now-sturdy branches of a childhood sadness.

Wanting to show me their "For Cynthia" (as her Gramma Gerry called it), Nora led me past the garden where David was planting peas and lettuce, around a corner of the house, and toward the forsythia spouting its fountain of gold. Above it, there was a clothesline pinned with crimson sweaters, maroon skirts, and scarlet stockings flapping in the wind like banners advertising a surge in the blood. Cynthia was pinning up a pair of rose-colored pants. "How can *all* your laundry be red?" I asked.

"I'm anal about two things only: my photographs and my laundry," Cynthia laughed. "I never mix my colors. That's why Nora won't wear red for weeks and then, all of a sudden, she's red every day. That's also why I take pictures of my laundry," she added, heading off to get her camera.

Inside the house, Nora seated me on her bed and introduced me to her stuffed animals, including a pair of platypuses, Buster and Lynne, and their new babies. Nora and her dad played platypus games on the weekends. That morning, with my visit on her mind, Nora had taken their game in a new direction. She told me, "Buster was giving the babies mollusk-digging lessons in the stream, and he decided to bathe them, and I thought, 'Wouldn't it be funny if we did a platypus *case?*' So while Buster was bathing them in the stream, Lynne came along and took some pictures because they looked so cute. When she took them to Beaver Mart, a beaver who worked there freaked out and took them to the police. My dad does this funny police voice all the time—Captain O'Reilly. He's Scottish. Anyway, Captain O'Reilly thought they were against the law, and that they were disgusting because the platypuses didn't have *clothes* on! They were only dressed in *fur!*"

"Have the platypus babies stayed calm, or are they pretty upset about the case?" I asked.

"Well, the babies are really upset. Captain O'Reilly wanted to take them to the police station, but they decided that they would get a lawyer first."

"What kind of lawyer?"

"I don't know yet. That's as far as we got this morning. It would be very funny, though, if they got Cheech, my red panda, for a lawyer. Cheech wakes me up every morning—well, my dad makes Cheech wake me up—and he has this high voice, and he tries to get me out of bed growling, 'Fear me!' He brags about how fearsome he is, but he's really totally unfearsome. To wake me up, my dad has him tickle my ear, so I wake up to '*shhhllllppp, shhhllllppp*' every morning. Usually I throw Cheech across the room and go back to sleep. But Cheech would be a good lawyer because he would make the judge fear him."

"Which animal do you think would make a good prosecutor?" I wondered.

"That's hard to say. I'm judging this partly by how my dad does their voices. Balto, my wolf, might be a good prosecutor. My dad does a hilarious Balto voice with a Russian accent, so Balto might be good."

As Nora gave me a tour of the house, she named all the bird feathers taped to the kitchen cabinets, including the roseate spoonbill feather her Gramma Freda had sent from Florida. She introduced me to the huge old wardrobe they called Gibraltar, the cats curled up in her father's office windows, and the nylon Grim Reaper that stayed up year-round in the stairwell, though its battery-powered laugh had run out Halloweens ago.

Heading back downstairs, we stopped to admire the WaWa gallery—framed photographs of the cat Nora used to call her sister. In her favorite picture, the tabby was stretched out on a shiny hardwood floor, and five-year-old Nora, wearing her sunflower dress, was stretched out, catlike, beside her. The grain of the wood, the swirls in WaWa's fur, and the round flowers on Nora's dress made patterns that echoed each other, as did the snuggling shapes of the cat and the child.

Nora said she was glad to have so many pictures of her past because it helped her remember her life. She said that was a gift from her mother. Then she paused and added, "I often wonder what it will be like to tell my own kids about the case. I sort of imagine it being led into from a conversation about pornography, and then I'll say, 'Well, you know, *my* mom—*your* gramma—was once accused of *being* a pornographer!' And then I'll go into it, though it may take several days on and off to get it all discussed. They'll keep asking, 'Tell us what the Children Services trial was like. Tell us how you felt.' And I'll tell them."

"What will you tell them?"

"I'll tell them how afraid I was. And how happy I was when it was over. I'll tell them how I was afraid my mother was going to go to jail for sixteen years, and how it really dented my faith in the justice system."

"But is there anything *good* that came out of the case that you would also want to tell them about?" I asked. "Children always like to hear the happy part of the story, too."

Nora sighed. "Well, I think even if Greg White didn't show it to the public—you know, just wanted to be Big Bad Greg White—I think he realized how much it hurt. Even though he'd never tell it to anyone, I think somewhere inside him he realized his mistake."

Nora had one more thing she wanted to show me. She took me into the dining room, with its towering boxes filled with thousands of photographs. Two snapshots were laid out on the dining room table.

Because her mother had been so sad last spring, Nora had asked her father to give her a disposable camera so that she could replace the two pictures that had been destroyed. Nora handed me the two pictures she had taken. I asked her to describe them to me. "Well," she said, pointing, "this one is the sunset sky with furry magnolia buds in the foreground. And this one is the ground under the Japanese maple when it's covered solid with leaves and the hyacinths are just peeking out—brown leaves with these tiny shoots of green."

She paused, gazing at them. "I know they'll never really replace the two my mother had to give up. But I wanted to give her a present she could always keep—a memory of spring and of life coming back."

AFTERWORD

In 2001, Jonathan Rosenbaum continued to generate headlines with his handling of several controversial prosecutions. In December, the *Plain Dealer* accused Rosenbaum of having "a penchant for overzealousness, a habit for making some of his prosecutions too personal" and sharply criticized White's continued loyalty to his chief assistant of nearly twenty years. A few weeks later, White fired Rosenbaum. Local editorials wondered if White had finally recognized that his partnership with Rosenbaum was jeopardizing his aspirations for higher political office.

Within a year, White was appointed U.S. attorney for the Northern District of Ohio by President George W. Bush. White served in that position from March 2003 until January 2008, when he accepted an appointment as a federal magistrate in Ohio.

After leaving the county prosecutor's office for good, Jonathan Rosenbaum returned to practicing law privately full time. In August 2008, he once again was in the headlines, this time tragically. An avid gun sportsman, Rosenbaum and his twenty-three-year-old son were shooting clay pigeons at a nearby gun club when Rosenbaum's son shot him in the back. The shooting would have been considered an accident except for the son's anguished 911 call, which was released by the county and posted on the Web (where, as of this writing, it still appears). Three minutes into the call, Rosenbaum, who was conscious, could be heard arguing with his son about whether the shooting had been intentional. In the slightly muffled exchange, Rosenbaum could be heard saying, "You shot me on purpose?" Then, "You fucking shot me on purpose?" Then, "You liar." The call was cut off, and the 911 dispatcher called back, trying to offer medical advice. Although Rosenbaum's son told the operator that his father did not want him to talk to her, the conversation continued until the ambulance arrived.

Rosenbaum survived the shooting but was paralyzed from the waist down. A Lorain County judge appointed a special prosecutor from outside the county to take over the legal inquiry into the incident. Rosenbaum testified to the grand jury that the shooting had been accidental, and the grand jury declined to indict the son.

Amy Wirtz and Kreig Brusnahan did not work together on another case, but they remained friends and professional colleagues. In the aftermath of Cynthia's prosecution, Amy became convinced that the legal system, at least in its approach to families and children, was broken. She could see that litigation was like war: two sides staked out positions and fought until one side was defeated. Often, in the process, everything of value—financial, emotional, relational—got destroyed. She longed to work toward solutions in family conflicts that preserved rather than destroyed family bonds.

In 2004, Amy joined a Cleveland law firm specializing in alternatives to litigation. With her new law partners, she became active in the Center for Principled Family Advocacy, an organization that trains lawyers in alternative resolution methods: mediation, collaboration, principled negotiation, and arbitration. She began to work jointly with therapists in helping families create their own resolutions and settlements during divorce and custody disputes. For her new office in a city high-rise, Amy bought a round bar-height table—a place where everyone could feel elevated and have an equal voice.

Karen, the mother who called Cynthia a few days after the ACLU ceremony, went to trial in Ravenna, Ohio, in late 2000. The assistant prosecutor in her county claimed that the three images of Karen's daughter mooning her were "sexual positions." Karen's lawyer argued that the photographs belonged in the context in which they had been shot: a high-spirited six-year-old girl playing in her mother's room after a bath. After more than two days of deliberation, the jury acquitted Karen on three of the five felony charges; they could not agree, however, on the last two charges and ended up with a mistrial. The county prosecutor immediately vowed to prosecute Karen again. The jury forewoman later introduced herself to Karen and became Karen's friend and supporter through the second trial. She was a Free Will Baptist who believed God had put her on the jury to see that a loving mother was declared innocent.

Karen's second criminal trial began in February 2001. After three days of testimony, the new jury, after deliberating for only a couple of hours, acquitted her on the two remaining charges. The family services case, however, dragged on for months, and Karen was not allowed to return home for more than a year after she had been separated from her children. By that time, she and her husband had spent on legal fees all the money they had saved to buy a house, and they were burdened with debt as well.

In 2004, after the failure of two appeals, the attorney for Nancy Smith, the Lorain County Head Start school bus driver who had been convicted of child molestation in 1994 and sentenced to thirty to ninety years in jail, referred her case to the Ohio Innocence Project of the University of Cincinnati College of Law. The OIP's research concluded that the case against Smith "was based on the testimony of very young children who had been coached by their parents" and that evidence of her innocence had been suppressed by the prosecutor— Jonathan Rosenbaum—and the judge. In 2007, after Smith had been imprisoned for thirteen years, the Ohio Innocence Project submitted to her parole board a strong package of materials outlining the flaws in the case against her. But because Smith still refused to admit to any wrongdoing, the parole board rejected her parole request and pronounced her "in denial."

In February 2009, Lorain County Common Pleas Judge James Burge, a defense attorney who had practiced law in Lorain County for more than thirty years and who had recently been elected to the judgeship, determined that the previous judge in the Smith case had made a clerical error in writing up Smith's sentence—an error that invalidated the sentence, according to Ohio state law. After fourteen and a half years in prison, Smith was freed on bond, pending a new sentencing from Judge Burge.

In July 2009, Smith and her lawyers appeared in court for a preliminary hearing in advance of the new sentencing. Judge Burge, in an extremely careful and measured twenty-minute speech, indicated that he had spent "countless hours" reviewing the original trial's evidence and testimony. He found the questioning of the children in taped pre-trial interviews "*so* suggestive" that their in-court testimony could not be credible or admissible as evidence. And since the defense had been denied access to those taped interviews, Burge declared that Smith had been deprived not only of exculpatory evidence but of "substantive evidence"— part of the overall police record, which a defendant can offer to prove fact.

The judge concluded, "I don't believe there was a human being in that courtroom in 1994 that was not there to do the best for his client—both defense counsel and counsel for the state of Ohio. Notwithstanding that, I have absolutely no confidence that these verdicts are correct." Then Burge stunned the courtroom—including Smith, her attorneys, and the prosecutors—by acquitting Smith on all charges.

In interviews afterward with local newspapers, Smith grieved over the years she had lost in prison, during which she had missed the weddings of her children, the death of her father, and the birth of her eight grandchildren. "Every night in prison," she told the *Plain Dealer*, "I cried myself to sleep. I woke up and couldn't believe that I was still there for something I didn't do." But, she continued, "I can't be bitter. I don't have time."

The Lorain County prosecutor's office quickly appealed Burge's decision, arguing that the judge did not have jurisdiction to even entertain an acquittal. As of this writing, there has been no final ruling on that appeal.

~~~

The stresses of Cynthia and David's legal ordeal took a heavy toll. In 2003, they separated. David stayed at Campeloupe, and Cynthia and Nora moved back to 82. David left his job at *The Nation*, earned an advanced degree in library science, and took a job in the audio book industry. In 2007, he married a longtime friend of the family's. They continue to live at Campeloupe, which they have remodeled and enlarged.

My son Jesse and Nora remained good friends through middle school. When Jesse changed to a different high school, they stayed in touch mainly through violin activities. The prosecution of Nora's mother, and our community's response to that crisis, influenced him deeply. By the time he was thirteen, Jesse was passionate about politics and had begun volunteering in electoral campaigns. At seventeen, he directed the Get Out The Vote operation in Oberlin for the Barack Obama presidential campaign, coordinating hundreds of volunteers in the weeks leading up to the 2008 election. Now studying government and economics at Hamilton College, Jesse continues to show a talent for political organizing and a gift for reaching across ideological divides.

In high school, Nora excelled in academics and extracurriculars: acing every class, starring in school plays, winning awards in art, serving as captain of the Academic Challenge Team, performing violin solos with a Suzuki Institute orchestra, taking Oberlin College classes in Latin and English literature and acing *them*, too. Even as she cheered Nora on, Cynthia worried that her daughter felt compelled to achieve in order to prove to Greg White—and to the rest of the world—that there was absolutely nothing wrong with her or with her mother. In the spring of 2009, Nora graduated from Oberlin High School as valedictorian of her class. In the fall of 2009, she entered Yale University, where she studies theater and Italian.

By Nora's eighteenth birthday, Cynthia had shot more than 3,700 rolls of film with her hand-me-down Nikon. Picture storage had become a gargantuan problem, but Cynthia waved away friends' suggestions that she switch to a digital camera. With Nora off to college, she hoped to find time to figure out where to put the boxes of photographs threatening to take over even her bed. Cynthia still resides at 82, drives her school bus, and stays in touch with Virginia Behner.

SOURCES

The sources for this book are many. Cynthia Stewart and David Perrotta gave me their full cooperation. Cynthia gave me many hours of her time during which I interviewed and re-interviewed her, going over every detail of the experience and combing through her files. David and Cynthia each kept extensive notes from the day the police first arrived at their door, and they gave me full access to those notes, which documented events as they were happening, their reactions to those events, the resources they were gathering, and the conversations they were having with their lawyers, the Children Services caseworker, Sally Mann, reporters, friends, supporters, advisors, and, once in Cynthia's case, with the county prosecutor. Along with their voluminous files, Cynthia and David also let me borrow: the roll of prints confiscated by the police, the photo album Cynthia submitted with her affidavit, the six binders of photographs Cynthia later submitted to the prosecutor, the shoe box of nude photographs of her daughter that Cynthia culled from her complete collection of photographs, the videotape of the interview of Nora conducted by the investigating caseworker from Children Services, a box of videotaped TV news reports, a box of newspaper and magazine clippings, two large grocery sacks of mail from across the nation, an audiotape of Nora telling her New Year's Eve nightmare, and fifteen hours' worth of saved phone messages on cassette tapes.

The criminal court filings were available from the Lorain County court clerk. The transcripts of the Children Services trial—443 pages' worth—were given to me by Cynthia, who paid with legal defense funds to have them reproduced by the court. Cynthia and Nora later viewed their family's case file at the Children Services office and took extensive notes, which they passed along to me.

Attorney Amy Wirtz was extremely generous with her time. I interviewed her numerous times about Cynthia's case, and she read the manuscript and gave me valuable feedback as well as some important corrections. Attorney Kreig Brusnahan, guardian ad litem Virginia Behner, and attorney Tom Theado also spoke with me frankly about their experiences during the case and their perspectives on the family and the prosecution. Sally Mann spoke with me about her own experiences as a photographer of her children and shared her thoughts on child pornography cases like—and unlike—Cynthia's.

I interviewed dozens of other people, including the citizens who met privately with the county prosecutor at the Oberlin church; the witnesses who testified on behalf of Cynthia at the Children Services hearing; the members of the "Politburo," along with others who took action on Cynthia's behalf; two of Cynthia's brothers; and Christine Link, the executive director of the Ohio ACLU. Because I was a participant in these events, I have also drawn on my own contemporaneous notes, correspondence, and recollections.

I was not able to interview a number of people whom I would like to have interviewed. When I contacted Greg White in 2006, he was serving as the U.S. Attorney for the Northern District of Ohio. He asked, with what I thought was surprising friendliness, how Cynthia and Nora were faring. But he said he could not talk to me about Cynthia's case because it had been "expunged," and, as a result, he was not supposed to even acknowledge the prosecution had ever taken place. I was taken aback by this news, since Cynthia had never mentioned expungement to me. I told White that Cynthia would be happy to give written permission for him to talk to me, but he insisted that legally he could not talk about the case and logistically it would be impossible since "all her court records have been destroyed."

"But I was able to find her case's court docket online recently," I pointed out.

White asked if I had submitted a public record request to the county prosecutor's office. When I said no, he said, "Well, try that. They should say they have no records for that case."

After we hung up, I called the Lorain County Prosecutor's office and gave the secretary Cynthia's case number. She typed something into her computer and confirmed, "That case was in Judge Zaleski's courtroom. I'll transfer you to the assistant prosecutor assigned to that courtroom." That assistant prosecutor's secretary told me to call the court records division. The court records division confirmed that the case file was available to the public at the courthouse.

When I contacted Cynthia and David the next day, neither of them knew anything about an expungement. With a little more research, I learned that expungement is a legal procedure that has to be initiated by a defendant (usually a first-time, non-violent offender) who has been convicted of a crime but who wants to expunge his or her record and start again with a clean slate. Expungement proceedings take place before a judge, and the prosecutor is given an opportunity to oppose or support the expungement. But Cynthia had never pled guilty to anything, had never been convicted of a crime, and had never initiated expungement proceedings—so her case could not have been expunged. I wrote White again, explaining that:

> I have followed up on our conversation and have confirmed that Cynthia's criminal case was never expunged, as you believed it had been. Nor have the records been sealed (which, as I understand it, would have been the appropriate procedure in Cynthia's case rather than expungement since she was never convicted of a crime). Cynthia never initiated the process to seal her records; they are still open to the public.
>
> As you suggested, I called the prosecutor's office, and they confirmed the case took place in 1999–2000. At the courthouse this week, I was able to view Cynthia's entire case file.
>
> I am writing to renew my request to speak with you about Cynthia's prosecution and its outcome. I hope you will feel free now under the law to speak with me about the case.

White never answered my letter, my follow-up fax, or my phone calls.

Soon after I viewed Cynthia's case file at the courthouse, Amy Wirtz went to view Cynthia's court records herself. The clerk told Amy, "That is a popular case file this week!" She explained that the Lorain County prosecutor's office had come in to get a copy of the complete file since they "seemed to have lost their copy."

Chief assistant prosecutor Jonathan Rosenbaum also refused to speak with me. I wrote him a letter, then followed up with a call to his office. He interrupted my first sentence with, "I'm not interested in talking to you. Why would I be interested in talking to you? You've already made up your mind this woman was abused by the system. You won't print anything I have to say, so goodbye"—then hung up the phone.

Executive director of Lorain County Children Services Gary Crow said curtly that he was "not interested" in talking with me. Magistrate Michele Arredondo and Children Services prosecutor Faye List did not answer my written requests for interviews. Judge Edward Zaleski felt that he could not comment on the case as long as he was still a sitting judge.

The customer relations manager at Fujicolor Processing Inc. in Mansfield, Ohio, the lab that had called the police about Cynthia's photos in the first place, refused to discuss Cynthia's case with me or to describe their procedure for deciding which photographs should be turned over to the police. "I'm sure you recognize the sensitive nature of this issue," he said. "I won't comment on anything." I suggested it might be helpful to parents taking snapshots of their children to understand what guidelines were being used to identify over-the-line pictures. "We get our guidelines from the federal government," he said. "That's all I'm going to say." And then he added, "And don't quote me on that."

So I called the FBI field office in Cleveland and asked for a copy of the federal guidelines on child pornography provided to film processors in Ohio. The FBI official said, "That person must be mistaken. I have never heard of any guidelines. I have no idea what he means."

He explained that the federal government would only be involved if there were transportation of child pornography across state lines or over the Internet. He suggested I call the U.S. Attorney's office in Cleveland (where Greg White was now U.S. Attorney). That office sent me to the office of the State Attorney General in Columbus, where I was routed to a Consumer Protection Specialist who said, "I have no idea what he's talking about. I don't know of any guidelines given by the state—other than the laws themselves." She suggested I call the corporate office of a large, Midwestern photographic retailer.

The man I spoke with at this corporate office was helpful but anxious that I not identify him or his company. I asked why both he and the spokesman at Fujicolor were so skittish about discussing the issue. "It's a taboo subject," he said. "We don't like to talk about it because our business is to promote positive family values."

I asked him if his company had received guidelines from the federal or state government to help evaluate photographs, and he said, "The law is our only guideline, and we use whichever law is most restrictive in a particular community: the federal or state law or some community ordinance. We try to abide by what the community standards are, but you can't get two communities to agree on what's pornographic. We're responsible to the community, but we're not in the censorship business, either. And you have to be careful, because a mistake can cause real damage to a family."

For every private conversation I describe, I had at least one source who was a participant in that conversation, and I have tried to make it clear from whose perspective the conversation has been reported. In the case of the group conversation with the prosecutor at the church, I was able to interview all five of the community representatives involved in that conversation and have tried to incorporate their perceptions into one scene. When I have written that a person "thought" or "believed" or "felt" something, it is because that person told me in an interview what he or she thought, believed, or felt.

In quoting from interviews, I have never put words into people's mouths. I have, however, sometimes cut long quotes into shorter ones in order to get to the gist of what was being said. I have worked hard to never change the import, tone, or context of a statement in my editing. Likewise, in the chapters documenting the Children Services trial, I have quoted directly from the transcripts, but I have sometimes edited out parts of a statement or dialogue for purposes of readability, brevity, and focus.

An important background source for this book was Kate Myers, an Ohio mother arrested in 1993 for child endangerment. She was the mother in the headlines as I worried about taking the Cupid snapshot of my son. A single mother from a prominent and affluent Akron family, Kate was charged with four felonies for nude pictures taken, without Kate's knowledge, by her six-year-old daughter and her daughter's playmate with her daughter's point-and-shoot camera. The Fujicolor lab in Mansfield turned the prints over to the Akron police, who staked out Kate's house for weeks, searched the house for child porn (during which they ransacked the rooms and threatened to shoot her dogs), arrested Kate, and took her daughter from school to the hospital for a vaginal exam to check for sexual abuse. The hospital staff refused to conduct the exam and called in the county children's services agency. Among the hundreds of photographs in Kate's house, the police found four of Kate's daughter at the age of two in which she was either naked or wearing no underwear. For those four pictures, Kate received two additional felony charges. For almost a year, Kate and her family endured sensational headlines and shunning from their community. Yet Kate refused to make any deals with the prosecutor, all of which would have required her to admit to wrongdoing. Kate's trial in January 1994 lasted one week. The jury deliberated for less than an hour and found her not guilty on all charges.

Kate's financial and personal resources enabled her to engage the best legal help available. Kate feared, though, that another mother, without those resources, might have been deprived of her civil liberties and the custody of her child. Although Kate's story did not ultimately fit within the frame of this book, it is a story every bit as compelling as the one I've told in *Framing Innocence*.

ACKNOWLEDGMENTS

My thanks begin where this book began: with gratitude to Cynthia, David, and Nora for trusting me with their family's story. I am grateful for their openness and for their willingness to have this story told fully.

This story also could not have been told without the generosity of the many people who allowed me to interview them. Some of those people are named in this book, some are quoted but not named, and still others do not appear in these pages, but behind the scenes (and sometimes off the record) they helped me understand complicated issues or provided key insights, verification, or background information. To those named and unnamed, thank you for your time, your belief in this project, and your candor. To those who read and checked my manuscript for accuracy, I am doubly grateful.

The Ohio Arts Council twice provided me with material support in the writing of *Framing Innocence*. In early 2007, they awarded me an Individual Excellence Award for this work while in progress, an award that provided both financial help and encouragement at a moment when I was particularly grateful for both. In the summer of 2008, the OAC sponsored a month-long residency for me at the Vermont Studio Center in Johnson, Vermont, just as I was facing a major edit of the manuscript. That month in the mountains, among fellow writers and artists, gave me the fresh eyes I needed to see my 500-page draft clearly, and then to cut and polish it into a readable book.

In her letter of thanks to her supporters, Cynthia wrote, "It takes a community of friends to right a wrong." My own version is, "It takes the critique of good writers and readers to turn a poet into a prose writer." It is only because I am blessed with a bounty of friends who are terrific writers and incisive readers—and generous with their time—that this book has made its way into print.

Susan Grimm read my first ragged chapters and encouraged me to keep going. Carter McAdams read my manuscript in more versions than anyone else and cheered me on. Jane Barnes defied jetlag to listen to an early draft of my first fifty pages—and to give me a reality check.

Martha Collins, Elton Glaser, Wendy Kozol, Lee Phillips, Michael Robertson, and Mimi Schwartz each read the manuscript in various forms, including, I'm embarrassed to say, its longest and most unwieldy incarnation. Each of them devoted hours to careful reading and to clarifying for me aspects of the writing that needed to be honed or rethought. To each of those writers, I owe a particular debt.

If I had not met Tony Dallas at the Vermont Studio Center in 2008, it's hard to imagine how I would have ever gotten from *there* to *here*. It took a playwright to help me grasp the narrative potential of a sentence and a paragraph. When sentences *move* in this book, and when there's salt in the meat of my prose, it's thanks to Tony Dallas.

Amy Sheon and Marvin Krislov read my manuscript in its nearly final form and identified passages that still needed clarity or cutting. Their enthusiasm for this book has been a big boost. A welcoming group of writers who gather yearly at Kelly's Island and monthly in Cleveland helped me finalize the book's opening pages the day before, as it turns out, my agent sent the manuscript to The New Press.

My agent Elizabeth Kaplan believed in this book long before my writing had earned it. She read numerous drafts and didn't mince words when the manuscript needed a good shakedown. Her commitment to this book and her patience with my process have been large gifts.

Ellen Adler, my editor and publisher, is my new role model for *grace under pressure*. For this book to move from acceptance to print in seven months, Ellen said we would need to "step lively," and she has done that without sacrificing patience or a healthy perfectionism. Her passion for this book, her attentive care to every aspect of its production, and her friendship through the process have been a writer's dream. The enthusiastic and capable New Press staff has been helpful at every lively step, as has Cinqué Hicks. My special thanks to Jyothi Natarajan as well as Maury Botton, whose design sense was so attuned to the story that *Framing Innocence* tells. I also want to thank Leon Friedman for his careful reading and equally careful suggestions.

As always, my family has been a source of great companionship and support. My parents, Bill and Joy Powell, read several versions of this book and remained my most buoyant fans. My brother Bill, his wife Amy, and their children Ida, Will, and Stewart Powell listened cheerfully to chapters at every family gathering and insisted they really and truly wanted to read the whole book! My sister-in-law Beth Stinebring jump-started me on this project by transcribing the tapes of my first round of interviews.

My husband, daughter, and son—Dan, Anna-Claire, and Jesse Stinebring—listened to me talk about this story at more dinners, parties, picnics, and family reunions than I care to admit. When I was at an impasse in my revision, Dan sequestered himself in his lab with my manuscript and a red pen—and emerged three days later with the last sixty pages I needed to trim. Anna-Claire, a wonderful writer herself, and I took many long walks and sat over many cups of tea talking about writing in ways that inspired me and strengthened my own work. Jesse brought his keen political instincts to bear upon my pages whenever he read any of them, including the week before the manuscript went to the copyeditor. Only Dan, Anna-Claire, and Jesse know what the writing of this book has asked of and has given to me. It is to them I dedicate this book with joy, gratitude, and infinite love.

PERMISSIONS

I am grateful for permission to reproduce the following material. Every effort has been made to contact all rights holders of material reprinted in *Framing Innocence*. If notified, the publisher of the book will be pleased to rectify omissions in future editions.

Correspondence on pages 88–89 and 268 is reprinted with permission from Sally Mann.

Excerpt from "Prosecuting Innocence" on pages 101–102 is reprinted with permission from Katha Pollitt and *The Nation*.

Letter from *The Nation* reader on page 102–103 is reprinted with permission from Matt Young.

Verse from legal defense fund contributor on page 103 is reprinted with permission from Bob Jones.

Letter to Katha Pollitt on page 105 is reprinted with permission from Warner Berthoff.

Editorial excerpt on pages 109–110 is reprinted with permission from Andy Young, editor, the *Chronicle-Telegram*.

Excerpt from "Reeducating Cynthia Stewart" on page 275–276 is reprinted with permission from Richard Cohen.

PHOTO BY CYNTHIA STEWART

Nora and Jesse at ages seven and almost-seven, taken just after their first grade violin recital in May 1998—one year before Cynthia took the photographs for which she would be arrested.

About the Author

Lynn Powell is the author of two books of poetry, *Old & New Testaments* and *The Zones of Paradise*, and has been awarded fellowships from the National Endowment for the Arts and the Ohio Arts Council. A native of East Tennessee, she has lived with her family in Oberlin, Ohio, since 1990.